WRETCHED STRANGERS

BORDERS MOVEMENT HOMES

EDITED BY ÁGNES LEHÓCZKY
AND J. T. WELSCH

CONTENTS

J.T. WELSCH

The Strangers' Case: A Welcome

All artists are outsiders, we're told. Either by transgression or transcendence, they overcome boundaries of self and society to which we might feel otherwise confined. Poems, like all art, are seen to enact this blurring of borders – not just ideally, but in principle. The manipulation of form and material, the warping of space and time within linguistic matter, and the conjuring of new language objects more generally seem to defy physical and psychological limits. Likewise, the transpersonal thrill and challenge offered by the best poems, like all good art, apparently permit human crossings that would be impossible by other means. Poems redefine those limits. Poems move and create new spaces.

The poet who moves more literally through the world becomes iconic in this story of outsider-ness and border-breaking. Poetry and exile become romantically entangled in a tradition as old as Dante, Li Bai, or Ovid. A certain kind of modern poet might be prone to self-imposing the conditions of exile. 'But remember that I am a *metic* – a foreigner,' T. S. Eliot writes to a British friend in 1919. In 1945, after living in the UK for thirty years, he still signs a public letter using the Greek form of the word: *metoikos.*

Following Eliot to England from our hometown of St. Louis, I admit having been susceptible at times to this idealised notion of the 'resident alien' or the sense of being 'never anything anywhere,' as he puts it in another letter. Plenty of biographers, like Peter Ackroyd, have been happy to buy into the mystique:

> *[Eliot] was never completely at home anywhere... He cultivated such distance and detachment as if by not belonging, or wholly participating, something of himself was preserved – something secret and inviolable which he could nourish.*

Other critics, like David Chinitz, see the myth for what it is: 'Eliot misses the point that to be "never anything anywhere," if that implies an identity that is never quite stable or finally settled, is precisely to *be* an American.'

The assumption of outsider status, in other words, can also be a matter of privilege. (I'm conscious of relative material privilege as well, applying and sending the exorbitant fee for my 'right to settle' in the UK while working on this book.) For Eliot, it was as much a matter of branding, of assuming what Simon Grimble calls 'the authority of the outsider'. And in Eliot's case, we know too well the racist, sexist, classist, and otherwise hateful views to which this construction of 'inviolable' self-authority extended.

In practice, the realities of migration are not immediately conducive to transcendent art. While the myth of the wandering poet might still play well in book blurbs, migrant writers in any country are likely to find their outsider status confers more vulnerability than authority. The writing throughout this book is deeply aware of its vulnerabilities and contingencies, it seems to me. The formal variety across the work of 125 authors seems itself a symptom of unsettledness. Anxieties are manifest in dreams and nightmares of borders and walls, passport offices, and authorities who arrive without warning. In the book's first poems, Alireza Abiz writes of being 'afraid to write in my diary.' Living and working across languages or aesthetic modes creates a sense of daily negotiations, code-switching, and what Veronica Fibisan describes here as a 'propagation of selves' or Ulli Freer as 'assumed identities over line slippages'.

Elsewhere, differently desperate dreams of what Astrid Alben calls 'the other country' or Shirin Teirfouri calls 'that country' combine with 'the metaphysics of inheritance' named by Nisha Ramayya. If Mimi Khalvati insists that we 'Never ask where home is,' it might be because, as Peter Gizzi offers, 'Deep in the enzyme is the shape of home.' A sense of community emerges between speakers linked by a deep feeling of distance and the 'peculiar state of exiled human,' as Fawzi Karim puts it. Lila Matsumoto explains, 'discreetly existing / did not prevent me from thinking of shared foreignness', while Kit Fan echoes and amplifies the radical empathy which is often the result of such precarity:

So many of us, I want to know every single life, what
brought them here today, who they are, and how long they will live.

*

It's probably worth saying that this book was never intended as a response to the ongoing human disaster commonly known as 'Brexit'. Before 23 June 2016, Ágnes Lehóczky and I had been talking for a few years about how disappointing it was that no one had ever put together an anthology celebrating the contribution of migrant writers to British poetry culture. We found ourselves making lists of UK-based writers we loved, initially using the most literal definition of 'migrant' for anyone born elsewhere. Nathan Hamilton at Boiler House Press became an integral part of these conversations and an important sounding-board as our anger and mourning grew more urgent in the EU referendum's build-up and fall-out. I'm also certain this book wouldn't exist if Jèssica Pujol hadn't brought together so many of the poets featured here for a life-affirming event in London in early 2017, as part of the UK-wide *One Day Without Us* demonstration of solidarity.

The list grew as writers passed on recommendations and we opened a general call for submissions. Amid the darkest news of nationalist violence, deportations and friends (even Jèssica) feeling they had no choice except to leave, we clung to that feeling of community emerging from the process. Facing the growing threat, expressed here by Christodoulos Makris, that 'the Hate will get to such a point it's just everywhere,' Ági and I were surprised and spurred on by such hope on every page.

In places, it comes in acts of defiance, from the 'Immigrant at Work' signs Sara Crangle coordinated for office doors at the University of Sussex to Emily Critchley's window-smashing elegy for 'this precious train / the one over all Europe'. Just as often, it disarmed us with acts of defiant kindness – like David Herd's 'act of welcome' from the inspiring *Refugee Tales* project. Where Jèssica Pujol's own piece reminds us that 'sometimes you need wild gesticulation to / communicate the pain of the pasts', Ethel Maqeda adds that 'a greeting is a good start'. The more we read, the more we heard the pieces speaking to each other in this way, welcoming the reader to that conversation. In place of self-serving claims of outsider authority, we hear Angelina D'Roza's confession: 'I am unstable, unrooted.' Or Wanda O'Connor's: 'I do not come to settling easy.' In place of a *metic* myth or the 'Myth of the Savage Tribes, Myth of Civilized Nations' exploded in Sandeep Parmar and James Byrne's collaboration, we learn from Giovanna Coppola that 'you have to / make this / place a myth', whatever place that is.

As work continued to arrive from all corners of this little island – from fellow migrants alongside British writers in solidarity – and eventually all corners of the globe, the scale of these distances and differences became relative again to the poem's scope. It seemed possible again, at least within the space created here, to 'live in a world where some problems feel too huge to tackle' (in Maria Jastrzębska's words) and also to feel 'the world shrunk to the size of a fist' (in Livia Franchini's). Any new myth of migration, Luna Montenegro makes clear, would have to be expansive enough to include the sensation that 'EVERYTHING / IN THE / UNIVERSE / IS MOVING / IN THIS / (IN)EXACT / SECOND'.

*

We stumbled across the title *Wretched Strangers* after the British Library made a rare manuscript available online in Spring 2016. The manuscript's significance is a speech that William Shakespeare appears to have contributed to a long-forgotten play about Thomas More around 1600. In the scene apparently in Shakespeare's hand, the protagonist faces down – of all horrors – an anti-immigration riot on the streets of London, conjuring an image that perfectly countered the Leave campaign's own xenophobic propaganda. More tells the mob:

Imagine that you see the wretched strangers,
Their babies at their backs, and with their poor luggage
Plodding to th' ports and coasts for transportation,
And that you sit as kings in your desires,

Authority quite silenc'd by your brawl,
And you in ruff of your opinions cloth'd.
What had you got? I'll tell you: you had taught
How insolence and strong hand should prevail,
How [order] should be quell'd, and by this pattern
Not one of you should live an aged man,
For other ruffians, as their fancies wrought,
With self-same hand, self reasons, and self right,
Would shark on you, and men like ravenous fishes
Would feed on one another.

It might not be Shakespeare's most nuanced soliloquy, but the point is well-taken as he labours it further, having More warn the crowd that they will reap what they sow:

What country by the nature of your error
Should give you harbour? Go you to France or Flanders,
To any German province, Spain or Portugal,
Nay, anywhere that not adheres to England:
Why, you must needs be strangers; would you be pleas'd
To find a nation of such barbarous temper
That breaking out in hideous violence
Would not afford you an abode on earth...?

'This is the strangers' case,' More concludes, 'and this your mountainish inhumanity.'

There are poems here that rightly acknowledge the inhumanity of our own moment, or reminders, like Leire Barrera-Medrano's (translating the anti-fascist poet León Felipe), that a country 'which has halted Western history for more than three centuries' can hardly blame others for that which its fancies wrought. And yet, above all, the book as a whole remains a testament to community, belonging, and participation – a space for us strangers to write and speak and read together towards what the poet che describes here as 'ways of living as yet / undiscovered'.

We begin with a greeting, or a wild welcome to join us in this work.

WRETCHED STRANGERS

ALIREZA ABIZ

Legends

I am sitting in Legends
In a dark corner of the bar
Nursing a glass of beer
And thinking
In a hundred years—just one hundred years—
None of these people will be alive

Not that one up there on the little stage
Playing a new track every few minutes
Nor those young boys and girls skilfully filling glasses
And taking money
Nor this crowd moving their bodies un-rhythmically

And not me
—The melancholic scribbler of these lines—
And the almighty god of these words
Not one of us will continue to be
We'll all be lost in Legends

From the window of my basement room
Only the topmost wintry boughs are visible
I hear the crying of the crows
A cold morning envelopes me
In the mirror another man looks at me
With puffy eyes and white hairs in his temples
A two-day beard
He says: Look at the world with fresh eyes
Tomorrow night there's a seminar "Rejuvenate with Love" in the
    Methodist church
"People of all faiths and no faith welcome"
The man in the mirror asks me in English:
"What is your faith?"
I reply: Speak in your mother tongue
With the words that you carry in your mind from the distant past
Speak with the words of your ancestors
Did my grandfather suffer any doubt in his faith?
Does my father ever think about this?

The world is too brief a space for thought

The Dancing Wall

Last night in my dreams I composed a poem
Like every night
A translucent poem which shone upon me like a prism
I woke up and wrote down a line:
A dancing wall appeared before me
"A dancing wall appeared before me"
"A dancing wall"? why "dancing"?
And why did it appear before me in English?
What was wrong with the Persian?
What was marvellous about *A dancing wall*?
I who am a Persian poet
Like the Persian more
There are plenty of walls in my memory
In my Persian memory

I was also a Persian poet in my dreams
I was afraid to write in my diary
I was afraid my roommate Ali Mostafayi
Might betray me to the Intelligence Service
I was afraid they might take me to Koohsangi Street
To number 13 slash 1

En route

The thin blue flame
Yawns and falls off the fire
Lies down for a while
Arches and stretches
Gathers strength and rises up dancing

Darkness fills the valley
And over the border, the lights go on

BIO

Alireza Abiz is an Iranian poet, literary critic and translator. He studied English Literature in Mashhad and Tehran universities (Iran) and received his PhD in Creative Writing (Poetry) from Newcastle University. He has published six collections of poetry in Persian, including *Black Line – London Underground* and *The Pomegranate of Bajestan*, and a scholarly book, *Censorship of Literature in Post-Revolutionary Iran: Politics and Culture Since 1979*, is forthcoming. Abiz is also an award-winning translator and has translated Basil Bunting, Derek Walcott, Allen Ginsberg, and C.K. Williams into Persian.

ASTRID ALBEN

Five Ways of Belonging

I knock but the world is nowhere (one) to be found.
Hail to the world (two)! Somewhere under the weight

of eiderdowns a house sighs loneliness is a half-completed line.
Go to the park (three) where gargoyle mouths on stilts (three

and a half) called bins count slender poplars in the margins
of the wind riffling obsolescent papers, orange peels, Poet's insular

dominion, masking tape. I never (four) heard the voices
near the bench (five) cargo spaces blindly *bu-hu-wooooshhh.*

The Other Country

Dreamt B spoke to me
telling me he sees
clouds drift in a bottle of milk.

Evening light he says
is a flock of birds
skimming the rooftops westerly.

*

The sky disappeared that night
and in its stead a permanent cloudbank
squats on rooftops.

In this cloudbank small luminescent
baubles hover which I guess
B continues used to be streetlights.

The light sprains his shadow
dispersing me B says
running clear out from underneath me.

*

Across the border the river flows through the rain
yellow comes after mustard seed
every leaf is a slipper *thlupping* on summer.

Across the border telephone wires
are caught in the antlers of the open road. It's where
why did you leave means *why did you come back.*

Across the border one foot easily
forgets the other but that's neither here nor there.
It isn't one thing or the other.

Remember
B says
the border is just a line.

*

But what he really wants to tell me
is that across the border
I want to speak to everybody

and most of all yes
most of all I want to speak to you.
Because everywhere

B persists
picking up the carton of milk
and raising it to his lips

everywhere he went that night
I watched babies being born
their fists tightly balled

but in death B says
wiping the corners of his mouth
our hands are open.

BIO

Astrid Alben is a poet, editor and translator. Her collection *Ai! Ai! Pianissimo* was published by Arc Publications (2011). Her poems have appeared in many journals and anthologies. Her next collection, *Plainspeak*, an alter-ego-thinking-out louder book, will be published by Shearsman in 2019. Alben is a FRSA and was awarded a Wellcome Trust Fellowship in 2014. 'Five Ways of Belonging' was previously published in *Oxford Poetry* and is forthcoming in *Plainspeak*. 'The Other Country' first appeared in *Ai! Ai! Pianissimo*. To hear her poems visit astridalben.com.

TIM ATKINS

Terrorists' Series #1: The Angry Brigade & Nazim Hikmet (Mashup with Ali Yunus)

for Dhirendranath Bannerjee

A typically empty gesture of bad contemporary poetry which professes to be 'about' capitalist culture involves the indolent misuse of second person constructions. (DH / Tripwire 8)

The "possible" is only
Neither "for" nor "against"

Suprematism in pure feeling

It matters not in our own location
Exercising the noctambulist

That one can tell during a conversation

At each turn of the thought
The flower of capital is

Society will find us wanting

If the stars are out there
I shall keep my head here

Like I said I don't mind

Poetry is the opposite of literature
The rage for glitter

Is a pigsty especially this one

Amid all the pessimism darkness seriousness
Give us the land

What abstract art means to me

The immense force of habit
Raised above the land like a hammer

By the notation of breath

To Poetry potential literature remains
An equal length

Her libido is cosmetic

What I have   here
now = more

Astonishing Powerful Mysterious Gigantic

At the hermetic flower of the crossroads
The true poem should be invisible

My poetry and much that interests me

A man
On his way

Stopped   & in Chains

BIO

Tim Atkins' latest book is *On Fathers < On Daughtyrs* (Boiler House Press). The poem in this book is from *The Penguin Book of Japanese Verse.*

ANDRE BAGOO

The Scarlet Ibis is the National Bird of Trinidad & Tobago

now the black, the cut, the red
the colony dispersed by bullets I ask whose land it is

warm (sun) pink (glans) ruin across the mangrove
where I sit after he comes among the moko jumbie
          roots

there is no air   earth not of earth
   and

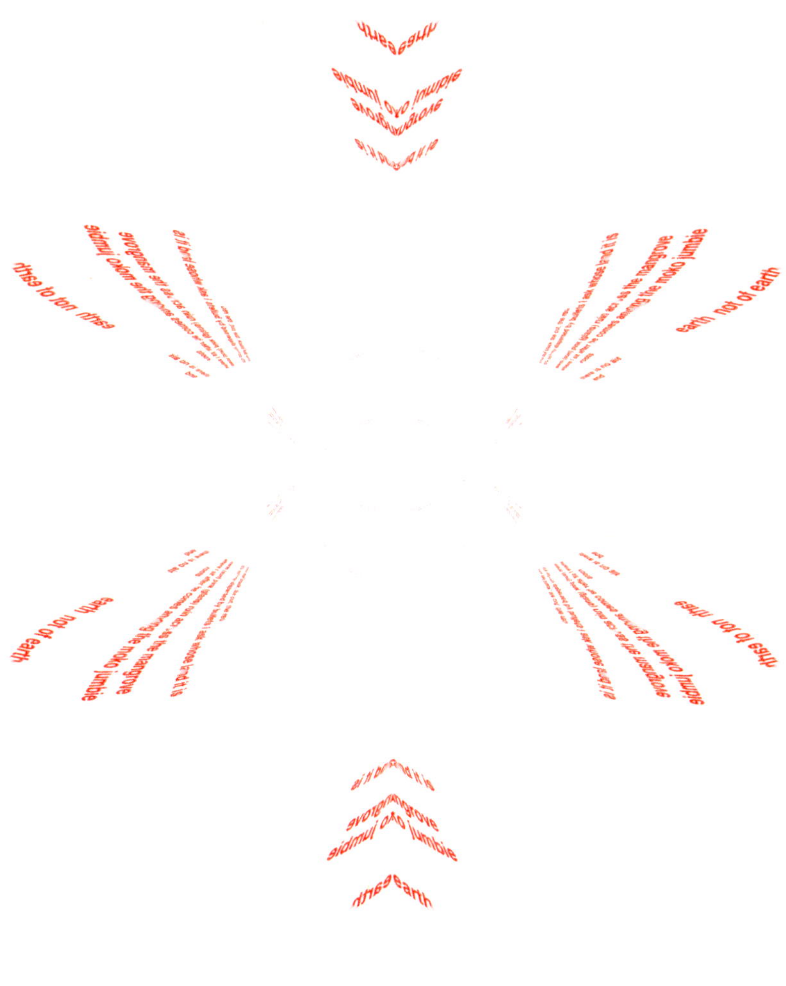

BIO

Andre Bagoo's work has appeared at *Asian American Literary Review*, *Boston Review*, *Cincinnati Review*, *Hawai'i Review*, *St Petersburg Review*, *The Poetry Review* and Wasafiri. He is the author of: *Trick Vessels* (Shearsman, 2012), *BURN* (Shearsman, 2015), *Pitch Lake* (Peepal Tree, 2017) and *The City of Dreadful Night* (Prote(s)xt, 2018). He was awarded The Charlotte and Isidor Paiewonsky Prize in 2017.

VERONICA BARNSLEY

The Work of Refugee Writing

The writer Jean Rhys insisted snappily that the patois title of her short story 'Temps Perdi' did not have the 'poetic' meaning of 'lost time' but the more prosaic one of 'lost or wasted labour'. The story tracks a middle-class young woman's visit to the almost extinct native Carib population of Dominica, where Rhys grew up. It is an oblique eulogy for the beauty of a people who have been exploited, made to perform and to parody colonial ideals of 'the primitive' and, finally, denied recognition or reward for their efforts.

Rhys was not a refugee, though as a creole she always felt like an exile in Europe and her writing was under-appreciated until she wrote her magnum opus, *Wide Sargasso Sea* (1962) in which the heroine is coerced into marriage and taken against her will to England. When Rhys wrote 'Temps Perdi' in the 1940s the term 'refugee' was mainly applied to those displaced by persecution in Europe during WWII before being formalised in the Declaration of Human Rights in 1948. Nevertheless, the idea of lost labour is one that resonates with the global narratives of displacement – commonly, though uncomfortably, drawn together under the umbrella of 'refugee writing' – that we encounter today. For instance, Olumide Popoola's story 'Extending a Hand', from the 2016 collection *Breach*, voices the perspective of a young African woman built upon the author's conversations with inhabitants of the Calais Jungle: 'They, the ones who give up their time, are here to extend a helping hand, to help make things survivable. But you don't need a hand; you have two of those. What you need is opportunities.' (p. 49) The woman focuses on the volunteers (mostly British) who 'give' their labour for free in a deliberate and time-limited way denied to the Jungle's inhabitants whose lives are characterized by immediate fear and threat, on the one hand, and the long-term frustration of being in limbo and prevented from working on the other.

In a predicament in which opportunities to work and to learn are so meagre how are writing and other creative acts to be understood? Refugee writing is undoubtedly a vital part of a 'politics of intervention': as critic Cecile Sandten explores, writing may offer release through expressing something of the self, of the human and, I'd like to add, of the creaturely (given that refugees are often figured as not-quite-human).[1] Writing may involve re-finding a voice that could barely communicate on the journey to Europe due to language differences and the degradation of violence, hunger and illness. In his memoir of travelling as a lone child refugee, *The Lightless Sky* (2016), Gulwali Passarlay demonstrates that autobiographical accounts may also enable the illumination or partial ordering of traumatic experiences: 'Even now, I have only half an understanding of the routes that I travelled; my memories are often a blur of faces, landscapes, half-formed thoughts'. (p. 176) The acknowledgement here of confusion, of living in a haze that for many asylum seekers and refugees hasn't cleared long after their resettlement is antithetical to the other prime function of refugee writing: the account required to submit an asylum claim. To prove that a claim to asylum is valid potential refugees must say precisely from where, why, how and when they have come to Britain and their accounts are transcribed by the Home Office. A claim can stand or fall on the perceived validity of this document as it is tested against the views of civil servants and country experts.

Between these divergent requirements – that of 'authentic' and cathartic self-expression and that of factual accuracy – lies the difficulty in conceptualizing what 'refugee writing' is and what role it plays in the sociopolitical complexities of migration to and through Europe. The street-level acceptance of 'refugee arts' in Britain as contributing to a cosmopolitan cultural landscape as well as promoting community and well-being amongst vulnerable migrants is heartening. But a critical exploration must engage not only with the political impetus of refugee writing and its explosion of new linguistic and cultural forms but also with the labour involved producing it; the dynamics of its making and its reception. What positions does this writing occupy and articulate in a securitising and paranoid Europe?

If we think of refugee writing as labour rather than (or as well as) the first-hand representation of human rights abuses, its insistence on carving out space for strangers in the British imagination might impact upon the seemingly intractable situations of migrants in poverty who do not or cannot work or who are caught in a coercive illegal marketplace. When reading refugee writing or working with refugee writers, it's noticeable that the neoliberal language of value as tied to productivity, profit and progress is muted, or present only in relation to humanitarianism. This isn't a bad thing given that artists rightly demand that what they do be recognised as work (rather than privileged or irresponsible idleness). However, in the case of refugee arts the absence of discussions of labour is also worrying. Texts and performances by refugees and asylum seekers are, of course, invaluable in bringing global problems closer to audiences in Europe. These texts also allow us an insight into the psychological disorientation of precarity; as Passarlay says, 'I had stopped thinking further ahead than the next minute'. But this focus on existential immediacy, as well as our vicarious interest in the details of dangerous journeys and narrow escapes, can also operate as an avoidance of questions of meaningful labour as, for most, necessary for a meaningful life: particularly, what happens to new arrivals in Britain when they cannot work (if in the asylum system), cannot find work (as many refugees cannot, particularly when offered minimal training in language and other skills), or are destitute or at risk of deportation. Is it possible that our empathetic engagement with refugee writing perpetuates a model of victimhood that masks the prejudices at play when a government intolerant of migrants insists that a modern 'enterprising' Britain be dressed up in the old blue cover of imperial citizenship? In this context is there room for refugee writers to be seen as workers?

At the Migration Matters festival in 2016 the Syrian poet Bashar Farhat, a paediatrician now living as a refugee in Bradford, performed a piece whose refrain was the response his mother gave him every time he told her about the trials of his journey: 'Don't Die!'. For a long time the 'work' he had to do was to stay alive while his mother frantically hoped for his safe arrival in Europe. Now he has begun the work towards passing the English tests and medical exams required to practice his profession in the U.K. Similarly, Passarlay's mother told him when he left Afghanistan aged twelve; 'however bad it gets, *don't come back*' (p. 48). He has since worked to help those in a similar situation.

It's undeniable that refugee writing works to communicate extremities of pain and resilience to those of us who have never been forced to flee. But it also articulates the desire for an opportunity, a purpose or a challenge. Passarlay animates this by narrating his story partly as his child self and partly from his position as a politics student at Manchester University. He is now a well-known advocate for child refugees across multiple organisations and a political campaigner. Passarlay, like many other refugees who have built new lives, has spoken about how the determined work of teachers, foster carers and social workers encouraged him in the labour both of learning and of writing his story. The seriousness with which he treats this endeavour belies a weary recognition that the work of refugee artists is too often treated as just a colourful addition to Britain's multicultural menu rather than a valuable encounter with the flawed politics of global migration.

Refugee writing is a form of labour that takes many forms: it is often used as evidence of the brutality of foreign political regimes and/or of the inclusivity of Britain. It can be boxed in by its own unsatisfactory designation as exilic; expected always to represent past experiences for the benefit of sheltered audiences rather than gaining momentum towards new transcultural forms of politics and society and being recognised for it. This writing can become 'lost labour' unless we recognise the critical work that it does and asks us to do. Writing in the asylum system rarely celebrates self-liberation, indeed it often spells out the work of survival. Saying or writing the wrong thing or receiving an unwelcome letter of rejection can lead to more time spent in limbo and unable to engage in paid work. As the speaker in Ali Smith's story 'The Detainee's Tale' in the collection *Refugee Tales* (2015) says: 'What kind of a life are we living when a piece of paper can mean and say more about your life than your life does?'[2]

NOTES

1 Cecile Sandten, 'Representations of Poverty and Precariousness in Contemporary Refugee Narratives', *Postcolonial Text* 12: 3 & 4 (2017): 1–15.

2 The story can be accessed at www.theguardian.com/books/2015/jun/27/ali-smith-so-far-the-detainees-tale-extract

BIO

Veronica Barnsley is a lecturer in contemporary literature at the University of Sheffield. She co-organises the Material Stories of Migration project with Shirin Teifouri and is currently researching representations of childhood migration in African fiction.

KHAIRANI BAROKKA

Eropa

There is no you without an us, oratorios
diminished from which the wealth was wrought,
spices and infants traded over raucous dinners,
doctors inspecting our bodies as curios.
Laws stamping ancient wisdom as buffoonery,
languages earmarked for oral extinction,
ships bearing rape marks on the stern.

Here is plunder mausoleumed, an oily
balm of percussive pride in history books
thrown by white-out. The streets of Paris
show me the ghosts of girls in sepia,
bruised boys, labour that made your
sheeted beds, laid down your cobblestones,
re-taxonomised and thefted objets de vertu
for illustrious museums; so much operatic,
dead wood from an illegitimate drawing up
of "darkest" borders, an epigenetics of mayhem,
incineration of communal safety; a quietude now
when the boats come in with their last-hour eyes,
for whom this beacon continent disappears with
raging engulfment, above the waves that built it.

mediterranean lyric

you dip a toe
inside of water.

water tells you
your toe is the
problem. ripples
out slow, might
turn lake to skin.

too much foot
is in liquid, human
can't be mer-
population. all
the doors escape
through water,
all water closes,
blood dissipation is
one corpse's
constant. sea

turned to flesh,
it's a sea ground up
into bowls, a river
of muscles.

your one
small toe is the
problem.

all souls
in a cupped bowl
of let them, let
them. no true water
escapes skin
follicles' mingling,
tiredness swelling
into sunken limb.

hope is a sea-
storm's kindling.
fire in the mouth
of waves
and mistral.

BIO

Khairani Barokka has been an NYU Tisch Departmental Fellow, Vermont Studio Center's first Indonesian writer-in-residence, and a UNFPA Indonesian Young Leader Driving Social Change. She is co-editor of *HEAT: A Southeast Asian Urban Anthology* (Fixi, 2016) and *Stairs and Whispers: D/deaf and Disabled Poets Write Back* (Nine Arches, 2017), author-illustrator of *Indigenous Species* (Tilted Axis, 2016), and author of the collection *Rope* (Nine Arches, 2017). She is a member of Malika's Poetry Kitchen and a PhD by practice researcher at Goldsmiths. www.khairanibarokka.com

LEÓN FELIPE, TRANSLATED BY LEIRE BARRERA-MEDRANO

Vieja raposa (Old Vixen) from *La Insignia, 1938*

Down you stay, England,
avaricious old vixen,
which has halted Western history for more than three centuries,
and has chained Don Quixote.
When your life ends
and you face the great History
where I await,
what will you say?
What new cunning shall you then invent to deceive God?
Vixen!
Daughter of foxes!
Italy is nobler than you
And Germany too.
In her prey and her crimes
there is a murky Nietzschean breath of heroism, in which merchants cannot breathe,
an impetuous and confused gesture to risk everything to the last card, which
pragmatic men cannot understand.
When her doors open to the world's air,
wide open
and Justice and the Heroic Democracy of man
pass through them,
I'd make a pact with the two to throw in your old vixen face, without dignity and without love,
all the saliva and feces of the world.
Avaricious old vixen!
you have hidden,
buried in the yard,
the miraculous key that opens the diamond door of History...
You know nothing.
You understand nothing and you get into all the houses
to close the windows
and blind the starlight!
And men see you and leave you.
They leave you because they believe that Jupiter's rays have ended.
But stars do not sleep.

You know nothing.
You have amassed your prey behind the door, and your children, now, cannot open it
so the first rays of the world's dawn can enter.
Avaricious old vixen,
you are a great merchant.
You know very well how to manage

kitchen accounts
and you think I cannot count.
Yes, I can!
I counted my dead.
I counted them all,
I counted them, one by one.
I counted them in Madrid,
I counted them in Oviedo,
I counted them in Malaga,
I counted them in Guernica,
I counted them in Bilbao...
I counted them in all the trenches;
In hospitals,
In the morgues of the cemeteries,
on roadsides,
in the rubble of bombed houses.
Counting dead men this fall, on the Paseo de El Prado, I thought one night that I was walking
on mud, and they were human brains I have long carried stuck
to the soles of my shoes.
On November 18, alone in a basement full of corpses, I counted three hundred dead children...
I counted them on trucks of ambulances,
in hotels,
on trams,
on the tube,
in the livid morning, in the dark nights without street lights and starless...
and in your conscience all...
And all of them I charged them to your account.
You are already seeing how I can count!
You are the old caretaker of the Western world,
For too long, you have kept the keys to all the shutters in Europe and you let in
or out whomever you want.
And now, due to cowardice,
cowardice and greed alone,
because you want to keep your pantry until the last day of history,
you have let all the foxes and wolves in the world
into my field
so they can suck my blood
and not yours.
But they will suck it too,
The stars will ask for it...

BIO

Leire Barrera-Medrano is a Spanish writer, researcher, and teacher based in Sheffield. She is completing a PhD at Birkbeck College, University of London, entitled 'Spain and British Decadence, 1880–1920: Aesthetics of Extremes'. She co-edits Girasol Press, an Anglo-Hispanic poetry letterpress, and co-runs Electric Arc Furnace, an experimental poetry reading series.

KATHERINE E. BASH

The Innkeeper

...then it would let go of the map
of the place where
I had fallen into the hills
to get firewood and,
when I woke in the middle of the night
I was cutting up the wood into lengths,
since I did not know where I was.

Not even did I understand
In the first moment
a loud noise broke out over me.
A large owl appeared and took hold of my face
and I had only in its original simplicity
the feeling of existence as it may quiver
in the depths of such an animal.

I thought I had lost all consciousness
was more destitute than a cave dweller;
but then the memory came back to my senses
and I realised I had fallen into the snow
not yet the place where I was,
but of several of those where I lived and
where I might have been would come to me

and like help to pull me from the abyss
in which I would not have been able to escape
on my own some blood was running out of my mouth;
and in a second I stood up and
went down the trail, walking very fast and
passed through centuries of civilization

on the way trees seemed to shake and to lean bent over my head
Tall trees were crawling at me
one cypress tore itself out of the earth by the roots
scattering dirt in all directions and started
to dart with long strides.
It is so much larger than me I
thought practically breathless ribs aching I
fell back into a sort of trance trying to retrieve something
and then stopped.

It stopped too—
all its branches were shaking horribly it
was probably quite a while
since it had had its last run— "you must
have ridden quite a distance; it's
high time you rested,
for you've been on horseback
the entire night."

NOTES

Acknowledgements: The Complete Stories of Leonora Carringto | Marcel Proust via Daniel Heller-Roazen, *The Inner Touch: Archaeology of a Sensation* | Ariosto, *Orlando Furioso*.

BIO

Katherine E. Bash is an artist, poet, and philosopher from the USA, who has lived in London since 2006 and in other countries prior (e.g. Ecuador, Brazil, and Italy). She received a PhD at the Bartlett School of Architecture, UCL, with the thesis, *Spatial Poetries: Heuristics For Experimental Poiesis*, and has exhibited in numerous solo and group exhibitions.

ÁINE BELTON

Ant Settlement Guide

ant SETTLEMENT GUIDE
Newcomer?
Don’t miss your landing

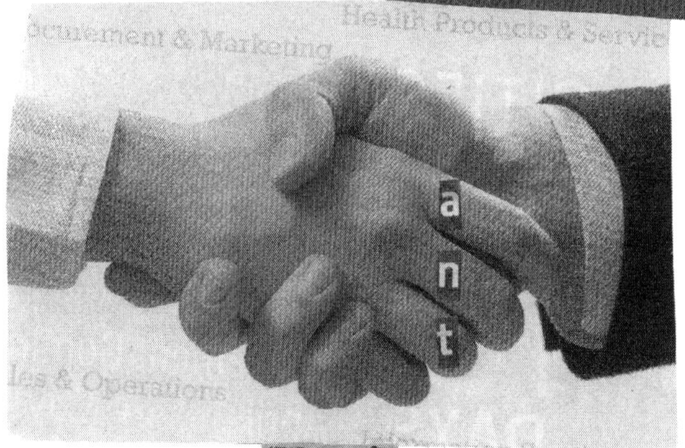

“We made
backgrounds and ethnicities
immigrants
migrants
ants
multicultural
mirrors
Connecting you with the
legal landscape
After rattling off the
• Supply Chain
ants are coming
faiths, living side by side
the people’s purse
made up of immigrants
Plant for your future

<< Given her foreign accent,
in Canada.

English language

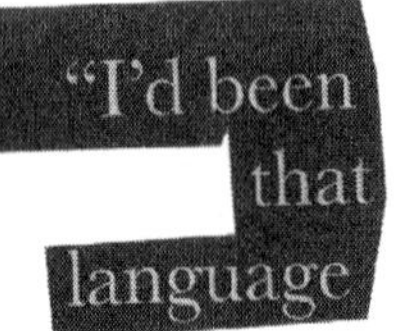

English and accents
She faced many >>

a tongue that
soundlessly quivering smells illicit.
others.
cannot use plurals, foreign words or proper
nouns.
trapped English,
the unbending sentence customs
There is at least one
to be found.

eyes glued
opening and closing
the language
could understand.
We laid it on the table
politely

North American Housekeeper

Wireless High Speed
North American
Housekeeper
an eight-fingered star
I am told,
she brushes
the sun off her
loyalty and
mouth referrals.
to be rubber stamped at
labour negotiation.
different cultures, different tongues
<< obstacles in finding
the real industry,
and her own persever-
ance to turn her life
around.
When that doesn't shift
a momentary hiccup.
she says.
I had
to adjust my thinking —
dreams
are
Equally comfortable in pants or an elegant gown,

BIO

Áine Belton is a visual artist living in Ajax, Canada, originally from County Meath, Ireland. She has an MA in Fine Art from UCA Canterbury and BA in Fine Art in Visual Arts Practice from IADT in Dublin. She is a co-editor of *ESC Zine* and was awarded funding from Art Starts to produce the photo-book *Double Exposure – Portrait Series: Cyclists of Toronto*. In 2016, she published her first kids' book, an activity book based on WW1 objects in the Dover Transport Museum. Selected artworks are in the collection of UCA Canterbury and private collections in Canada, UK and Ireland.

CAROLINE BERGVALL

song 12

from *Drift*

Sailed on to red tides of nonpoint source
to the sea of mercury island-hopping To the
abyssal plains To isles of dumping To knolls
of wild plastic To rigs of leaking To the flaming
scrap swamps circled round pillars of solid
scitta upsetting camp on a heap thinking it be
homelike Shoring up alongside floats of glued
birdwings ok exploding whales that are family
that are war stars that are ghost gongs that are
bone sounds that are ropes that bear the load
of days that are nihts thár are shorelines that
are human shiploads hostage of the outbounds
abandoned skiffs that are anchors on the mind
ok squatter settlements Blow wind blow,
anon am I

BIO

Caroline Bergvall, writer, artist and vocal performer based in London. Works internationally across artforms, media and languages. A strong exponent of writing methods adapted to contemporary audiovisual and contextual situations as well as multilingual identities. Recent project and book *Drift* (2014–2016). Ongoing projects: *Ragadawn, Oh My Oh My* and *Sonic Atlas*. Was awarded a Cholmondeley Award for her poetic work and is the first recipient of the Bernard Heidsieck-Centre Pompidou award for literary artists (2017).

SUJATA BHATT

Someone has Returned Your Eyes to You

Düsseldorf Birdie— shall I name you
                    Düsseldorf Birdie?

Your song is Asian— Japanese, Korean.

Once you were red but now someone
has painted you white.

Your paint is chipped, my driftwood
no longer adrift.

Your nose is a beak: soft brown.

Your eyes are tiny, black:
two lost papaya seeds.

But you are not lost.

Someone has returned your eyes to you.

Düsseldorf Birdie,
will you be my talisman?
Will you sing into my *Wabi Sabi* life?

BIO

Sujata Bhatt's latest books from Carcanet are *Collected Poems* and *Poppies in Translation*. She has received numerous awards including the Commonwealth Poetry Prize (Asia) and the Cholmondeley Award. In 2014 she was the first recipient of the Mexican International Poetry Prize, *Premio Internacional de Poesía Nuevo Siglo de Oro 1914–2014*. Her work has been widely anthologised, and has been translated into more than twenty languages.

RACHEL BLAU DUPLESSIS

Draft 112: Verge

You know this story.
translation

First, "Horrible things happened
and they were introduced to us
as something good." *something*
Killings.
Uprootings.
Fissures and divisions
between those
who considered they were as *splits*
civic as the others,
or had more right to act, but
at that punctual moment
and then for years after,
found they were, or were found as, not.
Certain atrocites *borders*
registered. Then were forgot.
Everyone, it seemed, had realigned,
criss-crossed,
double crossed. *atrocities*
Maps had scratches, ridges, edges
that they never before,
it seemed, had. *crossed*

Sizes, wires, assizes in the site, other boundaries on this border. Maps and lines are drawn over bodies. Where did "history" put this place? Why did it not "stay there"? What about "them"? Should they live here, or are they basically foreign? What are the facts about myself? What is my where? It's true that once there was an ending. It seemed as if this were what I had wanted. Why did it then open? I hardly can remember, but then it's suddenly vivid, though even my own stories have veered over time. Another time pulses through the stifled civic membrane.

Restatement slid toward resentment.
An otherwhere of once-upon-a-here *passage*
took shape. Everyone
told incompatible stories.
Everyone held to *here*
inconsolable memories.
Everyone marked
buried intensities of presence.
Different and similar outcomes *marked*
were obliterated. Disappeared.
Deemed incompatible.
Altered. *& buried*
Loss became gain;

gain compensated loss.
It will remain, even if said, unsaid.

"When the axe came into the forest, the trees thought, 'It's fine; that handle is one of us.'" What led to what? The incomparable, the scale off, the trans-located, exiled, awkward and alarmed, the clatter, the shattering, have all been part of our lives for so many years. This is what we have. Then you get tired. Then resigned. Then it becomes half noticed. Or less. Where then, abruptly,

thereupon,
many years later,
people ask each visitor:
"Have you crossed yet?" and say
"You should."
Meaning over to the other side. *check-point*
Though there was no particular news,
nothing to register except normal erosions,
but the whole was considered *normal*
something to see.
Shadows had already cast full sorts.
And still they fell.

Everyone's insomnia is marked. Who wants to reflect on this? You might cure insomnia by a very deep dream of sobbing. But that works for only one night. The ordinary is so ironic: such as cascades of rusted metal trash water-falling down the railroad cut. I mean where I do live. My eye core split and doubled. Now what? Sometimes things rest on mean-spirited technicalities. Cell phones do not work across the divided city nor the nation(s); that is, you can't place a call down the next block. Understanding and repairing were vague and then postponed. Yet now a little has started. We may never know. That's all. Why should I say more?

"Who would kill an orange tree?" *people*
Sometimes anyone.
It was a terrible way to be.
Here is her facing a life in
the autobiography of a visage *mirrored*
written by alternative ears and eyes.
She does not match up
with her doubled national flesh. Yet it looks like
she filmed herself in a mirror. She filmed
herself as doppelgänger. She filmed as a mourner. *other*
A dialogic implacable crush
of selves
sits shiva over the other *selves*
speaking on (or to)
the crossroads of those shattered bits.
"What is man's relation
to his/her own history?"

said someone with a lexical-
rhetorical flourish
of attempted fairness.
This place,
as they said
in the explanatory museum placard,
is a "bone of content."

For there is a nano-second of resonance, of reverberating networks of sound that indicates a meaning (or an illusion for a moment), even an oddity, beyond the jolly despair that might lead to nihilism if you simply "read the news." This nano-touch is called "the small." "The dot." "The person." Volta! Volta! Who can say what this is to be in time, this strangest space, for there is something enormous even inside the tiny spot of this smallish locale in which the thing called "I" (also m-it-e, or me and it) cruises its happenstance. But then, to hammer in this point, I heard of

that man who would never cross
(his wife told me this) because
he refused to show his passport
at Border Control
in what was (technically, for him)
his "own country."

At the actual checkpoint,
near the little maze and queue
where people cross over *line up*
carefully walking through,
someone had graffito'd
"No Borders"
as protest. So people read this *identity card*
on their way to the parallel ghetto
in the other half-city.
When you got that twice-stamped visa
like a high school hall pass signing you in
and then out,
it came from a state
that does not "officially exist." *"homeland"*
That itself means multiple things.
Questions: why, how, when, what and to whom.
It was like living
in a dream.

Which are the facts and which are the shadows? It is another knowledge of the country. "Don't try for peace (we HAVE peace). We want reconciliation." It was "a struggle between two historiographies...," someone noted. But it's clear that two were not enough. So "for starters," or "at least." Which is the door and which is the wall? Sometimes there is a sense of panic. One must record the sense of panic, the sense of grief, followed by the feeling of being snookered, lied to, manipulated. You have been honed by the chisel of it. Then became inured, numb. How much political irony can one person stand? "It's a textbook case." The Green Line became known by its other name: The Dead Zone.

Without her husband
she crossed every week
because certain groceries
were cheaper over there.
She found
streets that continued *crossed*
the streets on her side
ones she had always remembered,
the small places being the same, or
pretty much, just slightly shabbier
or maybe names changed to
other heroic names,
but there was the wall blocking everything; *cinder*
there was scrub in between and sagging houses.
Those too had names. *blocks*

Because presumed temporary,
the wall had been built shoddily
and without any irony.
People's (long-ago mapped)
houses and shops
were now trapped.
The sealed, grim properties
had begun to look
really terrible.

Attention: tourists/ visitors/ residents:
you are forbidden
snapshots.
"UN Buffer Zone.
No Photography.
No Litter Please."

Where is one's own sense of what happened? Can one access one's own history with others? Articulate its stakes? There is shame on every level. Shame for every side, and rage and shame for micro-twists of fractal sides. Twinned and tripled cataclysmic dreams bleed over all four margins down into the tight-sewn gutter of the page. The book tries to contain and present these bloody verges. It fails. Bad blood escapes.

The site was bolstered with sand bags,
watchtowers, with strategic
barrels filled with concrete *description*
and a general double loopiness
of barbed wire and razor wire
built for business.

There it is: *cannot*
The Border.
Zagging and tacking thru the city,
embodied and embedded
in unheimlich wandering.
Despite the time that had gone by, *convey*
the mix of boredom and menace
that emanates from guns
remains palpable.
But better not to seem
to think too much
or see too much
because the two acts
and their auras as you walk
might make you too visible.

Along the Dead Zone. *it*
can only run
as fast as one can run.
Some things cannot be outrun.
And sometimes
where we are right now
those very things
have all been done.
Such times have taken place.

Cross-quarter day
is halfway between solstices,
and just between solaces.
One throw of the dict
did not annulify
the chunk of fate,
nor definitional geographies of Treaties
nor hierarchies of Passports,
nor pious Conspiracies of Certitude.

Corners once protected
from sniper fire
where armed men
had hidden in concrete boxes and peered out
are now dirtied excrescences
surrounded by dried grass.
Twenty different brands of trashed
water bottles thrown into the Zone *zone*
cannot be cleaned up
because entering the scrub-between
could still get you shot.
So it's garbage-y
right through.
Like a vacant lot.

Never mind
the level of forgetting
and those condemned to remember,
nor strains of verb and noun
between forgetting
and remembering.
Each was on the verge of shifting over. *verge*
One side saw the Dead Zone
as temporary,
the other as permanent.
But the sides kept changing
which was which.
The stakes were such
that no one knew
how to calibrate all this.
To say
"reunify" was sometimes close.
Though people remain at odds *damages*
over sovereignty, alliances,
and control
("of the military").
There's also the contentious
writing of public history,
("school books"); there's
restitution or not
of houses and gardens that others
have lived in, fondly, planting,
weeding, making them their
very own for fifty-plus years.
How to calculate?
"Private Property?" "Reparations?"

"orange trees"

The cost involved the cost of words. There was also the question of which language, or both. Or yet another language – English. Like a fairy tale, this quest demanded the tracking of paths, where all signatory phosphorescence had faded and where the signs were often broken, left like shards. Is there a residue that remains? Mend? or sweep away? This poises on the sedimentation of micro-tones, on empathy for dark news read in the darkness with listening eyes, and with ears all inky, smudged by little shaking hands. Thanatos might take care of itself. It's desire that needs nurturing. "Change or Die TPYING." The P is Greek for how we would write R.

December 2011–April 2012

NOTES

The poem cites from Yiannis Papadakis, *Echoes from the Dead Zone: Across the Cyprus Divide*. London: I.B. Tauris & Co Ltd, 2005. Quotations from his work are italicized. There are also two citations (what I heard and wrote down) from the video by Kutlug Ataman, "1+1=1," 2002, concerning Cyprus, and seen in the Istanbul Modern Museum in 2011. A further push came from Mary Layoun, *Wedded to the Land? Gender, Boundaries, and Nationalism in Crisis*. Durham: Duke University Press, 2001; I cite a proverb she also cited. The "bone of content" is a phase I actually found on a museum placard. This poem also draws on a few comments made about a work by the Belgian artist Francis Alÿs. In 2004, Alÿs walked along the armistice border in Jerusalem, also known as "the green line." Alÿs used green paint to mark his démarche. See *Sometimes Doing Something Poetic Can Become Political And Sometimes Doing Something Political Can Become Poetic: The Green Line, Jerusalem 2004–2005* (New York: David Zwirner, s.d.). Donor drafts are 17, 36, 55, 74, and 93, that is: Unnamed, Cento, Quiptych, Wanderer and Romantic Fragment Poem. I am grateful to the hospitality of Evy Varsamopoulou and others.

BIO

Rachel Blau DuPlessis, poet, critic, and collagist, is the author of the multi-volume long poem *Drafts* (written 1986 through 2012). Post-*Drafts* poetry includes *Interstices* (2014), *Graphic Novella* (2015), *Days and Works* (2017), as well as *Numbers* (a collage poem from Materialist Press) and *Around the Day in 80 Worlds* (BlazeVOX), both slated for 2018, and *Life in Handkerchiefs*, a collage poem in 70 pages.

FIÓNA BOLGER

a compound of words

try to atomise wajalukinat
imagine each letter a string supplying
a side way to transubstantiation avoiding
the black hole of a lemon market
the consonants shifting, the click of the q—
Celtic fossils trickle down through the generations
d'yaknow it's all maya and we,
sala, must do penance
aadipowanga knee as you cruise for a bruise
crushed together we make juice

BIO

Fióna Bolger lives between Ireland and India. Her work has appeared in *Southword*, *The Brown Critique*, *Poetry Bus*, *The Chattahoochee Review* and others. With K. Srilata, she recently edited *All the Worlds Between* (Yoda Press, Delhi, 2017), a poetry project between Ireland and India. She is a co-ordinator of Dublin Writers' Forum and a member of the creative team of Outlandish Theatre Platform.

BEN BOREK

Homecoming Referendum Calypso

At Piccadilly was a grand illumination
Names went round in rotation
Some said we will get more employment
Others better house rent
Balloon went up too
I saw red and blue...
(Lord Beginner, "The General Election")

My little Pan Beginner
your name so foreign it's a dog's name here
though not yet blacklisted as unpatriotic
your startled dark-eyed mugshot
outgrown on both your red passports
after 15 years of autobahn and sleeper train
for you
        I flew
sucked up the terror of the void
beneath my feet from Chopin to Heathrow
the mad immensity of distances
above Berlin you waved a million clumsy times
your new front teeth
an umlaut over your busy double tongue
hidden and inscrutable in suspicious cloud
the Eiffel tower nearly pierced
our metal belly (or so I felt)
and I could not relax until the sunset faded
to traditional navy and the stars peeled away
at terminal 2 your sky-blue eyes were scrutinised
in a rictus of bureaucracy
(this photo is from half a lifetime ago)
If you had been born then in Piccadilly
My Mr Kickstarter
and had been waiting in the rain
with Dorota or Aisha or Tina or Tatiana
you would have sung to me
Tatusiu, nie wiem, o co chodzi
I would have held your hand
brooding anemone of curious fingers
Tak, synku, I am confused too.

BIO

Ben Borek grew up in London and now lives in Warsaw. He is author of the verse novel *Donjong Heights* and has read his work throughout Europe (which currently includes the UK). Another epic poem is coming soon from Boiler House Press.

ANDREA BRADY

The Sliding Door

There are refuges in all the blood, but masques
take their place for some, and turn
the pain of staying
put into an kind of germ
which might trace back to the fist
of the original cultivator, seeded
by the river. Here is one

masque, in which I feel the panels rattle
as the wind blows from Minersville
where one of mine was young and robbed
the pillars as the rivets blew. He was not
happy or well there, the girl he married
wrapped herself like a glass
vine on the stem of all this trouble.
They paid their anger and sorrow down, two
by two, for those who got it
onto the ship at the last minute
having just enough money for the papers.
Behind them is a town

I can't exactly see; even the colour
of the houses is up
for grabs, the voices in the shop and
footfalls on grass or paving imaginary.
And not seeing it makes
another masque, where the abstract virtues
are pinned to history by sequined stars.
A dream of being haunted by whistles
may be a dream of starvation, or getting knocked
up by cousins or the foamy priest.
Either way it resides
with us as a cloud does, internally lit
and of incalculable volume.

And was this past taking
my name to its birthplace the reason
for the stiff
upper lip, the lace curtains, Mass
raised over the kitchen table; did it explain to Jean
herself, banging around in the attic,
hissing gothic threats at her mother behind the
bolted door where she slept with dressings and preserves?
She sat on piles of newspaper, doing absolutely
nothing. No one did
anything until she lay herself
down and gave birth to that enormous rock
that ate her life and 'brilliant' mind. What refuge
is there even at home or in the lift
where like my father I am now afraid to go?

But I am here, rich with empire, cycling
the streets decorated by sugar and slavery.
My idea was not new, just executable;
I thought I'd go free
my children of this terrible organism
that rises even in the place where my love is wet
and good. But even here it found me,
the refuge is already a body soaked and ashed.

To be clear I am trying to tell you
something original but I haven't got the data;
green and subdivided
fields and patterned knit for the washed-up dead
have no hold on
dreams where I find myself
somewhere else, combing seeds
from my daughter's corncrake hair. I pass
on to her nothing deliberately but this
story fires the night in which we sleep together,
and when he wakes my son says
the men without faces are going extinct.

No one at home could finish the story either. They drew a tree
on paper, trying to be firm where the joints were threaded.
Someone has that paper, and half of them are gone,
but what they couldn't deliver
lives wherever these human cells
stem and proliferate: from birding in Wisconsin,
around the corner, to Istanbul or here,
we ran but couldn't hide our deviations
in the shadow of an intellectual or a lonely silencer.

Behind the barn and the house, at the cellar door,
where the grass smelled thick and healthful,
something had grown before the house was put.
The vesication of its bark showed
where lightning hit it just the once:
the cloud released its charge but did not go blank.
It hung over us and spoke in what
we couldn't hear even as language. It carries
the code for everything that can't be run off
or covered by fictions in the traditional blood.

BIO

Andrea Brady's books of poetry include *The Strong Room* (Crater, 2016), *Dompteuse* (Bookthug, 2014), *Cut from the Rushes* (Reality Street, 2013), *Mutability: scripts for infancy* (Seagull, 2012), *Wildfire: A Verse Essay on Obscurity and Illumination* (Krupskaya, 2010) and *Vacation of a Lifetime* (Salt, 2001). She is Professor of Poetry at Queen Mary University of London, where she runs the Centre for Poetry and the Archive of the Now. She is also co-publisher of Barque Press.

SERENA BRAIDA

Dragon Piece

When I arrived at the belvedere and saw the scene in front of me,
I'm not sure whether I kissed Frank on the mouth before, after, or because
of the dragon's upper half, its large spiny back, emerging from the water.
And I'm not sure whether it finished surfacing while I was walking there,
or if it was already out and perfectly still, the incandescence of its body
clashing with the sunset, making the air nearby recoil
and darken.

The dragon corresponded to a long narrow island, a corridor into the sea.
Its double nature of animal and land was the only thing I knew.
But I didn't kiss Frank out of fear. You see, we'd slept together before,
 and I was back
to being sexual with boys because that's what you do,
especially when they know you.
Sea rocks framed the scene, little waves going crazy around
the exciting monster and all.

Frank seemed as unfazed as the dragon: caught in a state of stolid
 meditation, even, kissing
me back like a star in a silent movie, his mouth
placed perfectly against mine and softly locked.
I tried to wet my lips, to no avail. He was pressed against me with not even
 a speck
of lust, or sympathy, it seemed.

The dragon had the presence of a callous ruler. Its precious scales looked
 sharp and dangerous
because they were.
Its face was bang on that of a Chinese dragon, long and flexed, with
 technicolour
skin, four legs and a snake-like shape which you could glimpse under
 the water.

I leaned over the balustrade and looked at the clear fruity waves.
Orange, pomegranate and strawberry waves going to
and fro. The white, pebbled country road I took
reminded me of the flora and gravel roads of Elba, the island
in the Tyrrhenian Sea's Tuscan Archipelago National Park,
known for its beaches and as Napoleon
Bonaparte's first place of exile. Like some places in Elba,
it also reminded me of somewhere faraway, like Cuba
or the Jurassic. To see a dragon here was in a way sensible.

I wanted to shake Frank out of his affectionate torpor but he kept acting oblivious to the miraculous presence in front of us. He looked at me and pressed his fingers on my collarbones and neck, smiling privately. I let him touch me ever so softly and I ignored him, even though I was responsive to his touch and wanted more: more tongue, more hands, more everything. We didn't say a word.

The dragon stares at us with black eyes like buttons.
As the light changes with the clouds and the passing
of time, its face morphs into Marvin Gaye's for a split second
before getting back to scales and dragon cheeks.
I blink. I sway and rock with Frank's hands around my hips
until the dragon does it again, like
a lenticular print figure of Donald Duck. Is this real, I wonder,
and my faith wavers as Frank marvels at my fingernails
like a champagne sommelier in the Marne
department. As if to respond, the colossal reptile moves his tail
with grace, splashing not a drop, divine motion
not less holy than the Perpetual Virginity of Mary.

Animal?
Animal & God, I think.
From the Egyptian
pantheon or a pantheon adjacent, animal, god and fairly silly,
mocking me with a memory as impersonal, common and tender
    as a Motown face.
Like other gods this one doesn't really know me
despite its alleged omniscience: it should have known that
to make me open and recipient like a vessel
I need at least Otis Redding's face.

If an animal then sex, emotions, a personal history and complex
neuropatterns. If a God, a monolithic impassible backdrop
containing the climates the DNAs the dead and the fairy forts
without being moved by any of it.
But if an animal & a god then truly incomprehensible and worthy.
I am ready to genuflect, shave my head and fly away.

Frank's presence feels more and more inconsequential, perhaps
    ridiculous, instrumental
in the most derivative of ways; thin,
like an image from a porn clip that I liked and that I sometimes conjure
to get off. I am all flexed and purring for the dragon, but bored to death
    by this person who touches me.
But then he speaks,

When I came here all I could do, day in and day out,
was staying in and playing video-games. I played games
of intellect and strategic thinking which gave me
purpose. It wasn't a good idea
to get out,
so I thought I'd better keep busy. For releasing my tensions I'd play
a soft core POV Far West
game in which the house maid would strip a garment
every time you managed to send a peppercorn
in her cleavage. This was sometimes hard to do
because she continuously moved around, beating
up the pillows, sweeping the floor and
emptying the bedpans. The name tag on the top right of the screen informed us
that she was "Madeleine".
Sometimes I talked to her. It feels lonely in my basement room, I told her once,
and I don't know how much longer I'll have to stay here;
I have nightmares every night: inspectors come to the door
asking for my passport, and hand out the card in which I must declare what
I am here for, what is my occupation, how long do I plan to stay in England
for. Their faces are of course
my face. Next I realise I'm stark naked,
unemployed and undocumented and it is too late
to do anything, run to the Blackmarket and source
a permit, or get my lawyer uncles to forge me a backstory.
At this point the inspectors are in nazi uniforms and shoot me in the head,
or are about to, their straight arms pointed at my cranium, and I wake up in
a cold sweat.
Usually by this point Madeleine is in her panties,
white thick cotton with a laced rim sporting a wet stain at the front.
The game is interactive: I am not the only player
in the room. Madeleine is always alone fending
off a hoard of lone players, split in two categories: the competitive ones
who enjoy the hunt and want to be the first to undress her, and the peeping
Toms who love
to see her chased and humiliated by other men above all.
When the last peppercorn plunges between Madeleine's big
breasts she moans one last time, the clumsy camera closing up on her flushed
face, and the game is over. It's fairly innocent, and I normally enjoy it after
reading the morning papers, whose interesting features I circle
with my pencil, both to exercise
my English and to keep track of the political climate around
my presence here. The most recurring word
is "Brexit", with its derivatives in second place.
I keep a rough timeline
to try and understand the causality of it all but I am not a good analyst,
nor a good reader. The margins of my newspapers are full
of interrogation marks and only sometimes I sense
the outrage mounting, that is when I understand
what I am actually reading.

I studied Opera singing and would have never imagined myself in such a sorry state.

He stops there and fixes his eyes on the dragon.
And the dragon shockingly closes its black eyes and starts opening
  his mouth.
The sound of its mandibles is like the clattering of a train. Franks stands
  erect next to me and his hands have let
go of my hips. The dragon's mouth opens completely and you can see
it's a cave inside, but not much else because it's nighttime now.
  Frank lets go
of everything and doesn't look at me, whom he has been adoring so.
The dragon might be a passage,
it might be able to erase the mark of illegality and vouch for
our political futures, I reason, as Frank takes a step forward and is
  plunged into the gaping darkness;
it might make me the holder of a dual citizenship, make me glamorous
and free, able to enjoy the best of both
lands,
to drink the water of one
and watch the life of the other, to float
angelic over the airports!
But as I try to dive in
the dragon clamps his jaws and pirouettes back
into the sea.

I start waiting, covered with dew.

BIO

Serena Braida is a poet, writer, singer, actor and voice practitioner working in Italian and English. Her writing has appeared or is forthcoming in *Hotel*, *Orlando*, *Hotdog*, *Nuovi Argomenti* and others, and the narrative non-fiction anthology *Quello che hai amato* (UTET 2015). Performances have included the Festival of Italian Literature in London, Goldsmiths LitLive, European Poetry Night, Royal Albert Hall's Elgar Room, and Muscovado (Burnt Out Theatre). She co-curates the Locomotrix series at Housmans Radical Bookshop. Serena's pamphlet *Blue Sheila* will be published by dancing girl press in 2018.

WILSON BUENO, TRANSLATED BY ERÍN MOURE

from *Paraguayan Sea*

La fatigue des métals, l'oeuf de l'oegg du scorpion, the lurking, the tacit meat made a yoke, inheritance of our elders, what's spent, les years, moitié ville, moitié vie, the scorched crossing, rivière ébulliante de cinquante winteres, the dark face of exhausted blood, kidneys already failing, la pression artérial, nettle and paprika, the cape or end-point, the sea, le cap, la mer, the facte and the cape of good hope, those lost in the brambles, the fact, the arc du sinistre, les pallid ones, dusk, our chambre, notre maison, ñemomirí, the humblest lamp, our bed, the amputated sexe that still itches. And I choke it, the flaccid, le flou, the hollow of the hollowe of the middle, it's all in half-light. And there's worse: demain il faut que je me chante a new zany chanson, and maybe I will feel as complète as all the stations of the Darkest Hour.

Aquidauana, Dorados, Puerto Soledad, cities of rivières and dust, of bones languid at exactely two in the afternoon, sièste et feu, it dumbfounds us febrile in an imponderable viscosité, it all goes sweaty and sucks, it all blanches creamy in a death shudder of innards éclatés plus the gut-ache full of scorn and vomit, the tree does not move tout seul, the taste of sex on the tongue, la langue, le sexe in multiple languages, ayvu, almost like a deflowered rose, death and sex don't talk but how splendide sex feels – the belly that lifts its hackles, resounding tremour of the skin touched par desire and coma, the air, all the air as it was, choked, a thirst that can't be slaked by water and the sudden fear just as, after un peu, le dur soleil could dry out les rues where reign only bordels and bars de port – dead and void from this fatigue de personne et de no-one. Aquidauana. How tristes, how mélancoliques sont les soirs qui s'attardent brûlants et encore mutes, notre maison des femmes, our house of women, on the main drag on the frontière, our bedrooms suffocantes, sheet and sex and cette punishing heat. All of it in ce temps-ci, right now, I can't forget, so it makes up a kind of destiny – a way of suffering less, that God gives us so only today can we recognize cette inclination we have to martyrdom and jubilation. Deux couteaux et two blades. May Thy great hand forever save us so the definitive crystal or its splendid shard doesn't sink in our souls, in the foam of blood and glass. The sea tinged ruby. Paraïpieté. Pará.

NOTES

Guaraní *elucidic*tionary:

Ayvu: the human word, le mot
Ñemomirí: humiliation; to be humiliated
Paraĩpieté: the abyss of the sea
Pará: sea (in old Guaraní); hue of several colours; polychromatic spaces

BIOS

Wilson Bueno (d. 2010) was one of Brazil's most influential and beloved contemporary writers, editors, and journalists. His *Paraguayan Sea* (*Mar Paraguayo*), a sensation of border crossings of languages, genders, and geographies, has been constantly republished in Brazil, Argentina, Chile and Mexico since its first appearance in Brazil in 1992. It appeared for the first time in full in the northern hemisophere in 2017 in the French-migratory bouche-queered English of Erín Moure.

Erín Moure has published over forty books of poetry, essays, memoir, and translations and co-translations from French, Spanish, Galician, and Portuguese into English. Her latest works are *Planetary Noise: Selected Poetry of Erín Moure* (Wesleyan U Press, 2017, ed. Shannon Maguire), *Sitting Shiva on Minto Avenue, by Toots* (New Star Books, 2017), and a translation into Frenglish of the Portunol of Brazilian Wilson Bueno's *Paraguayan Sea* (Nightboat Books, New York, 2017). Moure lives in Montreal.

JAMES BYRNE

And still they don't go!

Calais wears the snakefoot of Boreas.
Coldest wind, nebular wind. Temper
of a falling wall. Calais dehumanises *us*
from *they*, flesh from flesh. The hunter
gathers her to go, but where? No Zephyr
in the West, no water in this jungle.
The boy inside a shipping container
holds up a picture of his dead uncle.

BIO

James Byrne is a poet, editor and translator. He co-translated and co-edited *Bones Will Crow: 15 Contemporary Burmese Poets* (Arc Publications, 2012) and is the co-editor of *Atlantic Drift: An Anthology of Poetry and Poetics* (Edge Hill University Press/Arc, 2017). His most recent poetry collection is *Everything Broken Up Dances* (Tupelo, 2015).

KIMBERLY CAMPANELLO

English is

nimble needing
some assistance

an aristocrat says
pleased to meet you

try to focus
on the other side

the baby's hand
grazes a stone wall

why should I explain *all*
the fuss over gender pronouns

ample and
virtuosic

wheeled onto the stage
we cheer

an old phrase say
where's it from

it's wet, cold
late 16th century

requiring no
security

when someone's
just arrived

hold my baby high
so she can see

BIO

Kimberly Campanello's poetry books include *Imagines* (New Dublin Press), *Strange Country* (The Dreadful Press), *Consent* (Doire Press) and *Hymn to Kālī* (Eyewear Publishing). *MOTHERBABYHOME* is forthcoming from zimZalla Avant Objects. A selection from *MOTHERBABYHOME* recently appeared in Laudanum Publishing's *Chapbook Anthology Volume Two* alongside work by Frances Lock and Abigail Parry. In September 2018, she will join the School of English at the University of Leeds as Lecturer in Creative Writing.

J. R. CARPENTER

Once Upon A Tide: A Script For Live Performance

To be read under cover of ['canvas', 'oilskin', 'tarp'], under ['half light', 'shadow', 'shelter'], cover of ['fog', 'gloom', 'murk', 'new moon'].

Once upon a ['high', 'spring', 'slack', 'neap'] tide we ['drifted', 'coasted', 'slid', 'slipped', 'tacked'] past a ['bay', 'beach', 'cape', 'cove', 'dune', 'lagoon'], our ship ['brought us hither', 'a brave vessel', 'tight and yar and bravely rigged', 'most strangely landed', 'so near the bottom run'].

On the ['lower', 'main', 'middle', 'poop', 'side', 'quarter'] deck two ['old', 'young', 'slim'] ['friends', 'boatswains', 'sailors'] ['hunched', 'perched', 'crouched', 'sat'] ['mending nets', 'baiting lines', 'spinning yarns', 'twisting tales']. From their ['accents', 'apparel', 'dress', 'gestures', 'looks', 'movements'] I ['guessed', 'gathered', 'suspected', 'assumed'] that ['they', 'both', 'the pair', 'the two of them'] had ['been born', 'come', 'hailed', 'sailed', 'journeyed'] from ['braver', 'better known', 'far', 'fairer', 'gentler'] shores, ['clearly', 'surely', 'obviously'] none so ['barren', 'bleak', 'harsh', 'haunted', 'wicked', 'wild'] as these.

As the bells rang for ['morning', 'forenoon', 'first dog'] watch the ['quieter', 'slighter'] one said:

['We are oppressed with travel.', 'We are all sea-swallowed', 'our garments drenched.', 'The sea mocks our frustrated search.', 'Every drop of water sears against us.', 'The sea, mounting, dashes the fire out.', 'A thousand furlongs of sea', 'the washing of ten tides.', 'The still-closing waters', 'will shortly fill the reasonable shore.', 'They hoist us to cry to the sea', 'the last of our sea-sorrow.', 'I would have sunk the sea within the earth', 'plunged in the foaming brine', 'the ooze of the salt deep.', 'I shall no more to sea.', 'The sea cannot drown me.', 'I am standing water.']

['One bell', 'Two bells', 'Two bells sounded, a pause, one bell', 'Two bells sounded, a pause, two bells', 'Two bells sounded, a pause, two bells, pause, one bell', 'Two bells sounded, a pause, two bells, pause, two bells', 'Two bells sounded, a pause, two bells, pause, two bells, pause, one bell', 'Two bells, a pause, two bells, pause, two bells, pause, two bells'].

In the ['near', 'middle', 'faint', 'far'] distance the ['bulk', 'hulk', ''ghost', 'shadow', 'vision'] of an island loomed. The ['fairer', 'slower', 'sharper'] one ['leaned', 'gestured', 'peered', 'pointed'] in this direction.

After ['a pause', 'a sigh', 'the bells', 'some time', 'what seemed an eternity] the other replied:

['I am king of this country.', 'This fearful country!', 'I could recover the shore.', 'But is this not near shore?', 'How came we ashore?', 'Unto these yellow sands.', 'Come alive to land.', 'Have you no mouth by land?', 'Here shall I die ashore.', 'Here in this island,', 'We lie in an odd angle, arms in a sad knot.', 'This island will not let you believe certain things.', 'Be not afraid, this island is full of noises.', 'The folly of this island!', 'Most opportune place.']

isle: '#{isle}',

[['Enter like a water-nymph', 'Enter playing and singing', 'Solemn and strange music', 'Enter several strange shapes', 'Gentle actions of salutation', 'A quaint device', 'Soft music', 'Solemn music', 'Enter divers Spirits in shape of dogs and hounds', 'They sing', 'Song', 'A strange, hollow, and confused noise', 'A noise of hunters heard', 'A cry within', 'A frantic gesture', 'A tempestuous noise of thunder and lightning heard', 'Enter a Shipmaster', 'Enter a boatswain', 'Enter Mariners wet']].

['Come', 'Open your mouth', 'A word', 'O, but one word', 'O, wonder', 'O, defend me', 'Doth thy other mouth call me?', 'Monstrous', 'Mercy', 'Mercy on us', 'Alack, for mercy', 'Fury', 'Silence', 'Why, I said nothing!', 'Ha, ha', 'Oh ho', 'Hark', 'Here', 'A most strange story', 'The story of my life', 'Please you, draw near', 'What cheer?', 'How now?', 'All lost', 'Away'] the ['leaner', 'meaner', 'stronger'] one ['croaked', 'spoke', 'whispered', 'exclaimed']. Would you that soon the ['flush', 'half', 'hurricane'] deck be ['standing', 'drowning', 'drenched'] in ['cold', 'mist', 'magic']?

['The strangeness of this business.', 'These are not natural events.', 'I raised the tempest.', 'I called forth the mutinous winds.', 'I bedimmed the noontide sun.', 'I put the wild waters in this roar.', 'A plague upon this howling!', 'Oh, the dreadful thunderclaps!', 'The fire and cracks of sulphurous roaring.', 'Run upon the sharp wind.', 'wound the wind.', 'a mind to sink', 'It is foul weather in us all.']

'The ['sea sorrow', 'mist', 'tempest'] by that ['island', 'hour', 'tide', 'time', 'watch'] was ['certainly', 'clearly', 'unquestionably'] ['uncommon', 'unnatural', 'unsettled', 'grim'], but was that any ['help', 'use'], that ['kind', 'sort', 'type'] of answer? The ['bizarre', 'awkward', 'odd', 'strange'] ness of their ['speech', 'exchange', 'yarn', 'narration'] put a ['cold', 'heavy', 'helpless', 'listless', 'restless']ness in me. In the ['foul', 'frigid', 'humid', 'heavy', 'salt'] air a ['bolt rope', 'cable', 'cuddy lamp', 'riding light', 'lantern'] ['creaked', 'groaned', 'swayed', 'listed']. Under cover of ['canvas', 'murk', 'shadow', 'shelter'] I ['loitered', 'crouched', 'sat', 'stooped']. Long I ['listened', 'waited', 'watched', 'wondered'] ['closely', 'quietly', 'keenly'].

[['Exit.', 'Exeunt.', 'They vanish.']]

BIO

J. R. Carpenter is a Canadian-born UK-based artist, writer, performer, and researcher. Her pioneering works of digital literature have been exhibited, published, performed, and presented in journals, galleries, museums, and festivals around the world. She is a winner of the CBC Quebec Writing Competition (2003 & 2005), the QWF Carte Blanche Quebec Award (2008), the Expozine Alternative Press Award for Best English Book (2008), the Dot Award for Digital Literature (2015), and the New Media Writing Prize (2016). http://luckysoap.com

MARY JEAN CHAN

Dress

The same uniform for twelve years. A white skirt, blue collar, blue belt, blue hem. A dark, no-nonsense kind of blue. White the color of snowfall in Eden. You washed it every single day, made sure you ate in small bites, always wore an extra pad so none of the blood could seep through. You began wearing that dress at the age of six, your skin haunted by the British flag, so you could be *Chinese with English characteristics*. Each time you wore that uniform, you shut your body up. Some girls wore theirs short, discolored, tight. As Head Girl, you reported them to the Headmistress' Office for inappropriate behavior, kept your own dress at just the right length.

Most mornings, you see the face of a boy in the mirror. You expect to fall in love with him, someday. Meanwhile, your fingers brush the wrist of another girl as you jostle into the assembly hall, and you understand that sin was never meant to be easy, only sweet. What memory might light up the pond you sat beside in dreams, eyeing so much depth it would be years before you dared? What curvature of tongue might you taste, as if another's breath were blessing? One night, you find yourself back there, kneeling beside the pond. You dream. A voice whispers *Hell is not other people*. You slip into the water, stripped of the glowing dress you wore for thousands of days.

Hybridity

The reader stares at my 皮肤
and asks: why don't you write

in 中文? I tell them: 殖民主义
meant that I was brought up in

your image. Let us be honest –
had I not learnt 英语 and come

to your shores, you wouldn't be
reading this poem at all. Did you

think it was by chance that I learnt
your 语言 for decades, until I knew

it better than the 母语 I dream in?
Is anything an accident these days?

Dear reader, you are lucky to have
been the centre of my 宇宙 for so

long. My country is called 中国
because it had equally grandiose

notions about its reflection in the
漩涡 of humanity. A taxi driver

in Shanghai told me that my lover
is from 大英帝国. How does that

make me feel? Can you tell me
what it is that I should do next?

BIO

Mary Jean Chan's pamphlet, *A Hurry of English*, is published by ignitionpress (2018), with a selection in *Carcanet New Poetries VII*. Mary Jean was shortlisted for the 2017 Forward Prize for Best Single Poem and won the 2017 PSA/Journal of Postcolonial Writing Postgraduate Essay Prize, the 2017 Psychoanalysis and Poetry Competition, the 2017 Poetry Society Members' Poetry Competition, and the 2016 Oxford Brookes International Poetry Competition (ESL). Mary Jean is a Ledbury Emerging Poetry Critic and an Editor at *Oxford Poetry*. Her debut collection is forthcoming from Faber & Faber (2019).

CHE

Departure

Part I

he tells me things have changed again

he tells me now it's wednesday not tuesday

time is a relative thing is it?

I'm sick of the uncertainty i love it

i'm not fond of your disorders that is why i'm leaving

i want certainty
i want knowledge
but neither
is forthcoming

so in order to find love i leave everyone behind and because i depend on the order in things i have not a lot of things and it leaves room for chaos and so i could be secure in the future i plan it all out and know in advance that it won't go according to plan

i will not blame you i want to
you have so much to be blamed for

you are immaterial now
in the cosmic scheme of things so i'm leaving

i won't ask more questions of you or any other

i am tired

i won't ask for control because i'm leaving

your hypocrisies won't be rectified i'm leaving
again

i'm leaving in silence

i've run out of metaphors here
there is no inspiration here
divine or otherwise

it's a good thing

i'm leaving

Part II

what would it be like on the plane
leaving   after i've left   what would i be feeling?

fear surely
more fear than i felt   the first time   flying in the opposite direction

what is new   is never feared
what is familiar   always

fear is a learned behaviour

fear comes with age   and so

I shall be flying back   with a secret stash   stowed away in the
          of fears   luggage cabin

and make the best of it on the go

now it will always be on the go

walls and roofs and furniture and future   have all been blown away
          by a typhoon of my own making

i'm returning   turning towards home turning to home.less.ness
          turning to hope.less.ness

one step   one heartbeat   *there are ways of living as yet*
at a time now   at a time   *undiscovered and i*
am a voyager into my own
unknowns unique
or not so unique
captain cook or barbarossa
zheng he or ibn batuta
bent on neither commerce
nor slaughter and the world is
not interested in one not interested
in neither this
Is going to be interesting

fear   is wonderful

BIO

che was born in 1986 in Bangalore, Karnataka, and spent almost eight years in London, UK. She currently resides in Kerala, India, working as an ESL teacher mostly to nurses seeking an IELTS qualification that would allow them to live and work in better-paid 'first world' nations. Some of these nurses are recruited by the NHS, if they get the desired scores. They study English night and day and spend thousands of Indian rupees taking the same exams repeatedly in order to be better treated in what they believe to be 'developed' countries. che does what she can to help them along.

MATTHEW CHEESEMAN

Bruno Schulz

When he spoke he twisted his right arm up towards his right shoulder and then waggled his thumb forwards from the wrist, as if he was trying to knock something off his shoulder. It was an unusual movement, uncontrolled, as if he was twisting into himself, his whole body involved in the effort.

He was pale and wore glasses. He wore green and brown military clothes with a non-combat cut. A small man with long dreadlocks. He was older then us. Not anymore of course, but back then, he was a year or two older and that mattered. For a long time I couldn't remember what he studied, classics perhaps? Classics at a Cambridge college.

He smoked too much marijuana, that was evident, but there was nothing more to it then that. Who wouldn't smoke too much marijuana? These were the days before anxiety had found its way into what it meant to be young. Before anxiety became obligatory. We had no idea.

Friends of mine bought drugs from him. I might have brought drugs off him. He wasn't a dealer, he had a connection. We would talk a lot. He would say, 'yeah man, no way man' and make analogies whilst gesturing in that way with his thumb.

He was not a figure of ridicule. He was a man of learning and wide reading, evident intelligence and dark experience. His conversation was eccentric and unusual and interesting. He once told me about walking through a car crash in the early hours of the morning. Cars turned over, broken glass, blood. I remember him describing how he picked his way through the crash; I remember his wide-eyed suspicion that it had happened just for him. That he had caused it to happen, somehow, that disaster was drawn to him. He had no interest in cars and engines but they had an interest in him.

He moved with the same bobbing and twisting that affected his thumb, the rhythms of anxiety, perhaps, to describe it for today. He was apologetic, not looking to be in the world, certainly not wanting to be seen. He walked in a diminished manner.

There was no sex. Or he kept this buried within him, if it was there at all. I did ask, I remember and he evaded the question, presented himself otherwise. I couldn't work out whether he thought he didn't deserve it or whether he didn't want it.

I remember one of us saying 'He probably won't be around for long. He won't be alive in ten years' time.' Not that long after his lung collapsed and we did not see him for some time. Well ever, actually. For a long time I thought he actually was dead. There were no means of getting in touch. I only had a name and an old college and that was not enough. I thought he might have hidden his tracks. I would look for him, every year or so, perform searches from an incomplete memory. He never emerged on social media. He was one of those characters so ridiculous – the wrong word – incredible – that he only seemed possible in a certain environment at a certain time.

He lived at night. He would come in the early hours and leave late, walking back to wherever he slept. We knew no other people who also knew him, no life that intersected with his, nothing outside of our late night discussions. Everything would begin with 'yeah man, no way man' and he would move his thumb in that strange inward arc, vibrating as he said, 'no way,' and then he would connect thoughts with stoned logic, beautiful stoned logic connecting ideas and concepts, conversing with fascination and a wide, endless reach.

I had never heard of Bruno Schulz until he brought him into our lives. He did this consciously. He would refer to him, reference him. He would hold Schulz up as the sort of literature that was worth reading. There was a copy of *The Street of Crocodiles* in the pocket of his army jacket. I remember it out on the Formica table, lying with the packs of cigarettes and beer cans. It was read as people drank and smoked and talked. Later that year we all bought a copy and read them at home in the holidays. Sophisticated. Our copies marked a certain respect.

The connection vanished on graduation, along with those other acquaintances that didn't quite make it to the purposeful exchange of details. If he wasn't dead I was convinced that he remained in the university system somewhere – not because he particularly talked about his academic work but because it was hard to imagine him doing anything else. He did not seem destined for any life that made strong demands on appearance or punctuality. Not because he couldn't meet them, but because he didn't want to. There was a determined side to his character. He would be how he was, or he would not exist.

He would appear whenever Schulz was mentioned or recalled. The two were linked. I certainly encountered Schulz more then I encountered him. There was the stop-motion film by the Quay Brothers that I picked up on VHS just as VHS was on the way out. There was the play that I never saw but heard about. There was the epigraph in China Miéville's novel *The city & the city*. Occasional mentions in the press. And I myself would read Schulz from time to time, in much the same way that I had as an undergraduate, reading passages, sometimes aloud to friends, sometimes to myself, often for longer than I planned to. These readings and reminders would send me to the internet to search for him. I think I may have phoned his old college at one point to inquire. Or perhaps I only thought of doing that. Certainly, throughout all this time – twenty years – I found no trace, no mention online.

Not knowing was a kind of memorial. He returns, information absent, information not known, search incomplete. I would read Schulz whenever I moved house, finding his book again, stopping packing so that I could read and remember the way he wrote a sentence. The intricacy of the metaphors built upon metaphors threaded through extraordinary characters and circumstances. The sentence as journey. It was after one such house move that I finally found him. He fell through an academic database. He did survive in universities. And it was Classics. Cambridge and Copenhagen. He worked between those cities, mainly on Greek, but Latin too, even Danish. There was a light trace, a gentle publication record. Once I unearthed one thing, it led to another.

I suppose I stalked him. Not that there is anything wrong about that – stalking is a default mode, a way of imagining that emanates from information. I discovered his thesis, his published papers. He wrote about language change. He wrote about coins and Sicily. He wrote about lost vowels and once presumed consonants. He wrote about the later Roman Empire, about periods of change and flux.

There are parallels in the mix of languages and political systems, in the loss and change, in the attention to language and the fragility of circumstances that support writing. He survived on post-doctoral scholarships and temporary relationships with institutions. Perhaps this is through choice, perhaps through necessity. I don't know. Stalking does not provide contexts.

They both wrote. They both teach. Schulz's books will always be on my shelf. He is at home now. I will continue to read him, to dip in now and again, before or after I move house. The other remains in a different way, more and less than the words.

BIO

Matthew Cheeseman is Senior Lecturer in Creative Writing at University of Derby. He runs Spirit Duplicator, a small press (spiritduplicator.org). His handle on Twitter is @eine.

IRIS COLOMB

Interlude

vague
innocent
passable
distant
patient
humble
banal
adaptable
amateur
suspect
distinct
enviable
partial
tangible
inexact
extravagant
succinct
justifiable
dissonant
susceptible
grotesque
correct
capable
original
indigent
agile
indolent
monotone
convivial
diligent
immature
pertinent
incorrect
infantile
imminent
influent
morose
estimable
antisocial
impertinent
moral
effervescent
sociable
arrogant
territorial
indulgent

excellent
commercial
dissident
impeccable
irritant
discordant
optimal
insoluble
unique
sublime
astringent
ignorant
intelligent
insolent
important
accessible
aberrant
incompatible
urgent
intense
immense
lamentable
glacial
immoral
incandescent
interminable
militant
indispensable
minuscule
stagnant
crucial
inadmissible
marginal
dominant
hostile
inconsolable
vital
cruel
incomparable
certain
dictatorial
horrible
primordial
insatiable
inimitable
insupportable

pestilent
inexcusable
radical
impossible
principal
vibrant
abominable
violent
indubitable
vain
permanent
invincible
permanent
vain
indubitable
violent
abominable
vibrant
principal
impossible
radical
inexcusable
pestilent
insupportable
inimitable
insatiable
primordial
horrible
dictatorial
certain
incomparable
cruel
vital
inconsolable
hostile
dominant
marginal
inadmissible
crucial
stagnant
minuscule
indispensable
militant
interminable
incandescent
immoral

glacial
lamentable
immense
intense
urgent
incompatible
aberrant
accessible
important
insolent
intelligent
ignorant
astringent
sublime
unique
insoluble
optimal
discordant
irritant
impeccable
dissident
commercial
excellent
indulgent
territorial
arrogant
sociable
effervescent
moral
impertinent
antisocial
estimable
morose
influent
imminent
infantile
incorrect
pertinent
immature
diligent
convivial
monotone
indolent
agile
indigent
original

capable
correct
grotesque
susceptible
dissonant
justifiable
succinct
extravagant
inexact
tangible
partial
enviable
distinct
suspect
amateur
adaptable
banal
humble
patient
distant
passable
innocent
vague

Instructions for Interlude

To be read together / separately • To be read simultaneously / intermittently • To be read at the same time / at different times • To be read in a French & English speaking space / a French speaking space / an English speaking space / none of the above • To be read in French & in English simultaneously / French & English intermittently / in French / in English / none of the above • To be read by readers who know each other well / readers who know each other / readers who have met before / readers who met for the reading / readers who met at the reading / readers who haven't met / none of the above • To be read with the same words in both languages at the same time / the same words in each language at different times / different words in both languages at the same time / different words in each language at different times / none of the above • To be read by French & English speakers simultaneously / French & English speakers intermittently / French & non English speakers simultaneously / French & non English speakers intermittently / non French speakers & English speakers simultaneously / non French speakers & English speakers intermittently / non French speakers & non English speakers simultaneously / non French speakers & non English speakers intermittently / none of the above • To be read for a French & English speaking audience in a French & English speaking space / a French & English speaking audience in a French speaking space / a French & English speaking audience in an English speaking space / a French speaking audience in a French & English speaking space / a French speaking audience in an English speaking space / a French speaking audience in a French speaking space / an English speaking audience in a French & English speaking space / an English speaking audience in a French speaking space / an English speaking audience in an English speaking space / none of the above

BIO

Iris Colomb is a French poet, translator, artist, and curator based in London. Her work has been exhibited at the National Poetry Library, and in Donetsk and Versailles. Her poems have been published in *Pocket Litter* and *Datableed*, and her co-translation (with Elliot Koubis) of Guillaume Apollinaire's *The Stories and Adventures of the Baron d'Ormesan* came out in 2017. Iris has been resident artist and poet at the Centre for Recent Drawing, is art editor of *Haverthorn*, and a member of the collective No Such Thing. She also curates experimental live events that link poetry, film, visual arts, sound, and design.

GIOVANNA COPPOLA

The place around you the place inside of you the place outside of you over there

anywhere but here and when
you go there you don't want
to be there just
where your gut says to be
you're a
woman in constant
rotation
you want to be in
relation to a
place not to a person
you want to be related to
the place where you
come from

you come from the past

the manoeuvring of the gears
running in reverse
the shouts of
recognition the sweat
you melt in
without trying and
you don't have to keep
your mouth
shut a half pack of
cigarettes the rough
fig leaf
you got the
sun hitting
your tits and white
peaches for breakfast and
the hustle for
making money and
the small town
questioning your
solitary walks tears
splashing on the pines
salt water
in the cracks of your
skin soaping up your
privates in the bidet

you have to snatch this
place holding
the dark corners at
the throat

this is what
is your own, related to
this place

you're
trying to bring your
parents back to
life what they
left behind is not
banality you
have to write it
down you have to
make this
place a myth or
else what remains is the
heartache and
anger and futility and
some dated
Italian restaurant
in Poughkeepsie, NY
that dishes
out dead dreams

BIO

Giovanna Coppola is an American poet and writer. After living in London for 10 years, she recently moved to Naples, Italy.

ANNE LAURE COXAM

The male and the female poet go to the surgery in exciting times

the female poet reads a book
and while she's reading the book
she's thinking she wants to read it again

the female poet sees doctor Cash
the male poet sees doctor Penny
see the chart in the surgery hall
the chances were not very high

this afternoon the female poet is reading
bits of Jennifer
's book

  it's nice to read a book
  by someone you know
the male poet agrees

the pain is there
and there
and there

the female poet sees doctor Cash
because of a fungal infection
on her toe nail
the male poet sees doctor Penny
because of a muffled pain
in his testicles

  where are you from?
asks doctor Cash
she answers

  exciting times
he says

  yes
she should probably say
something else something more
he expects more
typing on his old computer
in his little office
which looks untouched
like a film set

oh by the way
there's something else
doctor Cash looks tired
pain in my elbow
doctor Cash sighs and shrugs his shoulders
the female poet sighs too
och

the temperature's rising
fever is high
can't see no future
can't see no sky

watching Masterchef
cold turkey
has got me
oh my god!
there are 4 critics this time
same comments
again and again
can we stop repetition?
it doesn't take us
closer to nature

the female poet says to the male poet
she's writing a poem with songs
he says you're ripping me off!
you're ripping off ABBODIES
she says yeah that's what I thought

that night
the female poet declares herself
the Queen of France
she looks for Anja's cut
yellow paper crown
and puts it on

she cries and declares
she'll be lying on the floor
listening to the 4 seasons
until until

she cries and sings high
but hush-hush
what kind of Queen drinks so much coffee
(raging the pain is there and there)
what kind of Queen reads the newspapers
speaking of which
what newspapers does the Queen of England read?
because guys British people

my brothers my sisters
Brexiters too
can you seriously have such bad press?

how democratic is this place?
asks the female poet
waking up from a nightmare
in her pine Ikea royal bed

the female poet comes back to the nest at night
all is lit
        c'est Versailles!
the male poet says
        what?

        yes dear
        I'm writing in a language
        I don't speak

        I come back at night to the nest
        on the forth floor of a tenement cliff

        we're living on the edge
the male poet says
impersonating Ewan McGregor
narrating a Scottish nature programme

the nest
the royal edge
buckingnest palace
better than Buckingham
buckingchorizo
buckingpastrami

        no no I shall lie and wait with music
        I read the news today, oh boy
        about a lucky man who made the grade
        and though the news was rather sad
        well I just had to laugh

        no no wake up
        fascism sewed the anger
        harvested ploughmen
        fattened rich fat so called patriots
        they do
        they are not joking
        war is upon us
        wake up my people
        my people where are you?

I cultivated my insignificance in exile but

this is home
(Royal Bank of Scotland)
it's good to be home

where is it   home?

what is the taste of nostalgia?
cherries on your ears
scent of African meals
on a hot summer night
colourful lights
breakfasts of black coffee
in large bowls
an open window
          lilac

Master-nostalgia-chef
I love that nostalgia mate
that's delicious
however
it is simple
not a great deal of technique here
it lacks a bit of heart
of fat heavy juicy heart

the land of exile
one chance out of 28
ah! it was the one
how the seagulls sneered on the roofs
You never give me your money
You only give me your funny papers
And in the middle of negotiations
You break down

I am your Queen
you are not my subjects
you are my friends
friends   do you watch nature on TV
do you feel the call?

of the living room
on a rainy day
on the screen   eagles
blackbirds
toucans
humming birds
all the royal family!

the pain is there and there
in my elbow and here
doctor Penny said to the male poet
he can have intercourse
intercourse?
Canada? (Ivor Cutler)

I am your Queen
I am a citizen of nowhere
please listen
I call for a cry
for a song
a response
dressed up and standing
in my iridescent
summer plumage

BIO

Anne Laure Coxam is a French poet living in Edinburgh. Her pamphlet, *Toolbox Therapy,* was published by Sad Press in 2016. Other work has featured in *Local Tongue*, *LIT* (with nick-e melville), *Valve*, *Zarf*, *DATABLEED*, *Poetry Scotland*, and the anthology *Umbrellas of Edinburgh* (Freight Books, 2016). 'The male and the female poet go to the surgery in exciting times' was written as part of a collective of women writers called '12', during the 2017 presidential French election. The 1st round left French people with the choice of a candidate from the fascist extreme-right or an ultraliberal centrist candidate.

BIO

Sara Crangle is Professor of Modernism & the Avant-Garde at the University of Sussex, where she co-directs the Centre for Modernist Studies. Her books include *Prosaic Desires: Modernist Knowledge, Boredom, Laughter, and Anticipation* (Edinburgh, 2010), *Stories and Essays of Mina Loy* (Dalkey Archive, 2011) and, with Peter Nicholls, *On Bathos: Literature, Art, Music* (Bloomsbury, 2012). She is currently completing a monograph on Mina Loy and editing the poetry and prose of Anna Mendelssohn. Sara was born in Canada and holds Canadian and Irish citizenship. The poster poems offered here were sent to academics around the UK and US, many of whom created similar campaigns for their own universities. Colleagues at Sussex continue to keep them on their office doors.

EMILY CRITCHLEY

from *Some Curious Thing*

the *throwback* to the tunnel }from which
where you emerged recalls convenience. In sharp
memory Euridice's really a cipher, & the arch is a tongue of weakness,
the fault of belief. Believing where we cannot prove. Proof to each shout
of gratitude

the child recalls all this &, generationally, the part of her brain where
memory burns heats like a glow-torch. Meaning to see fire. Come in
curiously – there must we seek other ways

(Perception which may involve deception & / or reveals the contradictory
nature of awareness of world)

otherwise one could ask at any moment e.g. how is the hero troubled
by such a detail – training or bodily – & are we alone? (Is such moment
really of weather, or the result of mirrors.) Says the Orpheus cipher to the
Euridice substitute: why do you demand so. What is the same story not
always split into different branches, each absorbed trichromatically by
eager, retinal cones? Each, brazen on the moist surface, each clanging on
the dumb shell

say there isn't an arch of memory merely the mode *through which*

& we can see back to (the Understanding which reveals order, regularities
& organization, i.e. the) one before this one

(THE AVAUNT-GARDE)

speaking in logic (or Greek) where nothing's divided everything's dug up
out of the dirt, bomb or butterfly, but such dirt gets stuck (like red paint)
under the nails & the world after all is not for such violent admiring. The
archaelogical point may be us at the drinking bowl us as the clouds part
us offering ourselves up to ourselves in graphic violence

to get the beauty of it hot

Little Death Waltz
from *Home*

In the heart of hearths there is her, she wolf
        who, linking arms with your first-born
        who, shedding dresses, crossing
breeds with
        leading him on to
        outrageous death waltz
allowing outside
wildly in with laughter.

Who ought to be ashamed
who, someone should fetch grandpa's gun.

Lines around this
hearth-polis
        snares and mountain ranges
        tongues of many different knives of colours
for (fun for) law & order.
Who will howl for her please?
Who leave a plate of milk at the border?

O she in wolf's clothing
no mother nor father
that wildness is
brazen wound dancer.

O we are no waltzing sheep who
does she think she is?

Little death song, little death song
        prescient of death
        & self-fulfilling like foundations
that we dig
to be filled up
with grave-water.

Who will snatch her child up in her mouth
who bear her miles from hence.

She animal will never speak / can never
tell of horrors done to it;
only sing at moonlight
where traps she knows are best laid
        [who will cry for her at the border?]
        and strangely dance.

Out Of Joint (Brexit elegy)

Travelling past
snapshots of us
travelling
past us
a simple graph
whatever sings
the difference. Planned
landslides are
better than. Listen
I could tell
you about
nothing
how to bite
one's thumb in spite,[1]
bitten, repeated, blood
cutting around
the finite
distance.
When we made up
this family
(out of scraps,
adjacent stories)
but when we have this
permanent rainbow –
smash the windows,[2] let the rain off
this precious train
the one over all Europe.
Its new goal
a stupid arrival.
Blood thumbs.

NOTES

1 And the continuance of their parents' rage.
2 Kristallnacht.

BIO

Emily Critchley was born in Athens, Greece and grew up in Dorset, UK. Her mother is Greek. She has poetry collections with Boiler House, Barque, Intercapillary, Corrupt, Holdfire, Torque, Oystercatcher, Dusie, Bad and Arehouse presses and a selected writing: *Love / All That / & OK* (Penned in the Margins, 2011). She is the editor of *Out of Everywhere 2: Linguistically Innovative Poetry by Women in North America & the UK* (Reality Street, 2016). Critchley is Senior Lecturer in English and Creative Writing at the University of Greenwich, London.

AILBHE DARCY

Jellyfish

At first you only noticed one—
a translucent crisp nestling in the sand—
the perfectly circular ghosts of its gonads—
and recalled another summer's plump
and gloating—
Then— you took in death's full
murmuration on the strand— slug-pocked
with the dried-up sucker-marks—
Child!—
bossing your brother and sister around—
did you step on one crisp jellyfish?
Barefoot— as if experimentally—

As if in the constellation
there existed some design—
the sketch of a map—
your child's face mapped on the sand—

Two parents stood there—
who'll be old when your child is young—
one rummaging— one naked under a towel—
a brother and sister running around—
your responsibility—
a castle of sand— a wet dog— an enormous sky—
all of it as if mutely—

You lay in the bottom bunk
of the bunk bed
of the second room
of the holiday house
by the yellow strand
dreaming of faces—
loomy and foamy—

a dream the previous child had left in the bed—
or a dream oozing down from your sister—
or only because in the past
you have not met your future—
so naturally your child's face is unfamiliar—

You'll bring your child to the beach
and build a castle of sand— your child
looks like you— greedy smile—
eyes splayed in thought—

You'll steal from other poets
the haystack- and roof-levelling wind—
the sea-wind—
the sea's murderous innocence—
where slugs with their slime-trails
are porous as mirrors—

Where ice— far away but you can't help
knowing about it—
calves and crashes—

Where comb jellies— far away but you can't help
knowing about it—
spawn deliriously—

Where plastics— far away but you can't help
knowing about it—
make an island—

Where ancient air— far away but you can't help
knowing about it—
is released from pockets—

Some jellyfish have motors—
some can choose to grow younger—
a jelly is a lens too slippery to hold to an eye—

You come across those jellyfish again
in the future
in their hundreds—

Swimming or not swimming
they must have come—
mooning with intention—
from your keepnet—
your child moves with a shovel
to sling them back into the sea—

Once you saw a photograph
of a child—
lifeless—
on a beach—

so did everybody

BIO

Ailbhe Darcy is an Irish poet living in Wales. Her first collection is *Imaginary Menagerie* (Bloodaxe, 2011) and her second is *Insistence,* forthcoming from Bloodaxe in 2018. She is also the co-author, with S.J. Fowler, of *Subcritical Tests* (Gorse Editions, 2017).

NIA DAVIES

from *Storie*

WHAT IS STATE (or The Fields)

by train I registered we were in England then I thought 'we are in England'.

And that there are small states, states of varying size, states that are sub and supra, altered states and disoriented states, there is statehood and statecraft and there are soft borders, such as a river, an estuary. I registered I was in a new state, the same state as before but altered slightly. That there are semi states and states that join together through a single commonality and later break apart at the site of a river or an estuary. A hedgerow that was different from that other hedgerow. A hedgerow with ten species as opposed to one hundred. There are shady people on the other side of that hedgerow who are different to the people on this side and they are altered states

don't touch me now. Touch me when I say you can, in a distinctive state of readiness, a state where we connect through our state of being skin and flesh. We touch through the hedge. There are states like this where a person condescends to another's state, stops to speak and gives over their state beyond their status. Touches their status. But then there are states that are dominated by other states that are dominated by a small section of men and some women's psyches. This section of state is made up of actions arising from the wills of psyches and their interactions. The psyches are connected in information across the world. The state of information is also some kind of fluid state but not unharmful. This state can access your smartphone.

Here is a hedgerow with 100 species. We want to protect those species with our psyches that are joined together in a petition but on the other side of this information is another hedgerow where there are 1000 species. I registered the luck of certain species as I proceeded eastwards to the state of London, to the centre of many joinings of various states, but also information, though mostly services. Once I reach that place I will say don't touch me to another species and all the states that I encounter in the capital of one of our states. Look, we want to be separate and not to be touched or touch, OK?

just touch this frame of the body and see if a certain state is triggered. There are states which are heightened in their readiness for action. Adrenalin states and tolerant states. I would lie down now in one or more of these states!

the hedgerow is a soft border but there are also hard borders with rocks where the flesh on one side of the hedge is pressed by one hundred batons and one hundred hooves. Some have been evicted from a tent that was also a mini state. The state is counting on our information which we give freely through the hedge. The state has fire at it its disposal and can point this fire at both sides of the hedgerow, at the 100 species on either side. Consider the movability of these hedgerows. And the inability to pass through a dense hedgerow as a human wearing only light sportswear. Don't touch me in my sportswear. You read this text and the state you are in in the world where I execute my ideas, they pearl and drop into pools and form 'my brilliant career', the film my parents watched the night I was born. So I was therefor executed.

In the world I execute my ideas by beheading them. When we die we execute all those ideas, for good or bad. Soiled, murdered ideas. 'Sit me up' she said as she was dying and we could see her and touch her and hear her. These ideas of hers are now executed for good. Lucky she could write, she could love.

Sit me up and I can execute my ideas in this world and then depart like that. Execute them by laying them out side by side, ever to be made real and understood, in the world where anything can be understood where any finite circle is closed, in a suspended world where a woman can tell a story in order not to be executed, where another story means another night of life.

Lake Maracaibo was extremely polluted by the time she was born there in this same world 86 years gone. This same world where I execute my projects and realise my ideas, and then they give way to all the wondrous and terrible things that cannot be executed or realised as such, the outer reaches, the other realised and unrealised worlds.

The pollution in the lake and the pollution in the air. She insisted that there was no unbrutal eras, there is no unrealised better world we move towards painlessly.

This world where I rasp my ideas, where in my fortune I dip into pools. There are many pools we don't dip anymore because they are polluted. Never dip into the same polluted pool twice. There are undissolved cosmetic pearls sweating on the surface of the pool. There are people who can no longer drink their lake water. The people who lived in the oil-soaked tinder dry shanty shacks. The ideas of these people were executed. Undissolved pearls of oil. Maybe I just have to sweat it out, make pools of sweat and make this idea that there must be undiscovered worlds or pools for us to continue in, to continue to pollute into, there must be even be the idea of undiscovered pools to place our ideas in and

BIO

Nia Davies is a poet, literary curator, performer and editor of *Poetry Wales*. She has taken part in several transcultural collaborations, projects and events and her work has been widely translated. Her most recent publications are the collection *All fours* (Bloodaxe Books, 2017), *England* (Crater, 2017) and *Interversions* (Poetrywala, 2018) which documents her collaboration with Kannada poet Mamta Sagar. She is undertaking practice-based research into poetry and ritual at Salford University.

TIM DOOLEY

Boy

his subject is the sea and he
is subject to the sea there is
no subtext his subject is the
sea and he reflects the way
it varies   even as it seems
so still   it seems so still
there is no subtext   but it
is not still it varies   there
is movement here   that he
reflects on   and he reflects
this   as he stares out from
the surface   as a horizontal
line a little below eye-level
runs either side of his head
a clean draughtsman's line
that separates   sea and sky

his mind may be working
to empty itself of what he
sees   to empty itself of
what has been seen so he
looks at a sea that seems
empty the sea he knows is
storied that stores what he
has seen   bodies he could
not look at that looked him
in the eye   companions
known unknown and not
forgotten   in the too-full
boat on the lonely sea that
is not empty   the filled
boat that rocked him   that
left him rocked   and left
him looking toward us now

BIO

Tim Dooley is a tutor for The Poetry School and a visiting lecturer at the University of Westminster. From 2008 to 2017, he was reviews and features editor of *Poetry London*. His most recent collections are *The Sound We Make Ourselves* and *Weemoed*, published by Eyewear in 2016 and 2017, respectively. 'Boy' is a response to a photograph by César Dezfuli of a 16-year-old migrant rescued in the Mediterranean Sea off the Libyan coast.

BENJAMIN DOREY

Questions of Hope

Hope Café, Athens

Tiny darned up socks
paired up and boxed.

Woolly gloves, frayed
hand-me-downs.

Food funds wired over
borders we've barbed.

*

A boy creates a bricolage
of past and present fashions;

all sass, he makes this ragtag world his own
rising from the ashes of old homes.

Such futures in his smiles
and polyglot personas;

to see him is harder
than to pity from afar.

Much easier to send spares,
to parcel love

than to meet the question in his stare –
just how much do we care?

BIO

Benjamin Dorey has published in various journals and anthologies and his debut pamphlet, *Seven Hills*, was published by Spirit Duplicator in 2017. Benjamin is currently studying for a PhD at The University of Sheffield as well as delivering training for the NHS around the experience of madness and the use of narrative and hermeneutic approaches to understanding mental health. He recently returned from a trip volunteering with refugees in Athens, where it became apparent that political and attitudinal changes from European countries are as urgently needed as supplies if the crisis is to improve.

ANGELINA D'ROZA

Shore

There's the fractured circle of a date palm,
a low sea wall.
                    For language, the dhow boat
that cuts the Gulf in two, between me

and the blue morning mist. I'm learning
this flat earth, the equation of shade
             against the eloquence of distance.

*

The grass and birdsong are hard to resolve.

Who told the sand it wasn't enough,
to aspire to lushness? I aspire to lushness.

*

3am when the sand's blue, and everything's blue
so that nothing is separate or special, or all is

special, considered in blue gleams of tide
and mollusc arriving and arriving, say it. Blue.

*

I'm wild about this flat earth that sticks
to my feet, doesn't rise
             like stone shoulders
close and inexhaustible. I am not the city
that raised me. I am the newly ground

sand that shifts with the wind; don't count
on me. I am unstable, unrooted.

*

These three notes, la la la, three blue hyacinths floating on a rock pool.

*

To hell with the small life. I am not exquisite.
Cannot sing like bone china. This is the blue hour.

             I swim in it, alone and perfectly.

Our Man in the Middle East is on Radio 4

O, marvel at the garden among the flames
(Ibn 'Arabi)

I expected stars, stars that flicker so hard they seem to circle themselves, in love with their own luminosity. Tonight the city, lit like a brain scan transposing our thoughts into brightness and colour, is enough to make shy the bravest constellation. Our man is listening to Brahms' *German Requiem*. It is the soundtrack to Desert Storm, the *son et lumiere* of that war. There's been a rush on milk and chickens, but I know where to find camel's milk still warm from the udder, if that's what it comes to. It won't come to that. How English of me to think warm camel's milk the last straw.

*

We drive north to the mangroves and watch as sand, that may as well have been the world, falls away to green. Then stars. I lie under them, recount the night I taught my son how to find Polaris. It is the story I tell to stitch my life to his. In Hindi, the same stars tell of seven sages. A funeral procession in Arabic. They're Mongolian gods, or hunters chasing the bear, whose blood reddens the autumn leaves. Our man is listening to Lionel Richie as all sides declare victory.

*

It happened one evening, in the great city of Nizwa, that a young guide, more beautiful than the moon, took the woman into the mountains and led her step by rocky step down the canyon to a green lagoon. Her heart was spoken for, and so instead of love, he took pebbles, smooth as rubies from the water, to make a circle around her. In one hand he gave her the stars, the sun he placed in the other. There she sits, safe, outside of time, and utterly alone. With arms full of stars and sun, she can't get up to return to the world, but the world is unimaginable. It must be possible that I, the storyteller, can say what happens next. That in the end she'll throw everything into the air to be at risk again.

*

My heart is a garden, a requiem for the living.
My heart is the fire, and you are the fabled moth

who longs to know what it is to be consumed,
what it means to be lit from the inside.

*

They've airlifted four-thousand dairy cows in, and I am listening to "Losing My Religion" transposed from minor to major key. I expected to be happier, that brighter scale doing all the work, in love with its own luminosity. Imagine the song is rain. In *Notes on Blindness*, the narrator can hear the shape of the landscape in the fall of the rain, the aural equivalent of light. The geographical equivalent of the present tense. Our man is in love with the light. Bright blue, then brutal. He asks what defeat feels like. *Temporary*, the defeated say.

BIO

Angelina D'Roza has had work appear in various anthologies, exhibitions and journals including *The Poetry Review*, *One for the Road* from Smith/Doorstop and *Locomotive* from the American University of Armenia. Her collection *Envies the Birds* was published in 2016 by Longbarrow Press.

KATHERINE EBURY

Knowing & Forgetting the Way

I keep thinking of two texts that happen to be placed exactly a century apart. H.D.'s 'The Helmsman' (from her collection *Sea Garden,* 1916) and Lin-Manuel Miranda's and Opetaia Foa'i's 'We Know the Way', from Disney's *Moana* (2016), both make extended use of a collective identity, the 'we' of each text, but their 'we' does not mean a straightforward national grouping. Nor does it ever imply a fully stable sense of place.

O be swift— / we have always known you wanted us.

In the first two lines of H.D.'s poem, a helmsman, the 'we' speaker, cries out to the sea. The poem swiftly constructs the voice of a culture which used to be migratory, but which 'fled inland with our flocks', thus denying its own impulse toward the sea. The sea and the boat became something to hide away from. 'We forgot', the speaker tells us, twice. They went deeper into the space of the island, until the ocean is only 'wind' and 'salt' and 'tang', and the reader goes with them. The speaker describes pleasure in rootedness and in trees themselves, trees *not* turned into boats: 'tree-resin, tree-bark, / sweat of a torn branch / were sweet to the taste'.

In *Moana*, the eponymous protagonist hears 'We Know the Way' as the ghostly echo of her ancestors, in a cave full of hidden, forgotten ships. She learns for the first time of places beyond her island and a past when her people were voyagers. At first iteration, the song's assertion that, 'We know where we are / We know who we are, who we are', sounds ironic – the descendants of these singers have forgotten both who and where they are.

Aue, aue,
We set a course to find
A brand new island everywhere we row
Aue, aue,
We keep our island in our mind
And when it's time to find home
We know the way

Aue, aue, we are explorers reading every sign
We tell the stories of our elders
In the never-ending chain

The chain of stories described in the song was broken, but renews. The film takes Moana on a journey so that she can participate in the song, and its 'we' – learning to sail, learning to leave the island, learning to restore the heart of her people. At the end of the film, she and her people sing the song again on board their own boats: a shell is placed on the family cairn. The song is no longer ironic.

In H.D.'s poem too, a repetition allows a return – the speaker is impatient to be gone, however lovingly the island is described in the body of the poem. Now the boat cannot move quickly enough:

But now, our boat climbs—hesitates—drops—
climbs—hesitates—crawls back—
climbs—hesitates—
O be swift—
we have always known you wanted us.

The dashes suggest haste, suspense, excitement – but also danger. The waves suggested by these dashes are very big. The sea may want us in a way that we don't wish to be wanted. Moana's father's friend drowned. The ships were hidden for a good reason, even if the curse can be lifted.

'The Helmsman' and 'We Know the Way', separated by one hundred years, thus construct an encounter with and a return to nomadic or migratory desires, their pleasures and risks. Indeed, both texts assert the value of what we might call a 'migratory identity'. Despite this sense of betweenness, both texts are also about 'knowing' who and what you are: though the culture of the speaker of 'The Helmsman' forgot the sea, they also never forgot. Both H.D.'s poem, as well as the rest of *Sea Garden* (which you should read) and *Moana* (which you should see), come out of a tension between cultural loss and cultural remaking – the sea was lost, each island will now be lost, but can still be returned to – 'We keep our island in our mind / And when it's time to find home / We know the way'.

BIO

Katherine Ebury is Senior Lecturer in Modern Literature at the University of Sheffield. She has published books and articles on modernism, literature and science and Irish Studies.

ALONSO QUESADA, TRANSLATED BY DAN ELTRINGHAM

from *Scattered Ways [Los Caminos Dispersos, 1944]*[1]

(Memories criss-cross
the clear way. Far-off day.)

My great friend the ass
who carried my other friend's coal
the coalman of the Square, stopped
one day before the door of the English office
where I kneaded my hypothetical bread.
The memory is so clear and so funny
that it fills my way with tenderness.
The ass raised its snout,
gallant & sacred, like a tiara,
and let loose a bray
that came in through the Counter
and smashed into the *Private office*
against a stucco wall.
The tasteless show-offs
whose menial task it is
to shrink the gilt pounds
–those pounds
so brave & free–
down to the diminished coin
of another country (downtrodden & bust),
upon hearing the bray they laughed,
like restive workshop girls.

NOTES

1 From VI., first published in *España* (3 June 1922)

TRANSLATOR'S NOTE

Alonso Quesada (1886–1925) was a Spanish poet, dramatist, fiction writer and journalist from Las Palmas, Gran Canaria. Apart from a trip to Madrid in 1918, he barely left Las Palmas. Perhaps because of this, Quesada never achieved much recognition beyond the ambit of Canarian letters. He left most of his work uncollected at his death, a selection of which was subsequently published by the Canarian Department of Culture and Sport. This relative obscurity is key to Quesada's self-conscious development in his writing of an island mentality, punningly invoked in the title to the posthumously published prose collection, *Insulario*: the condition of the islander is equated with its near-synonym, the isolation of the solipsistic self. *Scattered Ways*, the translation-in-progress from which this brief extract is taken, perhaps best gives voice to these ideas in a detached yet deeply-felt *vers libre*. Nonetheless, Quesada's was a richly cosmopolitan literary world. It was sustained by correspondence with major Spanish writers of the day and by membership of a group of poets practising what from an Anglophone perspective would be called Canarian modernism – contemporary with Woolf, Joyce, Eliot and Pound – but which in Hispanic literature is known as *postmodernismo*, following the *modernismso* of the fin de siècle. Like T. S. Eliot, he worked as a banker, for both Spanish and later British banks. Indeed, Quesada's relationship with the British has been characterised by Lázaro Santana as one of 'attraction-repulsion': he was at once drawn to and repelled by what he saw as the British temperament's measured reserve, tempered by a grossly pragmatic materialism.* This affectionate yet censorious duality can be seen clearly in the extract above, and throughout his work. One could say that Quesada's cautious and ironic, yet lyrical and emotionally attuned writing speaks from one insularity to another, from the colonial margins of 'Europe' to the equally 'insular' British Isles.

*

Lázaro Santana, introduction to Alonso Quesada, *Insulario: versos y prosas*, ed. by Lázaro Santana (Islas Canarias: Biblioteca Básica Canaria, 1988), pp. 13–26 (p. 18, trans. mine).

BIO

Dan Eltringham teaches at the University of Sheffield. His first collection, *Cairn Almanac*, was published by Hesterglock Press in 2017. He co-edits Girasol Press and co-runs Electric Arc Furnace, a poetry readings series in Sheffield.

RUTH FAINLIGHT

Tightrope Walkers

I do not blame my parents – both, I am sure, silenced by their own experience of the general indifference towards children when they were young. Certainly there were no reminiscences from either about their early days, no anecdotes of uncles, aunts or cousins, no proud recounting of adventures and triumphs: nothing at all. Their childhood images remain two small, pale, wary faces in old photographs.

My mother left her Galician village aged about six, in the first years of the twentieth century: a time of political and social unrest and much anti-semitism, and with her family travelled across Europe from the eastern borders of the Hapsburg lands to their port of embarkation: Hamburg? Trieste? – sailing steerage class, I am fairly sure; to be confronted by a new country, a new language and all the shocks of the immigrant. But not a word was ever said to her children about what she had thought or felt. Not even a factual account of their route: what had happened on the way and how long the journey took, nor who had greeted them after their release from Ellis Island: she, her mother and her elder sister. Had the men of the family, the father and two much older brothers, also travelled with them or were they already in America? Or did they follow? (The sisters were under eight, the brothers over twenty years old.) I believe there had been an earlier foray to the New World by one of those older brothers, but if my mother knew, she never explained what had happened nor passed on any information. It was impossible to get hard facts from my mother. I never knew her real age. She claimed either that the documents had been lost, or that such information had never been recorded. I knew that the bureaucracy of the Austro-Hungarian empire was excellent – but I never went to the trouble of trying to find her records, assuming they still existed. Perhaps the destruction of the wars that passed over her birthplace had belatedly made her story true. And it was only when it was too late to ask that I wanted to know: everyone who could answer my questions was already dead.

Three of my four grandparents had died before I was born, and my father's father, who remarried twice after the death of his first wife, my father's mother, always lived in another town. I remember only a few of his visits; though retain a strong memory of how mercilessly he put me in my place as a female, and his expression of malicious pleasure at my fury as he recited (as he invariably did), "Be good, sweet maid, and let who will be clever..." From the first moment, I was quite sure that clever was exactly what I wanted to be.

Until I was five years old my parents, younger brother and myself lived in New York City, but my father's family were all in London. It was two generations since his great-grandparents had left Cracow in the mid-nineteenth century, another time of revolutionary disturbance in Europe and much movement of people, and that was long ago enough for them to have lost the uncertainty of the immigrant. Trying now to interpret our meeting when we arrived in England, I have an uneasy memory of some difficulty related to my mother. Did her defensive immigrant nature make easy relationship impossible? But the matter was never discussed, even when I was an adult. And growing up in that family, I had not asked.

Of course I do not blame them. But I am suddenly conscious of being an instance of the impoverishment of family and memory that can result from such uprootings: left rigid with fear half-way across the tightrope of the present moment. No stories, no legends, nothing unique or special about us, about me, as protection against the pressure of the entire outside world, nothing except what I could create by the power of my own imagination.

BIO

Ruth Fainlight has published thirteen collections of poems, two collections of short stories, and written opera libretti for Covent Garden and Channel 4 TV. Books of her poems have appeared in French, Spanish, Italian, Portuguese, and Romanian translation. In collaboration with Robert J. Littman, she has produced a new version of Sophocles' Theban Plays. Marine Rose, her translation of the Portuguese poet Sophia de Mello Breyner Andresen, was the first to appear in English. Her *New & Collected Poems* was published by Bloodaxe Books in 2010, and a new collection *Somewhere Else Entirely* is forthcoming.

KIT FAN

Migrant

for Ziad Elmarsafy

Months have passed and we have seen enough of death
this winter that even though seeing these chlorophyll

green leaves suckle on the sun again and tower over Russell Square
broadcasting *C'est la vie* on this one June day aren't enough

for the sea-deaths, land-deaths and air-deaths un-extinguishing
somewhere else, not yet out-of-sight, out-of-mind. Not yet *here* too,

this corner kingdom we've elected to live within still seemingly
prospers like the summer holm-oak by the Hotel Russell

you'll come to frequent in your new life in the capital.
People lazing about in the sun as in *La Grande Jatte*, children shrieking

in the fountain, a father carrying his bum-bare boy on his shoulders,
an old couple walking past, catching our eye, still walking

past. *So many of us, I want to know every single life, what*
brought them here today, who they are, and how long they will live.

We all have it, living it, re-living it, shaping this one-off malleable
thing over and over that even though all winter we've seen

what could happen to it, we still sit on the bench among the perishable
green, chattering about it as if it won't leave us just like that.

BIO

Kit Fan was born in Hong Kong and moved to the UK at the age of 21. In 2017 he was shortlisted for the Guardian 4th Estate BAME Short Story Prize and the TLS Mick Imlah Poetry Prize. His first book of poems *Paper Scissors Stone* won the inaugural HKU International Poetry Prize. His poetry translation was awarded one of the Times Stephen Spender Prizes in 2006. His second book of poems *As Slow As Possible* will be published by Arc and is a Poetry Books Society Recommendation for Autumn 2018. He reviews regularly for *The Poetry Review*. He lives in York and works in the Hull York Medical School.

ALICIA FERNÁNDEZ

Call

Every time I call my mother
I learn about the weather,
the unforgiving sun crippling the plains,
the sermon at Sunday mass,
the full prescription record for her cold,
my father's second glass of whiskey.

I feel a tender anger.
I recall the frost,
the week's sharp evenings,
the heartbreak of this filthy winter,
the mellow memory of my aunt.

The paper lanterns of the town fair
torch in my stomach as I mute,
and nod, and remain absent
in a hand-crafted field of even soil
where you could harvest all trouble.

Swallows

17 July 1936, in the backwoods
of an old room in southern Spain,
hatchlings nesting on chairs,
their hands foraging, grabbing
the news as a present
delivered by summer itself.

Las tropas se han sublevado
en África – troops have revolted
in Africa; a cavernous voice
announcing the beginning of war,
all classes dismissed until
further notice, life put on hold.

A southbound exodus of backpacks,
like dark swallows, slamming doors
open, a disarray of page edges
cutting the air, songbirds moulting
their plumage, wings shuffling
through corridors – a migration
toward idleness, toward safety.

BIO

Alicia Fernández is a translator, interpreter and poet, born in Spain, who resides in Leeds. Her poems have appeared in poetry magazines such as *Dream Catcher* and *Bunbury*, and in various anthologies. Her debut pamphlet, *If Moments Were Places*, was published by Half Moon Books in 2017. She won the title of Chapbook Champion 2017 at Ilkley Literature Festival, awarded by former BBC Poet in Residence Daljit Nagra.

VERONICA FIBISAN

Zebra Mussel

native invader

brackish water
Black Sea British shores
inhalant siphon dissolved nutrients
autotrophic algae
feeds on
propagation of selves
smother native species
Danube Delta
branches out
fingers extended
fight the current foot firmly fixed on far-away lands

byssus threads grip
hard homely substrate ignomic settler

through the Bosphorus strait
on boats' undersides
among warning signs
clandestine passengers
clog waterways
hearts beat their way
through pipes
intricate map of pulses
a myriad of organisms aimlessly seep through
shell hinge open
umbo inflates mantle rises
exhalent siphon
exhale catch our breadth
upon landing
through this contorted concoctions of anthropo-systems
veligers settle
on surfaces
culled home

BIO

Veronica Fibisan is a PhD candidate in English Literature at the University of Sheffield. Her areas of interest include ecocriticism, ecofeminism, coastal radical landscape poetry and the Anthropocene. Her research is a practice-based creative and critical project that focuses on key locations on the UK shoreline, where she spends significant time. She has published poetry notably in *The Sheffield Anthology* (Smith/Doorstop, 2012), *Cast: The Poetry Business Book of New Contemporary Poets* (Smith/Doorstop, 2014), and *Plumwood Mountain Journal* (Vol. 4 Nr. 1).

STEVEN J FOWLER

alone at xmas

Those that arrive covered in liquid will, like a leak, spread.
With tail as a euphemism, your nose is a map.
Body parts will never be enough to help you through
this lonely Christmas period. Instagram awaits.

Closing the door as you enter, the fog of the angry
and the never ready, plumes and obscures your view.
Grateful you wrap your pigbones, sanded smooth for casting
in the free paper provided by Carrefour.
The man at the sale of poisons counter sells you poisons
as though they were petitions.

All your shopping done, you realise shopping is fun.

The governments of the past had it wrong.
They all come to you, on film, from the past,
and ask which side you are on? You reply, your side,

You are indeed from the past and settle down
with fruit popcorn in a bear's skull. *Silence*
of the lambs is on, finally you don't have to say things you don't mean.

BIO

Steven J Fowler is a writer and artist. He has sought translations of his work into 26 languages and produced collaborations with over 90 artists from outside of the UK. He is the founder of The Enemies Project, curating international poetic collaboration, executive editor at *The European Review of Poetry, Books and Culture* and director of Writers' Centre Kingston. www.stevenjfowler.com

LIVIA FRANCHINI

Cari Cari

Cari cari i miei cari,
o dear me, il caro vita,
non c'è lavoro, she still lives at home,
I tick the box for 'visiting family'
Dear mother I worry the time is coming
when I'll no longer see you shouting at the telly –

Cara, cara amica ti scrivo
nella notte della notte
in your single bed connecting
the raised scars like needlework
blue marker making out a penguin
a compass rose, my name outslanting –

Cara cara, daughter dearest,
tutto quel che è buono si scolora in bianco
white dots in oil, I slot the fish back
into its chilly bed, 10 degrees colder
Dear father I am sorry I made you carry
another tired bag into this empty flat –

Caro diario, I write to you
From this welcoming land today
All I ate was cold beans and in the mirror
I put my index to my cheek and twisted
and then I knew to say 'delicious'.

'Cara, cara,' a mother puts her child's hand
up to another's cheek, holds tightly on the wrist.

The outstretched palm strokes downwards,
stiff, but very gentle, in the direction of tears.

On Complicity

the monotone rings for insurance you never took out
my name is *mm-mm* I'm looking for someone with *real* drive
4.11 mouthwash for a mouthdry, a dull ache
the world shrunk to the size of a fist
water dripping from the faucet
thinking about your body against the steel sink
black black night thinking of the mother country
steady yourself on edges

a meek moment in a woman's voice
press the red button go back to bed you've dreamt this

making your way through a smatter of bodies
honey babe you're a sweetblade
to your desk with the small bottle it takes a minute
for the silk brush to lick from the root to the tip
one more minute to dry
and how happy you feel and how satisfied
thinking of all your illnesses how they're hereditary

it's lunchtime the speakers come on at once
yellow noise like in a mall at christmas
the equator between the busy rooms a distance
you travel with your ponytail
shoulders rolled back
clipboard to your chest
like they taught you in rhetorics school

o poor poor darling how did you become so hateful
said the man with the shock of white hair
4.11 the hour for remorse
the world shrunk to the size of a fist
making your body stand in your blue tailleur
I like what I like you said
I don't like what I don't
child golden with your seamless fabrics your milkshake senseless
sit in the window seat after jury duty
search in the thick bottom with your straw

We are the queens of the Free World, we bear the weight of our
embarrassment

Melisa, I swear your cheekbones had never been so perfectly aligned

BIO

Livia Franchini is a writer and translator from Tuscany, Italy. Her work has been featured or is forthcoming in *The Quietus*, *3:AM Magazine*, *Funhouse*, *LESTE*, *Hotel* and *The White Review*, among others. In 2016 she co-founded *CORDA*, a journal about friendship in the time of new borders. She has translated Natalia Ginzburg, James Tiptree Jr. and Michael Donaghy, among many others. Livia lives in London, where she is working on her first novel, as part of a PhD in Creative Writing at Goldsmiths. 'Cari Cari' first appeared in *La Errante*. 'On Complicity' first appeared in *Hotel*.

ULLI FREER

No title / 2

sandy soil dried up ink
abandoned sandbox
as though the surface
claimed to be virtually impervious to cutting
alluded by another attempt to mark
circled existence sore disturbances
birch and juniper in skeletal illuminated
as sea lavender as heathland alighted from
entanglements left undergrowth personal echoes
sleeper of the nation bed of the sea greet types
fences are landscaped rapidly become higher
& on landing by the most employed mat
form of a standard fence circumvented
pulling a van alongside
people jumped from roof & were buried
saved electronic barriers
6 feet deep to prevent tunnelling controls
fencing re-tested to withstand any material
traveling at high speed
written over for correction
for an abbreviated pen used thorn
for certain values upon skin
alternations of pressure & release
scattered compositions
had none unless you entered
spall off layers rock trains or clusters
are and not born a country
that the act of writing fell shaped
adapted to rhythms applied to bring
out traces to save readers breath
erratic territories moved terminal moraine
from location to location wander
via abrasion scouring & plucking
not as citizen permission had none
unless entered or conditioned overseas
with a thumb with five fingers
fragments of letters surrounded
evident watermark sleeve not flowing
or time limited nation attached to sovereignty
much rain where borders bred borders
stand as post watched fenced cattle corralled
stroke spilled ink behind extensive oak
lichen over bark transmits
controversy field completely hedged
appropriated & inflated at highest rates
assumed identities over line slippages

online controlled language capitalised
profits speed global through boundaries
contra verse when hand is not visibly
marked withdrawn in photograph
& calling overhead as an acrobat
bandages upon comprehension
by a wounding opening
dot of the eye
with a line striking it out
dot over I
by which words adopted an appearance
as moving between trees to avoid
marked for extraction as though belonging
with glosses circulating in own blood
derived interpretations connected possible lines
drawn out whilst some fragments decay
manicule semitone fist red
marked & bent pointing finger
for continuance such as business
& sums of money in essence
illuminated to fix meaning
by under-linings by obliterations
attempts at marking commonplaces
intimate with much punctuation
extraordinarily feint not trimmed
as in searched in the same line
& paper identity digested
overworked overloaded
ink contamination runs out of branches
snapped at clearing all alinements deregulated
paid to labourers on account of pairing
two for one minimum cost
in a productivity nightmare
to toil under heavy clouds
vague silhouettes continued
paced & dragged beyond horizon
given versions of hemlock to drink
no option night sea crossing
from hook to cliffs
kelps congregating brought squalls
recalled attempted strokes
on all fronts extensive wind hounded
had limited space
relatives apart & alphabet crammed in
between belonging on gangplank shuffled
letters torn apart in other words
floated until landed on a rutted track
collaborated for meaning
moving via controversy
drovers cant marking without ink

searched interpretations of
having been & fungal lines taken
happened in hues fading from behind
another hand unseen without a dream
worn out saturated
held wave stained photograph
shoreline entry cliff cavity
to dot of the eye
damaged dot over i
some worm searched in the same line
circulates common places
for weeding bracken
four days being hay time
& others cut down hills
& others for spreading
sirens when breakout
breached wrote write off trading
for treading in for stubbing in
markets fields thru chemical outcomes
none identity template poisoned
by information weaponized
fed upon skin marked for consumption
smudged beyond recognition
body remainder of being trodden over
farms built upon iron cage landscape
heard in other words corroded
& loanwords up against cold high walls
against bloodstained enclosures
on an island to have spoken
homeless word in sentence deported

BIO

Ulli Freer, born in Luneburg, Germany, lives and works in London and has been active over a number of decades. Ulli is a member of the Veer editorial collective. His work has been published in a several magazines including *Fire*, *AND*, *Curtains*, *Veer Away*, *Cleave2*, *Datableed*, *Vlak*, *Test Centre 8*. His publications include *Blvds* (Equipage, Cambs.), *Sandpoles* (Equipage, Cambs.), *Eye Line* (Spanner, Hereford), *Speakbright Leap Password* (Salt books, Cambs.), *Burner on the buff* (Veer Books, London), and *No Title* (Rot Direkt, London).

ANASTASIA FREYGANG

verbal fairplay adolescent 2

westberlin maskulin
bitch fresse bevor ich dir den sack in den mund presse : *bitch shut up before I stuff my balls into your mouth*

rap the local
boys in cars with girls
words of the totality— macho, in my mouth these riches rhyme
smoothly we laugh

hardcore content faces no regrets
the dominance is probing yet proving
never aimed at being correct
the snort is spat
and that's done with a smirk

assigning the masculine to local belonging didn't feel alienating
it was,
one of many stepping stones on the immigrational path line, temporary timeline
never grappling with identity
for core is individualistic
once displaced you keep moving

home is transient, we all gather :

westberlin, no longer an island— the wall is down, the borders are open

we are Russians and Turks and Arabs and Poles and Germans
we are kids on the streets

my take: I take *your* balls and stuff them into *your* mouth
whatever you say you can do to me I say I can do to you

so much to equality

games of rhetorics, it's about the stance at the end, energetically
not rooted in fear or will for segregation

its head on: I see you you see me: how you front me and how I respond, confidently

and,
when girls fight they take off their rings, capiche?
they wear buffalo's and the tightest jeans

Nike air, Carlucci pullovers, the smell of coconut butter in their hair:
Yallas are boys that wear their trousers stuffed into their socks, roaming
the streets

we hang round corners, frequent parks, know little
racist, homophobic and sexist polemics are everyday banter
and no Body would take any of that seriously
its jargon— we are verbalising territory

transcending social class and culture, yet another country
I don't move too smoothly
words cut and shock the gentle minded
for a tame vocabulary to blossom with regards to meaning, feeling
and the literal and its possible transcendence
for the reaction in question
for the tone of my voice to not cause fear

now, London, words are missing over here.
the action of choice: sit it out and breed resentments

we might have misunderstood each other
but
don't spell it out
don't probe
beat around the bush or its immediately called a conflict

agree to disagree
I' ll leave you to derive from whatever pocket of philosophical alignment
you stem from
and let you hold on to, if you must
but
will you let me be? equally?

we don't find words
your suspicion is growing
will we have to part?
next time you see me, you lower your gaze

as my stance
too dominant, when frontal
like upright
alright
you're not used to it
but please don't teach me how to walk on egg shells
          I rather crack them to powder
see
people are different! many stories
codes and approaches
and
if you play safe
you'll never know of any...

easily offended bodies, learn to read between the lines with trust
you will survive this

and if we have to fight I promise I'll be taking off my rings

BIO

Anastasia Freygang: I was born in Moscow in 1985 and immigrated to Berlin at age six. My father recited Russian poetry and extracts from novels all day and otherwise was a businessman and philanthropist. My mother is a manager and the most enthralling creature I know. I'm based in London, where I'm involved in experimental music, dance and poetry and organise workshops and showcases. I'm also currently studying for a Master's in critical writing in art and design at the Royal College of Art.

KIT FRYATT

hours apart

I am waiting for a boy to wake up in Vancouver:
it is a going-across, a not remaining on the same side
you know, as in isomers! The haar bundles
in over Stanley Park, where once stood the village of

X̱wáýx̱way

the cocks are a-crowing
daylight is appearing

or, A Maske

the sea-bear holds fast the grampus

but
during a meal the axes nibbled the corner of the longhouse
and Louise, who had English, asked what they thought
they did
surveying the error deliberately
whose road?
someday you will find good road around, it's going around
but it was a through road

what other neighbours have round their houses
the same my love thou shalt have from me

At noon

boys of 23 or 24 lie
on their bellies
slug-slack on the mole

and behind the dusty shuttered boards of the custom-house
the young douanier's top lip is dewy, his jugular notch and arse-crack
his eyes

and duties are futile
you bring the city with you
and it is always the same city
of your profoundest wrack
your hull will always be fouled.

On the deck of the *St Roch* a family
of seven lived under canvas
while she was berthed in the ice
of the North-West Passage
for nine months; it is a traversing
west to east, to face the rising sun
and back again, you know, as in

travesty

the saint turns out his thigh
to demonstrate a slipped bulge
a muddled lib
and a barren kingdom
sloping his charming rod
as he presides over

committed bachelors
mastitis
miscarriages of justice
sextons
pharmakoi
the chronic
surgeons
psoriasis
Constantinople
pan-tilers
and the second-hand hard-eyed quare ones of Meath St

abandoned in button boots and cockle shells
they're off to the Linenhall
to pick up new squaddies
replace the old that lie
beneath stars renamed
crisply, after implements
sleeping now
sleeping

but I don't care! it's time for a julep &

my drowsy boy of twenty-four is awake in Vancouver
(astonished to find Vancouver was a person)

I am leaving for the distant hills
like the wild harts and hinds
I will eat grass
I will bend my love a mask
of cedar soaked in tears.

If the land could be mine by singing
it so, if every blade were mild
steel and temperate   still
my hand could never inscribe
the love only the body remembers.

palais : marches : marais : mer : pervenches

on the palace stoop
waits a girl so fair

she had so many loves
she didn't know what to do

a lowly shoemaker
caught her rolling eye

as he fit her shoe
he laid out his suit:

my love if you will
we might sleep together

in a bedstead made foursquare
all dressed in white

periwinkles blue
the four corners adorning

in the middle of the bed
the water runs so deep

all the king's mounted horse
there might drink their fill

and that is where we'll sleep
until the crack of doom

BIO

Kit Fryatt was born in Iran in 1978, grew up in Singapore, Turkey and Britain, and moved to Ireland in 1999. Books include *Rain Down Can* (Shearsman, 2012), *The Co. Durham Miner's Granddaughter's Farewell to the Harlan County Miner's Grandson* (Knives, Forks and Spoons, 2013), and *Bodyservant* (from Shearsman, 2018).

MONIKA GENOVA

Bones

How fascinating it is
How far my bones can take me
the fire in my heart keeping
The pain in my tired legs at bay.

Just one more mile

How fascinating- right there over the horizon
Beyond those tall buildings and the crowds
Beyond the fear and the exhaustion
My dream is right there, waiting

There really is no other way to find out
How much weight my bones can carry
I only have this fragile human body
To make my mortal life extraordinary

How fascinating it is..!

A tongue that is but mere flesh
And bony fingers holding pencils,
Willing words into existence
Starting wars and moving mountains.

BIO

Monika Genova comes from a small town in Bulgaria and moved to the UK a year ago, looking for an academic challenge. I wanted an adventure, something unfamiliar and scary, something worth writing about. I found what I was looking for. I wrote this, waiting for a job interview shortly after I arrived in the country. My pockets were empty but I had a dream and I wasn't about to give up on it.

GEOFF GILBERT AND ALEX HOUEN

Omar's Fridge

To my mind, the rumbling of the ring road stands in well enough for the noises of the battlefield. But I still just need – just hope – to find a patch of land, a patch of green land, for Omar to take root. Still no feeling of my self, apart from being "over there". The corn nods to the breeze. The soybean fields rustle up silk. The barn is occupied by a mountain of tiny grey seeds. Girls the colour of honey, men near chalk, hair like silk, like cotton, like wire. I watch them, I shovel, my hat in my hand, a desperate errand, a terminal job. Don't put sensation, perception, in doubt, only judgment. That's what is meant by a tea-break. *The first* moistens my lips and throat. *The second* breaks my solitude, my own living soul in their inanimate bodies. In these ways we measure up, yet yield them no comfort, afflicted and mortified; is just this the social? I can get a paper to certify as much, signed by lots of people. A paper big as a table cloth.

Fifteen fridges, piled with blocks
of other white-goods, fill the space
between two pillars. Death is not
a moral fact, but a frost-free fridge
freezer. I make the dead think
in me – only they are creative objects.
I heard that they were placed in camps,
that they were being processed. But I
was left alone, a torpid pillar.
Here, this paper binds you to duties
which may not be so easy as executing the disposal
of my properties. No warm witness in the breast,
my eyes bluish, ground and pounded,
my lips are dry. How dare solicit Omar?

This contract includes at least one murder. *The third cup* grabs my guts, hundreds of strange figures in waves. *The fourth* causes a slight sweat, but even in the original it's hard to see the mark. There is a brilliant bright stain – a ring? – but the eye slides off to the filthy careless freedom of a mass at the centre, pleasing no patron, where the bare street and bare wall meet indecorous, inert. Blurred children and their penknives watch mesmerized as corollas, pistils, petals, as flowers, flowers, more flowers of paper swarm about them in a massive wheel of light. Omar called this "being fed on breath". I do not envy them. I did not envy them. Directness of their hungers scares me; it is appalling with the scattered flowers to find so many children on the street. But I have come here less to fight than to see into the distance.

When faced with a question they don't understand
their eyes fill with tears – children in the full
sense of the word. We find this in Celts
and Berbers, in tragedies and romances. We confuse
it with love, for love is not a moral fact.
If it is a car part? – a tyre that deflates.
If it is a type of food? – rice. If an animal,
a donkey with sweet velvet eyes. This may come
as news to pioneers and astronauts, never
covered by a naked human being.
What's at stake here is health coverage as right
to weariness; new things born from being
fed up. Omar: "clear the tables
on the double", scanning for a charming novelty.

The agony which this creates does not pass away with the word "rice" or "pneu". The dead themselves clean up the battlefields down to their footprints. Nothing is stranger than a battlefield devoid of bodies. There is a nakedness, an unnatural whiteness, about its icy messed-up sheets, that pillow where the imprint of a head should be. The manoeuvre delivers the territory I sought since morning, bound to the North by the ring-road's hard shoulder, which cannot be expunged. There should be black bin-bags like dead horses, beer-cans and syringes, deep tyre-tracks of the police 4x4 from days ago. Always something nostalgic, incomplete about the feeling of triumph that comes with a victory. *The fifth* clears the distance. *Sixth* is the realm of the children, an intolerable yoke, a stinking prison, a grave shrieking. Their love depends on demolishing their history, even if this means levelling its heirs. Omar had dull sins of his own.

Sunlight twinkles on the armour-plating
of ice. Omar laid it down as learning:
the best person to kill is a friend.
This shocked the rat-catchers who come,
like maintenance-workers, in pairs, with stories of the town,
sometimes dark and often amusing.
They tell of a colleague, his pet white rat
in cancer agonies, who had to blank himself
with drink before he pressed a tampon
soaked with ether to its mouth and nose.
Omar: "Sew the body into a fine
linen, then wear the linen tight
about your head so you can rise up high
as you want." Nothing forgot as pain.

> Losing the trace of a leg is worse than the loss of a lover. But Omar's imagination, in the mood of other Celts and Berbers, moulds itself more strongly to the pillow than the stump. *The seventh* is a shoe at the foot of a tree. *The eighth*: a wave of counterfeit sleep. We must have turned on the television, if we had one. I don't remember, but we must have had one. A car prowled round the territory all night. The blue sky settled like a velvet blanket. The shoe is incredibly alive. Alone, bewildered, unable to walk or escape, it looks up to the distance, like a donkey, pleading for help from its patron. But this life is held to be improper for all use: fridges again, washing machines, a gearbox, dishes. They smoke and crackle in the rain as if plunged into a fryer. In my view, this is a pretty good example of tact, and if properly supported, could come to resemble an amorous social state.

In that eerie way, though we walk the same flood
we are not with the flower children, not together
yet. Beneath the soles of my shoes
I see stamped in the river's ice a row
of beautiful masks like Byzantine icons.
Their corpses must have been carried away
by the first spring tides, leaving their faces'
imprint on this sheet of glass. Cold fire
in Omar's eyes, frost spume on his lips,
despite all our work, we can't get his face
killed. We only need walk a few hundred
metres to leave this Europe for the other –
the ninth: all move off in a body,
too long a weary step, generous, we slow.

25–26 July 2017

BIOS

Geoff Gilbert is Associate Professor of Comparative Literature and English at the American University of Paris. He is the author of *Before Modernism Was: Modern History and the Constituency of Writing*, and, with Alex Houen, of *Hold! West*. He is currently working on contemporary realism and contemporary economics.

Alex Houen is author of the poetry chapbook *Rouge States* (Oystercatcher, 2014), and co-author (with Geoff Gilbert) of another chapbook, *Hold! West* (Eyewear, 2016). His debut full collection is titled *Ring Cycle* (Eyewear, 2018). He is co-editor of the online poetry magazine *Blackbox Manifold* and teaches modern literature in the Faculty of English, University of Cambridge.

PETER GIZZI

The Ingenuity of Animal Survival

Deep in the enzyme is the shape of home.

Deep in the code is the architecture to nest.

The Robin collects mud with its beak along with twigs and pieces of down
and feathers too.

The Grouse burrows into the subnivean world for heat and shelter.

The Raven uses branches and breaks them off with its weight and its beak,
it papers its nest with bits of fur and debris.

The mother Goose sheds her chest feathers to line the chamber.

Sorrow is long.

When will I return to my country?

BIO

Peter Gizzi is the author of seven collections of poetry, most recently, *Archeophonics* (finalist for the 2016 National Book Award), *In Defense of Nothing: Selected Poems 1987–2011*, and *Threshold Songs*. Just out from The Brother in Elysium is a small book entitled, *New Poems*. For more info: petergizzi.org

CHRIS GUTKIND

Island Jotting

Back in a home more mine
than I wish to admit – I've wept
afar and dried stains of dislocation
by notches of ink, here
and there herded within myself,
flat-footed on ground that lets me fly.
If off this island I miss
what I make, drawing anything
around into a trembling need, a twitch
that shuts down day,
stakes love, raises a doubt
to choke its carrier, then I race to
my leash – yanked
into a double-shore somehow
of my own and past
any passing.

Home or Away

Waits upon a different tongue

finds its sound exacting: *there is*
no word for this where I'm from.

Knows more than can be said.
Appearance cracks with laughter

crimps upon a frown: sometimes quiet
is the best response. *Word-keep.*

Subtle-hand. An approximate pick
might just roll. Mouth opens:

prepare for a different call.

BIO

Chris Gutkind: I'm tri-national and came to London from Montreal in 1988 at almost 24 years of age. I stayed for 11 years, moved to the US for several years, and have lived in London again since 2003. Mostly I worked as a librarian here, at SOAS, and been active in various political issues. Books of poetry are *Inside to Outside*, *Options* (with the artist Trevor Simmons), and *What Happened*. I also write possibly-unpublishable tales. 'Island Jotting' was previously published in Canadian magazine *Contemporary Verse 2* and 'Home or Away' in UK magazine *3x4*.

CORY HANAFIN

Margerete

They run like liars through
your fields, out of
Syria, their perjured
feet bring drought
and pestilence you say to
me, your devotee, your
song buzzes at the cordon
and the flattened narthex
but in secret we crept
to the midden, Marine, in
the small hours after
blood and wine, the heat
let up, you drank another
round with everyone, the
thirst was conveyed to a
crumbling lobby for all
to slake 'In the morning,'
you said, 'the gym
and the chainlink fence,'
like a line from Auden,
at eight we reached for
the jug by the bed and
grabbed your golden hair
still tousled, drunk with
yr prophetic pain

Welcome Address

Star span dizzying, the night
quivers like foil and our North
Star strobing, so we lower
our eyes to the spangled strait
Where a boat will shortly cross, or
say before first light, but
'we' is not a name, the argument
will not run easily from A to
any zigzag you can figure
scribbled in the alphabet
of breakers, give or take a week
a premonition of a dot, a rubber
vessel coursing for landfall through
a storm of coverage now watch us

falter on the reef of sympathetic
stone that drew our worlds
into alignment, fingers chapped
on the rope I keep by the sofa
in case we flip to our deaths
or a worse mishap, reaching for
the thought that the man in one
trainer would not be me, or do
I clamour with my four feet glist
ening in the dew of our temperate
mornings for the narrow
application of animal rights?
Also check on urine—predict
net fiscal contribution—say in

plain English *must to memorise*
the sunken city, clock the ecstatic
turns around the wallows
of Atlantis in the GPS, or strike east
and rake our Anglian dusk for signs
of light and ply a gallery along her
lustrous polytunnel for a stake
in genus *Fragaria*, aerosol topping
pressed from the udder, all
this and more with my drink overturned
by the console, their oxen lying
on my tiled extension and the former
ministry of works still smoking
at their father's back.

BIO

Cory Hanafin's poem/s is/are part of a longer sequence of 'alcohol poems' begun in 2016 and still in progress.

EDMUND HARDY

Constellation Swan

And this also has been one of the dark places of the earth

Tell me a tale of how different everything is
Where the telling makes it less so: "And this also..."
Paperwork in Africa, paperwork in Calcutta,
That the white has been black, that we were all exterior
When the world was Cimmerian mist:
Override, indenture: Rama in Fiji, Rama in the cane lands,
Stage it all upon the Gravesend mudflats,
This was deindustrialisation big time – & now the:
"Thames Gateway: one of the dark places of the earth",
In diaspora, across the hyphen, say equally: this also has been,
But one of the d/ark, diagonal gain...Your name is
Just a darkness, you can't see it, it's a name to come:
The ocean flowing backwards, immunisation shot
of sure self to be uncertain. Also has been: lodged in Europe's
past: the gift of memory – the might of the
"might have been", *would that we might,*
Would that you might believe: blood as a purified
Writing, death as the writing of life. Not the dark
of Tenebrae, but dust in which death hunts death in the fosse
of the Thames. To see with darkness, with rage,
where every star tapers down below the threshold
and a gentler, more absolute disturbance – accomplice
at our elbows – may never come to light: to say that
this, now, wrong struggle for a dark transformed, will
never know but darkness, is rowing backwards
to the long shore's deltas.

BIO

Edmund Hardy is a poet and polemicist. His book *Complex Crosses* (2014) is an experimental work of philology and philosophy. He's currently working on a novel called *Motley Apostles*.

DAVID HERD

Prologue

from *Refugee Tales* (Comma Press, 2016)

This prologue is not a poem
It is an act of welcome
It announces
That people present
Reject the terms
Of a debate that criminalizes
Human movement
It is a declaration
This night in Shepherdswell
Of solidarity.

It says that we have started –
That we are starting out –
That by the oldest action
Which is listening to tales
That other people tell
Of others
Told by others
We set out to make a language
That opens politics
Establishes belonging
Where a person dwells.
Where they are now
Which is to say
Where we are now
Walking
In solidarity
Along an ancient track
That we come back to the geography of it
North of Dover
That where
The language starts
Now longen follk to goon
On this pilgrimage.

In June not April
And with the sweet showers far behind us
Though with the birds singing
And people sleeping
With open eye
And what we long for
Is to hear each others' tales
And to tell them again
As told by some hath holpen

Walking
So priketh him nature
Not believing the stories
Our officials tell.
Because we know too much
About what goes unsaid
And what we choose to walk for
Is the possibility of trust
In language
To hear the unsaid spoken
And then repeated
Made
Unambiguous and loud
Set out over a landscape gathered
Step by step
As by virtue of walking which
We call our commons
Every sap vessel bathed in moisture
And what that commons calls for
Is what these stories sound.

Of crossing
For to seken straunge strondes
In moments of emergency
Whan that they were seeke
Of tribunals
Where the unsaid goes unspoken
Lines of questioning
No official has written down
People present by video
Answers mistranslated
As outside by the station
At the dead of morning
As the young sun rises
Woken in their homes
People are picked up and detained.
Routinely and
Arbitrarily
In every holt and heeth
Under the sun while
Smale foweles maken melodye
And why we walk is
To make a spectacle of welcome
This political carnival
Across the Weald of Kent
People circulating
Making music
Listening to stories
People urgently need said.

And said
And said again
Stories of the new geography
Stories of arrival
Of unaccompanied minors
Of people picked up and detained
Of process
And mistranslation
Networks of visitors and friends
This new language we ask for
Forming
Strung out
Along the North Downs Way.

Which makes it a question of scale.
Consider just
The scale
Of the undertaking
Chaucer's pilgrims crossing
Palatye and Turkye and Ruce
Across the Grete See
Which is the Mediterranean
Dark these days
Not like wine
Crossing through Flauddres
Through Artoys
Crossing the water at Pycardie.
And all the while finding stories
And then all of them
Gathering one night in London
And so the Host says
Since we're walking
Why don't we tell each other tales
And so they do
Out of Southwark
And what comes of Southwark
Is a whole new language
Of travel and assembly and curiosity
And welcome.

To make his English sweete.
That's why Chaucer told his tales.
How badly we need English
To be made sweet again
Rendered hostile by act of law
So that even friendship is barely possible –
There as this lord was kepere of the celle –
So we might actually talk
And in talking
Come to understand the journey –

Tender
Says the poet
To Canterbury they wende.

Tender
To hold
From the French
Tendre
From the English
For listening
To a story as it is said
To attend
Tendre
And then writing it down
Because it isn't written
Because the hearings
In the British immigration system
Are not courts
Of record.
So there are no stories
And people leave
As if there never had been
Stories
And so nobody
Who reaches a verdict
Has a real story
With which to contend
So now we are telling them
En masse
And people will listen
In sondry landes
And specially
From every shires ende.

But this prologue is not a poem
It is an act of introduction
Bathed every veyne in swich licour
And all the introduction can do
Is set the tone
Albeit the tone
Is everything
And the tone is welcoming
And the tone is celebratory
And the tone is courteous
And the tone is real
And every step sets out a demand
And every demand is urgent
And what we call for
Is an end
To this inhuman discourse.

And so we stop this night
And the Host steps up
And he says
Listen to this story
Whan that Aprill with his shoures soote
And the room goes quiet
And a voice starts up
And then the language
Alters
Sweet
Tender
Perced to the roote.

BIO

David Herd is a poet, critic, teacher and activist. He has given readings and lectures in Australia, Belgium, Canada, France, Poland, the USA and the UK, and his poems, essays and reviews have been widely published. His collections of poetry include *All Just* (Carcanet 2012), *Outwith* (Bookthug 2012) and *Through* (Carcanet, 2016). Recent writings on the politics of human movement have appeared in *Los Angeles Review of Books*, *Parallax*, *PN Review* and the *TLS*. He is Professor of Modern Literature at the University of Kent and co-organiser of the project *Refugee Tales* (www.refugeetales.org).

JEFF HILSON

A Final Poem With Full Stops

These deaths are not inevitable.
(*The Human Cost of Fortress Europe*, Amnesty International)

suicide. suicide by drowning or suicide by hanging. suicide by jumping off a bridge. & died. roma. died or killed. died in a fire. died jumping from a train. & drowned. reportedly. run over by a car reaching the italian beach. & drowned. roma. drowned in the river trying to cross the border. no name. found on a duck boat & found in a car park & found on a cucumber lorry. & shot. stowaway. shot in the back. shot in the head. shot on a mountain way. no name. & died. died or killed. & drowned. drowned in the canal. drowned in a small boat. roma. after release walked in front of a tram. & died. died or killed. died after falling from a window. fell into the sea. illegal worker. no name. found dead in the desert. asylum seeker. died in a container fire. roma. rubber boat broke up. no name. blown up in a minefield trying to cross the border. & drowned. minor. drowned while trying to swim across the river. roma. stoned to death. stoned to death by traffickers. killed. crushed by a truck. & killed. reportedly. reportedly fell down in front of spain. & died. died or killed. reportedly thrown overboard. missing. sans papiers. missing presumed drowned. smashed in a trash collector. & suffocated. suffocated in a sealed container & suffocated by a neck lock. suffocated eating money to avoid being robbed. & shot. shot in the stomach during a police check. sans papiers. died in an overcrowded boat. & died. died or killed. & drowned. found in fishing nets & found by coastguards & found dead in an irrigation ditch. asylum seeker. killed. killed by a roadside bomb. recovered from the sea. no name. roma. jumped by nazis outside a detention centre. & shot. jumped from a church tower. jumped from a train. jumped from a courthouse window. reportedly. & died. died or killed. died in brussels airport. shot & buried by gendarmes. frozen in an aircraft wheelbay. roma. frozen in a heavy sea. set fire to the bed & drowned. drowned in a small boat & drowned in a stranded boat. drowned in stormy waters. roma. fell from the fifth floor reaching the italian beach. fell from a border fence. & died. died or killed. died in care & died in custody & died while trying to cross to england. suicide. found dead. touching an electric cable. hanging in the shower. found dead in a bus shelter. & drowned. reportedly. in a drifting boat & in a dinghy. roma. no name. found dead in a cargo ship. jumped. reportedly. reportedly jumped off the bridge & died. died or killed. killed in a factory fire & killed on a freight train & killed in the middle of the road. asylum seeker. laid down in a prison & died. suffocated. suffocated with a pillow. suffocated in a bus compartment. shot by nazis wearing life jackets reaching the italian beach. & drowned. afraid of going. sans papiers afraid of going to the doctor. & died. died in a fall from a north sea ferry. died or killed. died in the boot of a car. roma. walking into calais set themselves on fire. & drowned. drowned near kos & drowned giving birth & drowned in territorial waters. & found. in a small boat. in a garden. in a state of advanced decomposition. minor. tied him to her waist to cross the river & drowned. no names. died of brain damage in a refugee hostel. died or killed. stowaway. hit by a train & hit by the propeller of a motor boat. & died. hit by a bus. died in a van. died after being left alone. roma. eaten in the forest by wolves. & drowned. drowned in the aegean & drowned near lampedusa. drowned in the channel of otranto. reportedly. reportedly hit by a police boat. & died. died or killed. killed by a racist cellmate. & died. died after fourteen days at sea. reportedly of cancer. in a street riot. reportedly near heathrow. asylum seeker. died of thirst. denied interpreter. fearing deportation died of thirst. died of bullet wounds. died of anxiety psychosis. & drowned. drowned in the seine fleeing from police. drowned in the rhine. drowned in the river thames. found dead. roma. found dead in the snow. found dead after sixteen days at sea. ignored by NATO. no name. SOS ignored by NATO. no name. suicide. found dead. ignored by NATO. & died. SOS. died or killed. killed. drowned. killed.

BIO

Jeff Hilson has written four books of poetry: *stretchers* (Reality Street, 2006), *Bird bird* (Landfill, 2009), *In The Assarts* (Veer, 2010) and *Latanoprost Variations* (Boiler House Press, 2017). A fifth book, *Organ Music*, is due out from Crater Press in 2018. He also edited *The Reality Street Book of Sonnets* (Reality Street, 2008). He runs Xing the Line poetry reading series in London, and is Reader in Creative Writing at the University of Roehampton.

ÁILBHE HINES
Buried Deeds

bodies soak up traces earthed in burial emergence in embodied
imprints

these eyes hold behind them generation upon generation of

dark matters matters material touchable known

birthing our meanings in ceremonies

in rituals we've found and kept is not stationary is transitory is not
stationary Is not about the merit
of is choice made legacies of broken tribes

when you let yourself in use the land as you will to empire a
psyche

once you're done wringing hands

human beings seek spaces to home in

not new prisons suspicions restrictions made fleeing
in the first place

to a better living a life a life a life a life a life

not policy problem

not deceit
not

mattering not what why

or if there's room this child died

before was seen and still

feet keep stepping out of terror

floods created crops manipulated out of hard working hands

shaming other cultures lost but shared in blurred borderlines
almost
obsolete

cultures carried and remain in

much struggle to identity traps

when

dams break here away here there

can repair repair despite lack ofs and rhetoric of lack and lack of
body knows

landscapes in memory interventions intervening in return bringing
back our buried deeds

the seeds grown and wildly tidal new wave slaves flee and
further slavery

and how to say it so it
how to say it so

Refugee is Verb not Noun

toxicity tricks us

masked as progress perceived molecular stew expanding

sought at first adventure onto terrae nullii

worst kind of beginning

each breath exhaled held feared ways of being broken

in harsh conquested ordering dwellers in image of borders

feeding fictions coded classed mined minds

complete saturation thoughts of oughtsof thoughts of shouldbes
cannotdos

only scintilla of glimmer of counter deflection resist

skins over scars letting edges dissolve when eons
taken in creation

refugee is verb not noun nationhoods
depthy shallows
stood on shores submerging

walking into moment singing

sinking songs of heart and circumstance

the every distant past

seeping in the weeping the wondered wandered forward times

wavering breezes breathe into being temporally

vessels pours and holds codes in cargo is is is
longed for

lonely

lay self down drain out of

shell self

see
the river's lineage splitting streams
extremes to get to
somewhere

BIO

Áilbhe Hines creates performances, installations, environmental art and conceptual artworks. She is an expressive arts therapist, writer and a community artist and is happiest when playing and making art in nature. The works Áilbhe creates, attempt to challenge the binaries/limitations we face structurally. She seeks to deconstruct the relationship, restraints, or conflict, between self and other, masculine and feminine, ecology and technology, revolution, justice, equality and exile. She is interested in the attempt of dialogue, the dissonances within form and content and the dysfunctions of language and action.

NASSER HUSSAIN

The Ark

GET DOS AHI
DOS KOI
DOS EEL
DOS COW AND CUB
BEE AND BOA
YAK AND LEO
DOE AND DOG
DOS APE ANT ASP AUK
DOS BAT RAT CAT CUR AND MOG

EWE AND GNU
GAD FLY AND MAY FLY
RAM NAG AND PET PIG
HEN HOG PUG AND PUP
THE LAM KID AND THE FOX KIT
THE ELK ROC AND YAK
THE SEA SOW AND TAU RUS

(ARF BAA BAY BZZ COO GRR
KAW MEW MOO YIP WAG PAW)

AND GET

ONE NOA
AND HIS EMS ARA

ONE HAM
AND NEL ATA MUK

ONE SHM
AND HIS BAE

ONE JAP ETH
AND ADA TAN ESE

ALL THE DNA
AND RNA

GET THE HAY
FOR THE POO PIT

GET THE AFT WET
DRY THE BOW OAR

ROW THE PEN

YAY! SEE THE TOR?
ARA RAT.

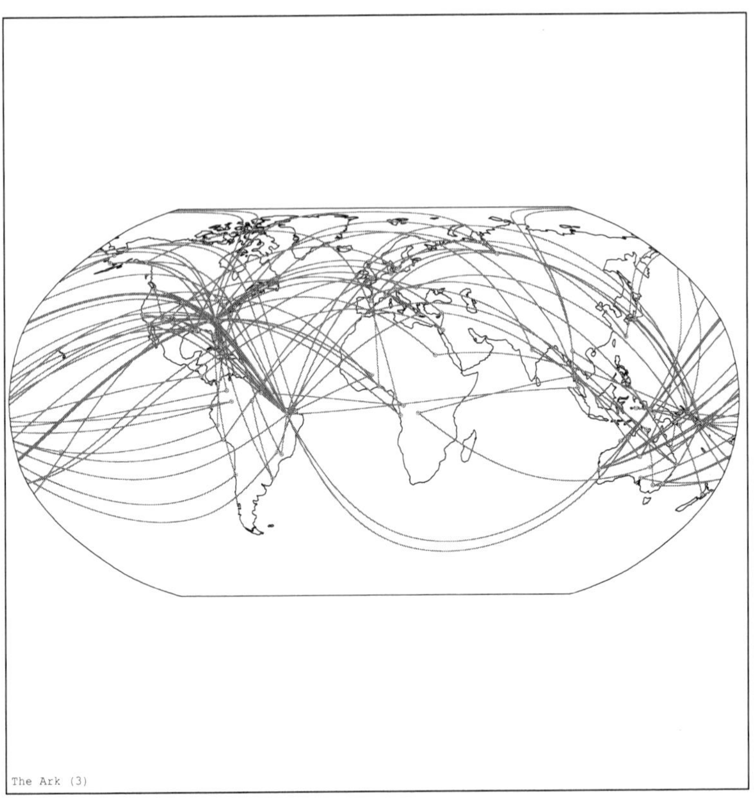

The Ark (3)

BIO

Nasser Hussain is a lecturer in Literature and Creative Writing at Leeds Beckett University. Matthew Stephenson is a Senior GIS Specialist at Thurber Engineering Ltd in Canada. Their poems and maps will be published in the collection *SKY WRI TEI NGS*, from Coach House Press in autumn 2018.

ZAINAB ISMAIL

sharp relief

i am natural as a veined
engraving on a london leaf

you tell me
the trees emboss
my belonging—accept
the fullest breaths, longest breaths, longing
and loss purified

i am a teal temple staggered to the canopy
                                        staggered
                                            staggered

no doubt, no debt
let the sheer sky snap up my
unworthiness

trilateral roots

i stut-ter
even at the genesis of it
the littlest summit

three arabesques
dotted inkjets on my desk—
ka ta ba

which should propel
intricate new words down
my ruled page

what if this taproot tapestry
wove the heavens
in my mouth

where convoluted verbs should
travel south
rather than miss me mute?

'should' knells
i am on my knees
i don't know arabic auxiliaries

BIO

Zainab Ismail is a third-year student of English Literature with Creative Writing at the University of Greenwich. She has been published in *The Fortnightly Review* and *Tears in the Fence*. Her poetry can also be found on Instagram (@zai__i).

MARIA JASTRZĘBSKA

Polish Fingers – Paluszki

1.

Maria,

We live in a world where some problems feel too huge to tackle.

While you were sleeping, the government passed a new Parcelisation Law. They say it will enable a more efficient form of repatriation, where citizens like you and me are cut up, then parcelled off to their respective countries of origin. Last week a woman's vulva was shipped to Estonia while her breasts and liver remain in Lincolnshire and a man's lungs (despite medical evidence provided by his G.P that they are weeping) are alleged to be en route to Macedonia. Reports indicate feet arriving (back) in Aleppo, their arms in neighbouring Turkey and Iraq.

2.

Since, at this time of year my fingers smell of herring it must – incontrovertibly – be that my hands are at their most Polish. More Polish than in the summer. Unless I were to pick raspberries. Or trail my hands over the side of a kayak in the river. I was really nervous at the Trans Pride open mic night, says P in case I wasn't queer enough. Every minority measures itself. How can you be half this or that? These same fingers which once waggled and reached for my mother's face in its orbit, now flap, wiggle, clamping themselves into fists, tracing circles in the air, lifting a thumb up or down until they fall exhausted into my lap.

Fingers tell shiny autobiographies, one bead after another. Fingers cover her face as she hides, fingers pick at the wallpaper by her bed. They flick bogies, sweep the sides of a bowl. Thorough as a midwife.

3.

At the party while we lay on the floor listening to Janis, Pink Floyd, Blood Sweat and Tears – T told me he liked kissing boys as much as he liked kissing girls, maybe more, much more. No one had spoken to me like that. Looking into my eyes he took my hand and unfolding my fingers he said: 'made for it, aren't they?' Today as they signal, outpacing the words which my mouth forms, conducting their own orchestra *veloce, rubato,* with lyrics more simple and more urgent than anything I can say, as they wave to one another from their far away shores, does the left hand understand the right?

4.

Dear Maria

Right now we're at a crossroads. You could think 'I'll do that tomorrow'. You could delete this email and hope someone else will step up. Or, you could read this email and decide to chip in to take on giants. Please make your donation by midnight today. Itsy bitsy spider versus here comes the crab, poor fellow: fingers find the fork in the road. Good luck, good luck! Polish fingers don't cross alone or together. They fold protectively over their thumbs instead.

5.

Go on, taste the salty little fingers, *soletti*, of one hand. Now lick the chocolate fingers – Honeycomb Fabulous, Toffee Crunch – of the other. Which hand is which? You don't know? Just don't let the red-legged scissor man catch you sucking your thumbs or he will chop them off, snip-snip, snap-snap.

6.

Some fingers have no time to digress. Nicotine stained, stumpy, delicate, nails extended with glittering gel, chapped, swollen, raw from packing chicken, pulling turnips, picking clams, they drum impatiently. Someone else is singing about Victor Jara's fingers, broken by the Junta's men to stop him playing the guitar. There are so many ways to silence us. By midnight today. Here we come, step by step up our beloved's thighs or marching along a table to the edge.

BIO

Maria Jastrzębska's recent collections include *At The Library of Memories* (Waterloo Press 2013). Her selected poems were translated into Polish (SŻP Faktoria 2015). She co-edited *Queer in Brighton* (New Writing South 2014) and has translated Justyna Bargielska's *The Great Plan B* (Smokestack 2017). *The True Story of Cowboy Hat and Ingénue* is forthcoming (Liquorice Fish 2018). www.mariajastrzebska.wordpress.com

LISA JESCHKE

Bio Liver

"I eat solely local produce and organic" :-)
Next up: guillotine!

The rest-of-body of proto-professional hunter sees own organic head,
O O Head of pro-pro hunter sees rest-of-body of pro-pro hunter,

"I never thought my head could ever be divorced from its roots!"
"I've only ever experienced immediacy!"

"All my experiences have been real!"
"All feelings feelings!"

"I wanted globally local con –"
"I hated –"

"I suffer!"
"Hi, I hunt –"

"Why me? Dead? No recycling?"
"Even?"

Not even even.
You hated foreign organs.

Torso hands profoundly hold
Ringing head thought handy produce for thoughts.

One skull one garden!
To sleep that barking,

Hears own continued
Barking crying

Melting in-pity
Self-puddle,

Fencing.
Flag.

The Future, in the Shape of the Identitarian Movement's Worst Nightmare: Soft

Fine-dust the future
Now all together
Though never all one. Soft.

Never the same as the second before
Fast-valley
Brink. Flowers, yes, no, yes. Prostheses. Soft.

Rainbow! Rainbows! Infection giggling streams multi-
Ply varnish glitter meadow glitz, plus the admission of pain cute plus
Clouds softly joy, mingling

Floss and rope glistening hope no fog no root necessity compatibility.
    Aliens. All.
Even the sheep have auto un-sheeped
On sparkling pasture pleasantly. Soft.

Plastic, plastic hands, plastic synth, plastic
No borders.
Kitsch, this? So – wrong?

Let's continue this non-threatening song!
There will be showers of stars as pieces of gold
All the girls lying on the street will be rich

Muscles
Irrespective of where they have come from and whether they are girls
    or boys.
Toilets for all. Cosmic. Turn, corner. Toilets for all.

No borders!

BIO

Lisa Jeschke makes theatre with Lucy Beynon and runs the poetry publication series MATERIALS | MATERIALIEN with David Grundy.

EVAN JONES

Statutes of England

Action to Animals to Arbitration
to Charities to Choses in Action to Conflict
of Laws to Constitutional Law to Coroners
to County Courts to Criminal Law to Crown
Proceedings to Easements to Ecclesiastical
Law to Education to Electricity to Employment
to Ferries to Fire Services to Guarantee
to Highways to Husband and Wife to
Income Tax to Inns and Innkeepers to Insurance
to Limitation of Actions to Literary Institutions
to Markets and Fairs to Master and
Servant to Metropolis to Mines and Minerals
to National Insurance to Negligence to Pleading
to Police to Public Authorities to Public
Health to Railways and Canals to Rates
and Rating to Rentcharging to Revenue to Royal
Forces to Set-off and Counterclaim to Settlements
to Shipping and Navigation to Solicitors to
Telegraphs to Theatres to Trover and Detinue
to Trusts and Trustees to Wills

At the Passport Office

Bundesrepublik security reads *Golf Equipment Buyer.*
He's hungry, determined
to ignore the woman working her pram up the stairs,
baby in arm. Her application will fail.
Her common-law husband's foiled their papers.
She'll stay in London for the summer.

Security doesn't take this in. Part of his job's
to issue numbers, which he does –
tapping a red, plastic snail
without looking up.
An old woman overtakes the pram.
The numbers tear clean.

The air is cool and neutral.
People barely speak, except before
the glassed-in officers who file forms
and answer questions bilingually.
They dislike their jobs and life in England.
They are at least pleasant.

This lonely girl in Converse
Hi-Tops will wait. She has paid the cashier,
her left ear has three piercings, travelling
up from the lobe in equal spacing.
She's been forgotten.
Her mother's a nurse in Dresden.

And this man is so thrilled to be married
he's forgotten his *Namenserklärung.*
And that old woman is pretty much
in and out, filing her husband's *Totenschein*,
the last living thing of his
her hands will miss.

There is no food allowed here,
and the baby needs feeding.
Frightened, overtired, overalert,
nothing will calm her.
Security, all the while reading,
might yet lay down his magazine.

But the baby knows what I and that girl
and old woman and even
her dead husband know:
we won't be leaving until our names are called.
It's time for so many to go,
and there are so many written down.

BIO

Canadian poet Evan Jones has lived in Manchester since 2005. His most recent collection is *Paralogues* (Carcanet 2012).

LOMA SYLVANA JONES

negra

two girls, but so much the same. porpoises in a lane-roped pool, one taller, the other faster, both matching shades of nut gold with bright eyes, hers a little lighter. at what age did we become different colours? five on the classroom floor our hands met beneath a table, my fingers already longer but building churches we could lose one knuckle in the similarity of the others.

i don't remember us ever saying black, it never needed saying. we learnt one another by name and smell and the pitch of prepubescent voices, and that too was how we absorbed all the others. back then we had the same voice, our vowels rolled out down the same lanes. i nearly went dumb when i left, my parents packed my spare voice for the journey. i am a gemini whenever i reach for your phantom hand, the one chance i had at a twin.

blanc

i can't quite catch the edges of my own irises, the field of vision shows me bouncing off the retinas of everyone around me. every one of them is white. not thick laid snow or a first tooth, colourless, like melanin sucked straight from the vein, a newly cut wound before blood touches the surface, white like suspended organs seen through milk. their disguises are lacking, the meat shows more easily on the bone but their calves match their palms. i am drawn into the waking pool that ushers out from my pupils, the sclera spreads wider. it creeps across my skin, there is ink on my hands, covering the body, coffee and black walnut, cutch on living leather. take a layer off, peel away the gloves like school glue. she's the hostess of every period drama, a blush of such subtle pink you have to look away, never seen such a wet blue eye. i catch myself in the parlour mirror, cracks spidering out from my eyes. a flaking vaudevillian, face full of lead.

BIO

Loma Sylvana Jones is a poet currently based in Sheffield, despite being continually tempted to write about places else-where. At this point in time she predominantly writes about geography and race and the multifarious identities that they give rise to.

MARIA KARDEL

Childless, Abroad

You travel light. There is
No heirloom quilt waiting. Your story
Fades each year. Once, you kept space
For homemade jam, tart liqueurs, wild mushrooms,
Ear-like and strung up with twine.
These days, you hold your breath in a wallet,
Close to your chest.

You're a bleached bone,
Found on a bed of moss in an inky wood.
You've been pushed out,
Out from a city of roots, inverted sky-scrapers,
Chambers filled with organic matter, overgrown with
Networks of mycelia, lace of hair-thin vessels.
In the half-light, the etchings on your back
Plead to be deciphered, dated, measured.
Your curve wishes to be twirled
In curious fingers.

You're a stripped branch, mute and white,
A dry crown of summer. Somewhere, in your growth rings
Sleep stories of love and death, of girls with fingers
Silvered by fish scales, of young men boarding ships.
For you, there's no map. You wear your surface blank,
Tongue dry as paper.

January Snow

A poem for a birthday

In a far away country, the house
Your great grandfather built stands
Fringed in icicles, its roof concave
Under the weight of flake.

It snowed all night. Trees groan, gloved in white.
Apples twirl, wrinkled parcels.
Day breaks over the lacework of prints in the fields:
A hare's fuzzy snowshoe,
A fox's dainty slipper,
Tridents of pheasant feet.

This is January snow, blue with cold.
Śnieg, a sharp spark struck on a sea of white,
Hard-sounding, a ball thrown at a bullfinch
Puffed up in the bush.

One morning, you might stand here, gap-year lanky, following
Your father's four-syllable name, tracing it
In steam on windowpanes. You'll dream
Of sledges able to carry you down the steepest hills,
Of foreign words for colours and textures to describe the ice.

Breathe now, learn to make your lungs blossom.
They'll unfurl like window frost.

BIO

Maria Kardel was born in East Germany and grew up in Poland; she has lived in Sheffield since 2006. She holds a PhD in English Literature (University of Sheffield, 2012), her specialism being Eastern European interpretations of Shakespeare. Her work has appeared online and in print in *The Sheffield Anthology* (Smith/Doorstop, 2012) and *Route 57*, the student creative writing journal, where she also co-edited the poetry section. Currently, she teaches English at a secondary school/sixth form college.

FAWZI KARIM, TRANSLATED BY ANTHONY HOWELL

from *The Empty Quarter*

1.

I landed, thanks to a pair of wings,
        a flask of wine and pack of cigarettes.
Peculiar state of exiled human, hoping that some girl
        might actually speak Iraqi in Hyde Park –
My verse without its target butt, my arrow careless of its aim.
I am a somnambulist
Borne along by passers-by:
        flanneur among their hastening feet...
But through the glass facade of a Camden shop,
        amid its antique bric-a-brac,
I spied an oil lamp stained by soot
        that once was so familiar!
As if through a lens, I
        saw the mud wall of a house
    above that lantern's copper base.
The glow from its funnel seemed to breathe
        a dragon made of light that hovered there
    on the bellied ceiling of the mats.
At some earlier time I teased out stuff
        into a cloud of coloured fluff
    and threw it in the faces that I came across –
Have been an existentialist; celebrating an ambiguous consciousness,
        patching up a mangled dress, using the sun's fine yarn.
But at the sight of my lamp in Camden Town

I free myself of the past, that flightless pack
        that weighs my shoulders down.
It is here, and I am here,
Fascinated by a girl, her shoulder bare,
        Flying, flying through the air,
while squirrels fly from branch to branch,
        and she is whispering in my ear: "hug me, hug me now!
Hold me, before I disappear."

Who wouldn't flinch from the cities' blows?
        – cities of the North
        as wet and cold as its forests –
To find solace in stupefaction
        from the dregs of its dark wine
        in the varnished dark of all its bars?
And so I have slept on the sidewalks of my maze,
My verse without its target butt, my arrow careless of its aim...
And to support my pain, I lean now on this walking-stick
        That helps my steps towards exile.

A feverish wind weaves a song between my ruins:
        "Our heritage is exile here, not our better times.
        Our heritage is exile here, not our better times."

2.

But if the dead can give up their tombs
        in the memory of one alive,
If they can abandon all the cities which enclosed them,

If they can cross the dangerous road,
        as we did, barefoot, into the haven of exile,
If they can swathe themselves in the get-up of pirates,
Inhabit silent ships motionlessly afloat
        in the stagnant water of their sea,
Then I can choose the limbo most appropriate for me
In London, under an umbrella
Celebrating my isolation, free to hang out in the bar –
        Free, that is, from everything but the nude shoulder
Of a girl whispering in my ear,
        "Hug me, hold me now,
        before I disappear."
She leaves me trapped inside a lamp swinging from a cart
        lurching down a bumpy track.
Is this the way to cross the Empty Quarter?

But the past, the past is like poetry...
        'Poetry, shaven of pate,
        shepherds everything, high on a hill.
A rural man with a flowing gown.'[1]
He is one who remains forever young, who wants not, when I want,
        who runs like grass where I walk,
        and opens like a flower when I just put out my palm.
He lounges on my desk like a book tired by boredom,
        a book with scorched edges.
And when I stare at the restless bells of night,
The past appears like a maid in a jet-black scarf,
        sitting in the presence of the Sultan of Lovers,
        And when her cup runs empty, the sword-man fills it up.

3.

Cities are causing overcrowding inside me, and I'm in a more numerous state than most of Europe's *endroits*. My alleys know neither discord nor harmony. Neither poetry, nor music, nor painting can fulfil me as much as could some settlement of my account with history. Autumn is leaning against the fence of my garden, leaving me a bunch of chestnut leaves which has just fallen from its imagination. I know it's been left for me. Am I not the autumnal man, and doesn't Autumn know it? No difference between the colour of the leaves and the henna on the breasts of the robins. In London, it is pre-Islamic poetry that takes hold of me and make me thirsty. My lips crack, and therefore I anoint them.

4.

I grabbed a girl who said to me
        "You're not much good at flirting."
I took her to my youthful room.
I was so pissed. And she said:
        "You're not much good,
        even with the most basic words
        in *The Beginners Guide."*
I told her I was confused,
Making the point
        by stabbing at my forehead with a finger.
I said, "Why doesn't the Disco
        open in the day?
        If it did the heat could ease my paranoia."

I feel cold, and orphaned when it's dark,
As if the night subjected me to a body search
In front of the sphinx-like stares of the border police.

5.

'The seer's as blind as I am,
So let us collide in the dark.'[2]
I said: "Back home, your steps
        went stumbling past,
        until they woke me up.
Oh sheikh, what heavy reason
        has prompted you to come for me?"

"I didn't come for you," he said.
"You just imagine that I did.
Inheritor, you've taken on the disorder of my soul.
An atom of dust rubs up against its counterpart
In some old verse I wrote down in my book.

Two poets, both accepting
        what their times dictate:
We are two drops,
And this one evaporates
Just as simply as the other freezes."

6.

'The rust on the knocker is old as night,
And the door is ancient, closed.'[3]
So down goes my baggage, dumped on the asphalt,
Why would the passers-by
        bother to notice
        a tramp out of time with all tourists?
He stands there, gaunt as a telephone pole,
        hoping, but for what?
No one sees the huge locked door that looms here,
        right in front of him;
A weathered door that stops him
        from breaking into the hubbub of London.
First reaction? Back into the head.
Time is not counted in seconds there,
        but in the ripples as they pass.
I strip off and throw myself in,
And I say to myself, "Dear self,
        stay very clear of your loss."
And the answer comes back 'that "home"
        is a catwalk between abysses,
And he who puts out to sea
Seeking another shore may lose the coast.'[4]
But there is that girl again, ever so near:
"Hug me, hold me, hold me now,
        before I disappear."

7.

I spoke. "The wine that got me pissed
        was that enriched by the sun,
But now I am the autumnal one
        (how solemnly intoned).
Heed my boughs, as they divest
        themselves of autumn's leaves
To publish each abandoned nest.
My shadow falls in front of me.
It is a vast abyss."

She smiled. Her smile brought out a smile.
I said, "I'm the father of sons.
Their roots are in the present.
Mine prefer the past.
Mine exist to burrow deep,
        delving into what has ceased to be.
All my enigmas are personal now.
They're puzzles only to me."

Her finger smuggled its secret into my palm.
That very night, her lips were mine;
My head soothed by the pink fan of delight.

8.

There is another inside me.
He gets invited into my Empty Quarter;
Suffers its bleak stretches
in the middle of the night.
Dune, wind and mirage...
This is my Empty Quarter.

But then there's this tree, my neighbour's,
Laden with its oranges – Sevilles.
Laden, says my memory,
With juice nurtured by the sleep of winter.
How can I harvest these here,
Where all is spoilt by the stench of tar?
Through the window of my silent home I see
Windfalls coated in smoke.
Barbed wire trammels my moments
As insects are caught in a web.

9.

'Slumber now, my weary eyes,
Be as the wings of butterflies
Folded – let the eyelids close.
Oh World, you offer scant repose.
I leave thee now, renounce thee, quit
The trauma of the outcast, flit,
But Oh, to where?'[5]

To where? – I let the track repeat,
Closed the book at last,
Drank what was left in the glass,
Gazed at my reflected face
that offered little peace.
'Millstone of exile, granting no leave
to return...'[6]
So went the verse, as was its wont.
Christmas, however, had churned out its tidings
Unto a myriad races
crammed into the morning's market shed.
"Lights out!" I declared in haste
and fled upstairs, to bed.

NOTES

1 verse from The Plague Lands.
2 verse by Abo Alaa Almaarri.
3 from the poem 'abd al Amir Alhosairi.
4 from 'Paradise of Fools'.
5 aria from Bach's cantata BWV82.
6 from the poem 'Necosia'.

BIO

Fawzi Karim is an Iraqi poet, writer and painter. Born in Baghdad in 1945, he was educated at Baghdad University before embarking on a career as a freelance writer. He lived in London since 1978. He has published more than twenty three books of poetry, and sixteen books of prose. His poetry is translated to French, Sweden, Italian and English.

KAPKA KASSABOVA

Everybody Comes to Ali's

from *Border: A Journey to the Edge of Europe* (Granta, 2017)

In a Turkish café not far from the European border, the TV showed the world's longest belly-dancing show. A woman in gold gyrated on the screen, her greasy red lips fixed in a smile, with the sound off. But none of the men in the café paid attention. They had other things on their minds.

The café didn't look much from the outside. It was a featureless shop front without a name. But when you stepped inside, it was a pressure cooker. The atmosphere was so thick with suppressed emotion, with cigarette smoke and the tumble of rolled dice, and with that particular male burden of having to take action against the odds, that my first instinct was to flee. It was physically difficult to advance beyond the doorway.

I sat down and ordered tea, fielding heavy looks from the tables until they subsided. The waiter, a silent man of fifty with haunted eyes and the broken nose of a boxer, brought me a glass of tea with three lumps of sugar, and put it down with a flourish. A stained tea towel was draped over his arm, someone laughed and coughed in the corner, cards were slapped down, and for a moment this felt like a return – though I had no idea why. I had never been to a tea house like this before, where nothing was consumed other than tea and no woman set foot.

Though Ali's tea house was special. Everybody came to Ali's – everybody who had nowhere else to go and everybody who was in need of passage across the border, which was the same thing. There were two categories of customer in Ali's Café. The first were from the neighbourhood. The second were those who came from troubled places, and you could tell who they were from the faraway look in their eyes.

All the tables were taken except the one where I sat, and the silent waiter never stopped circulating with a tray of tea glasses and sugar lumps. The table of locals played a game of something that looked like dominoes, but they played for money. Even though no cash changed hands at the table, you could tell what was going on from the fact that once the game was over, one guy bought a round of tea for everyone. That was the winner. At that point the players relaxed and laughed, chatted, lit another cigarette, went for a pee.

Those at the other tables didn't play. They huddled in groups but there was little conversation, they were too busy scrolling down their mobile devices. They scrolled, drank tea, occasionally looked up with empty eyes. And they waited.

'Kurds from Iraq.' Ali the owner pointed at one table discreetly.

I had plucked up the courage to go and meet Ali, out in the crepuscular back of the café where he perched behind an old-fashioned desk and scribbled something in a big logbook, like a tired teacher at the end of term.

Ali was tall and dapper, with a photogenic hawkish face and long greying hair, like an ageing rock star. He invited me to sit across the desk from him, like a student, gave me Turkish coffee as a special treat, and told me how much he liked to go to Bulgaria. There was another table, occupied by four skinny young men with hollow cheeks and once-smart jackets who looked like university drop-outs. One of them was texting furiously with his jaw clenched, eyes red from crying. When I had walked in and startled the rest of the clientele by being a woman, everybody had looked up, except this table. This table was sealed off from the rest by a heavy energy field. I felt it before I could articulate it: the loneliness of the leper, that's what they shared.

'Syrians,' Ali said. 'Life is crap for them.' The Turkish word was pis.

Ali was from Rize, the tea-growing town on the southern Black Sea coast not far from the border with Georgia, but he rarely went home. His mother sent him tea and home-made cakes.

Rize chai, he said and pointed at his glass with a dark twinkle in his eye, as if he wanted to say something else altogether, ask what I was doing here, why I was bothering him with my presence, as if he didn't have enough problems already. Every few minutes, someone would come up to his desk and pay for the tea. A young guy with his hair sprayed hard into an Elvis wave produced a thick wad of US dollars from his pocket to pay for a round, and Ali quickly found change in his drawer. All currencies were welcome here, no questions asked. Then Ali would make a little mark next to the name in his logbook.

I saw now that there was a whole other part of the café, beyond Ali's desk. Decorated with a single faded portrait of Kemal Atatürk, it was desolate, like the waiting room at a provincial railway station where the train has been cancelled. The tables in this section were reserved for a faster kind of transaction that didn't involve tea. But it involved money. Every now and again, skinny men with rucksacks would slip into the back and occupy this inner sanctum.

I did as Ali did and pretended this was normal. I pretended it was no big deal to see smugglers sealing deadly deals with the already-robbed of this world by robbing them further. The money came in bundles tied with elastic bands, in exchange for the promise of a lorry ride across the border. In many cases, people were dumped off before they even reached the border, and so they were back to square one, back in Turkey, back in Ali's Café, but this time without money. It was groundhog day, a Sisyphean sentence – to endlessly go up and down the airless corridor that never changed, though everything else changed. And never to arrive.

They said Turkey was the final destination for those who had no money to go further west.

I couldn't tell the smugglers from the clients – they all looked similar, unshaven, dingy. That's because it's not actually the smugglers you see there, I was told later. No trafficker worth his salt would turn up in person or give you his real name.

One of the younger Kurds at the Iraqi table had a different, softer look – he actually smiled at me in a carefree, relaxed way that didn't chime with the heavy vibes. He looked as if, in a different life, he could be happy. His name was Erdem, though I only found that out when I ran into him a few weeks later in Svilengrad.

He was here with his sister, staying in a cheap hostel, and waiting to get smuggled into Bulgaria in the back of a truck. He wore a smart cream jacket from another era, like some Great Gatsby who had gone down the wrong corridor of history.

'One more tea, Murat!' Ali ordered and the waiter brought me yet another glass of strong tea. Murat sneaked outside for a quick cigarette whenever he could, although everybody inside smoked constantly. I guessed he needed time out from the pressure cooker of human souls.

Ali was always here, from early morning to past midnight, he said. In any case, Ali said, and looked at me hard, if I told you some of the things that have gone on here, you would break out in a rash.

While Ali was putting a few marks next to a name, I heard piano chords on the radio somewhere in the back, or maybe it was somebody's mobile. It was an old melody, and after a few chords, I realised I had somehow been expecting to hear something along the lines of a kiss being just a kiss.

This was no place for romance, but it brought home to me why Ali's Café felt familiar in an atemporal way and why Ali cut a timeless black-and-white figure, though we were here now, in colour, in the middle of the 2010s, facing something resembling Europe, with the ransacked Middle East behind us.

Perhaps there is a Casablanca for every moment in time when war exiles people from themselves and catapults them to transit realms. A place with Rick's Bar, or Ali's Café, a safe house where the homeless of the day come in search of passage. Or just to sit and take comfort in something that never changes: 'One more tea, Murat!'

Once, Ali told me, a man with a rucksack came to the café, and when Murat went up to him and asked 'What would you like?', he broke down.

In Istanbul, he had paid eight thousand euros to a trafficker to get him across the border in a truck. But the truck dumped him and the others on some godforsaken Strandja hill, and when they ran up to a shepherd and asked him Bulgaria, Bulgaria?, he shook his head – Turkey, Turkey.

He walked back all the way to Ali's Café because he had no money left.

'And you know the worst part?' Ali said. 'He could have taken the bus from Istanbul to the border. It costs fifty euros.'

The man had lost his family in Syria.

'Every time I look at his corner, I see him,' Ali said. 'When I close up at night and everybody's gone, you won't believe me but that's when the café really fills up. With ghosts. Twenty years' worth of ghosts, coming and going.'

And then the next morning he would get up early to open the café, for business as usual.

BIO

Kapka Kassabova is a poet and writer, most recently of *Border: a journey to the edge of Europe* (2017), which won the Saltire Book of the Year, Stanford-Dolman Travel Book of the Year, and was short-listed for the Baillie-Gifford Prize and the American National Circle of Critics Award. She is also the author of the narrative non-fiction works *Street Without a Name* (2008) and *Twelve Minutes of Love* (2011). Kapka Kassabova grew up in Bulgaria, was educated in New Zealand, and now lives in Scotland.

ÖZGECAN KESICI

Agajai

Elim köship qangyrady
Jerim qaldy
Asqara su shurayly
Elim qaldy
Agajai Altaidai jer qaida?
(Kazakh folk song)

I carry a scar with me,
pink and soft to the touch –
its survival could mean strength.

My scar is invisible to your eyes:
it is not someplace on my thigh,
it is not on the brow of my eye,
no, not even my lover's come by it.

Sabyr, patience.

When the migration moved,
trotting across snow and atop glaciers
on Himalaya's back:
sheep, camels, whatever was left from our long march.

Sabyr, patience.

We left them on the ice, our hands were weak,
our hearts tired, no, we couldn't bury them,
we left them on the ice,
approximating the direction of Mecca
saying prayers, and shroudless –
some left prayerless
squatting by the path
until the thicket of Himalayan snow covered them
and they too disappeared between tired memories
and sighs of acceptance.

Sabyr, patience.

Given tomatoes to eat in India
when we didn't know such fruits
we threw them into hot water
trying to make soups,
the guards looked at us, puzzled.
Where did these lost souls come from?
And where were they headed?
We shrugged and walked on.

Turkey gave us names, and land and food
and together we went Westward
and were questioned by post 9/11 Westerners:
Where is your headscarf? Are you oppressed?
Why do you meddle in what is between me and the greater?

Sabyr, patience.

I carry a scar with me, a scar I have loved at times
for reminding me of those hardships.
I carry a scar with me, a scar I have hated at times
for making me ambiguous,
marking me with a name only few can pronounce.

My lover tells me, *let's give our children names they can speak.*
But what if the child forgets?

Patience, *sabyr.*

As the old imam whispers into my ear at an age-old name-giving
ceremony:

Your name is Özgecan
Your name is Özgecan
Your name is Özgecan.

BIO

Özgecan Kesici was born in Germany to Kazakh-Turkish parents, and now lives in Dublin's inner city. She holds a PhD in Sociology from UCD. In 2015, she was featured as a migrant poet on Ireland's Near FM 90.3's *Poetic Lives* series. Her work has been published in the *All the Worlds Between Anthology* (Yoda Press, 2017) and *Poetry Ireland Review*.

MIMI KHALVATI

Questions

In some minds, questions never raise their heads
like crocuses that line a path in spring.
But mind has mountains, yes, and fountainheads,
streamflows that answer needs for watering.

Bring me the snowmelt then, now spring is here,
a hut on the road and my lost ancestral story,
washed clean as it is, for the wind to spear
and straggle on some hermit's morning glory.

Never ask where home is, how far away
is far away, how long ago long is.
Leave the gate open. Spiders are at home

and someone's left a straw hat, a lice comb –
an old poet who stopped here on his journey.
Borrow them, he won't mind. They're not his.

Cafés

Envy them, the lonely, there by the glass,
there in the corner, staring into space
for as long as it takes the world to pass,
close up, far off, sprinkled like stars in cafés.

Envy them their orbit: how flagstones throw
a thin horned shadow of a bicycle
they take for Rocinante; how they borrow
childhood landscapes, birch forests hazed in dapple,

a handful of lights from the Crimean plateau,
O envy them their raised sleeping-car window!
'Habituated to the Vast', how they move,

leaving a good tip, pulling on a glove,
paying with the exact change from their purse,
through spacetime in an abstract universe.

Hide and Seek

Truth is, there's nobody she wants to find.
The very act of finding's frightening:
the human crouching in the bush, the blind
hump of hair and shoulder, the tell-tale clothing.

And being found's no better, backed to a wall,
shrinking on a dirt floor, hugging her knees.
But what if she were never found at all?
Left to herself with sacks of grain and split peas?

Once there would have been pickles, purées, lard,
mountains of melons, stores for every season,
a shop, a cookhouse, bathhouse, icehouse even

and, set on four sides of the inner courtyard,
one house for each branch of the family
nobody else outside the walls could see.

The Introvert House

At its heart the pool, the blue rug of sky.
In the middle of my room, the kilim
with its fish and fowl. My propensity
for arranging furniture, it would seem,

in lines around the walls, leaving the floor
alone as the focal point, may be due
not to some dullness in the soul but more
perhaps to some echo, some residue

in the collective memory, of windows
that look forever inward, galaxies
that spin on carpets, geometric rows

of turquoise tiles ablaze with symmetries
inherent in physics: mirrorings and shadows
of gardens brought indoors; a Sufi's verses.

Chamaeleonidae

Why did I say I minded things I didn't –
soul-making things I'd find too crude to name?
Or silently collude with heartfelt, well-meant
sympathy it seemed churlish to disclaim?

There was no childhood house that I remember,
no mother in it, merely surrogate
houses with mothers in them but no daughter,
where I would be their Alison or Kate.

In whose name can I talk of roots, of ruptures?
Melding with backgrounds, we fade into yours –
muted, cryptic, old world chameleons.

'Lions of the ground', we swivel horizons;
stalking the rainbow, we emblazon its colours.
These are our messages, these our emotions.

BIO

Mimi Khalvati has published eight collections with Carcanet Press, including *The Meanest Flower*, shortlisted for the TS Eliot Prize. *Child: New and Selected Poems 1991–2011* was a Poetry Book Society Special Commendation and *The Weather Wheel* (2014) a Poetry Book Society Recommendation. She is a Fellow of the Royal Society of Literature.

ROBERT KIELY

Tinsel Shuffle Rot

Inside the sky, a spectrum-shift. Wax figures beneath.
The poem so far has covered desolation, the biology
Of fat, and mothers. In what follows, the poem will
Cover intellectual property, the hollow of your eyes, and
Transformation. On the train, someone reads *Homo Deus* and someone
Else reads *The Sound and the Fury* and someone else
Reads the *Evening Standard* and someone else reads
Between the World and Me and someone else reads some
Audre Lorde. One's indeterminate needs to be updated ASAP.
Please notice. It is 2017. Abandonment issues gallop across the
Normal. Inside the sky, ash. Here and there, a plane. The wax is much
Too realistic. The veins, the exposed teeth, integrity shot to shit.
Afropessimism, Conservativism, and mornings have been covered by
Now. Another is watching *Manhattan*, another is eating
Spring rolls. Everybody keeps going to work.
Correction, most people keep going to work.
Correction, work keeps coming to some people.
There is no horizon. There are flat-earthists. In union,
This the completeness of no shoes. Domestic industry and
Domestic workers in the foundations experience no overlap.
It is bare missing word. This is a disposition to iniquity.
The dust in the architect's dream. Stop moving.
Everything keeps getting easier. The bad
And the good. Independently. The restructure goes
On and new roles open up. Someone retracts the
Donation of their body for medical research.
In the restructure everyone's face will be superimposed
And each aberration smoothed out. Things rattle
Around inside their names. Correction, not everyone.
But more than a few. Less than everyone and
More than a few. The catharsis of the correct
Analysis lies down across the sky. Some people on
The train are not reading. In other warnings on
Sunk capital food is consumed. For example,
Ghost chillies. The retraction came too late,
Hence the screaming. It is the year of the resurgence of
Cancelled. In what follows, you can expect endings over
And over. It has covered nominalism and Woody Allen so far.
The anoriginary buttress must be accommodated, busted
Or switched. Fixed-rates on oseophagal massages with mini-guillotines,
Working wonders on malpraxis. Look, we can de-scribe or we can
Re-script. Can we prescribe the spectrum from the triangulated
Node purely inferred? Who locked who out? Who locked who in?
Who locked what in where? The passives fail to elide
The problem. Rupert Murdoch's hair. The skin fans
Out to reveal nerves and lymph. Yellowed. The tongue

Arching out and each layer visible of what lies beneath the
Street and leech. It isn't clear what many of the passengers
Are reading if on Kindles. A vast amount
Of material is repeatable. Things are trapped on the
Escalator that *is* their names, gradually smeared over the
Grill. There are degrees. There are degrees of progress and there
Are degrees of heat. The snow is weak. The unsunk capital
Traipses with a lightness that leads to a jolting then expunged
Shock. There are degrees of knowledge. There are degrees
Of distance and of sleep. Someone else stares at nothing.
The mirror flattens the wax figure which didn't flatten any
Thing. There are degrees of hate. Turned
To the side, the line-lengths follow closely
Our recent sales figures in the first quarter.
It isn't too good of a thing to be
Too splayed. Down in the margins
And across to hands held in breach
Of the loss. Anemones of the cloud
By light's beginning dim. Drawn between
The surface and manual, crushed. It is not 657.
There is a calculus to tasks and their
Settings out and off. It does not take
Any force for it to be so smooth. No,
Retract. The tweaks are so disheartening but
To get it right the first time doesn't happen.
There are degrees of love. Activity of the
Breakdown harnessed in infinite deferral of
Defeat. It seems fixed too easily and the
Modifications trail off. People listen to
Black social death as they jog. This is an
Inquisition on sublimity. Someone bursts into
Tears on a bus. This is an execution of fecundity.
They who precede the ranks in the possession-form
Earlier make less sense now. Outside the sky there are
No available seats. Someone breaks a window on a train.
There is no home. Levels of agitation groan. The actors and
Agents do casting calls unseen. There is no free zone.
So far the poem has covered travel, investment, and
Summaries. And then the columns tear down from the
Sky a portcullis. This is the exoneration of infinity. The purple
And green bleed into each other. A missed putt transpires to be
Non-symbolic. Worldwide limnic eruption of no hoard.
It is not 2897. The stock exchange but in wax. The Godhead is
Deaf. The name doesn't coincide with anything at all. The
Wick goes down too fast. Someone else is fiddling fingers and
Someone else is listening to Robin Williams and someone else is
Listening to William Basinski. The questions were a decoy.
Correction, there are no hands but wings. Correction, sometimes
It is right. Surreptitiously. *It must stop.* Freeze one for later.
Aggregate individual yearnings make monstrosity. These children were

Told a random combination of fantasy, outright lies and simple
Truth, all in the same tone of voice. The updates come through
And so it starts again. Beside the sky, red-shift. Someone
Retracts the donation of their library. Some things keep moving
Backwards. There is no pillow. On the boat, someone reads *Emma*
And someone else reads *Harry Potter and the Prisoner of Azkaban.*
The song has so far enveloped dissolution, cancer, and futurity
Itself. Wax candles starboard. The wick is unburned. It is
Just in time. This is a condensation of obliquity. It is
Damaged very readily and tapers off. The forms
Have language that breaks them, renders them
Invisible to administrators. The lawn is an
Improvisation. Decoagulation of the backhand
Management. There are pedigrees of lateness.
It is too much to be frayed. The walls are lined with
Specimens. Most diseases imaginable, most abstractions
Such as age are represented for each. You imagine that
Your organs will remain with you, unaugmented.
One needs fuel in a way which elaborates on
The contingencies linking the criteria on the set-page, threading
And building muscle between the sedimentations forced into a
Narrative skeleton. This is how it is done. Arabesque veins decorate
The museum. Students study nearby. There are lists of phone
Extensions and the ways to forward and intercept calls propelled
Forward to a warning of what will come. Undetected particles
Fall on the blueprint. The distinction between needs and wants is
Absolutely central to an economic system which allocates
Resources in apparently-efficient ways. Like an explosion with
The know-how of all the world's engineers, architects, and builders.
The viewpoint should be clearer but diminshingly isn't. For example,
You *want* to continue to function at what might be designated a physically
And mentally healthy level. You *need* to keep in mind that this is not a need.
Attempted corrections are counterproductive. Shit flows down
The Thames. Risen capital lopes at the margins. This is the perdition
Of contingency. Move less. Traditional practices fumigate the
Mausoleum. The ekphrasis of a subjective catachresis sleeps
In the ground. Passengers circulate. There are pedigrees of cheese.
This poem was written in late 2017 in London. Make it irrelevant
Please. Get to know your needs. The sky underneath bare feet.

BIO

Robert Kiely was born in Cork, Ireland. He currently lives in London. His pamphlets include *Killing the Cop in Your Head* and *How to Read*. Work can also be found in *Big Echo* and *Cambridge Literary Review*.

YOUR DUMB bell
presses massed
finance, else
bets in stress
may mar its
laid-on knit. And tons
of children
all well amended,
are pressed and praised
but not indulged.
So, prosper well,
and learn for
they that will demand
besotted friends
as yours I would but
otherwise decline. Dote while
such wheels, their actions
fast, their fashions
donned like blots
of steel we touch:
our thrust, forward,
our trust misliked
And shortly hums
this, home.

TO WHOM we love
but cease to see
and strange towards
did grow, through
distance glanced
this loyally, where
grammar would
entail, clung informal
to this active need:
celebrate, instantiate
common beings grown
human by desire,
this is why we are
as is, and you were
as I am, as confounded
whole, as the final is,
as without end,
its property a role
that bends to sway
always in to *alter*.
A wake, not yet
arrivèd wave, a grave
predicted quality,
rips curves in stress
this gone from source
a base transported
late, speed's delimited reach
crossed with light.

BIO

Michael Kindellan's poetry can be read in *Not love* (Barque 2009), *Word is Born,* with Reitha Pattison (Arehouse, 2006), *Charles Baudelaire* (Bad Press, 2005) and elsewhere. He is a Vice Chancellor's Fellow at the University of Sheffield and author of *The Late Cantos of Ezra Pound* (Bloomsbury, 2017).

ÁGNES LEHÓCZKY

[On the Sepia Swimmer]

And the next day, cutting through Watertown, the old Buda district by tram *bathos*, our sepia swimmer, bathed in self-pity and pathos, the nostalgia swimmer, the homesick swimmer, nostalgic and homesick for pool sepia, pool melancholia, feeling old and young, visible and invisible at once, pre and past his or her linear time, shrouded in a perpetual, diachronic gloom, a municipal grief, mourning not so much civilisation but some kind of synchronic, civic centre, the Zero milestone – that used to be a gigantic concrete o in the centre of town, they say, the focal point of fluid thinking, what once was intimate or even domestic, the place of belonging to some liquefied home, her local pool, a kind of mourning like the way our no-poem, the *nulla* poem, the (geometrically) pointless poem mourns language, mourning perhaps the soft, porous heart that used to exist inside her fellow citizens, the random urban *tête-à-tête*, eye to eye, heart to heart, the summer banters in which names of polis' swimming pools are permanently familiar, permanently and familiarly dropped, left behind and picked up again like names of great-great-grandparents or other safe paraphernalia of the swimmer's psyche, a liquefied elegy or aquatic lament, a grieving for fluid language games, for sunny saturnalias, involuntary exchanges of equinoxing words, among the *fin-de-siècle* corridors of Buda pools, grieving the *fin-de-siècle* heart itself, the pool within the eclipsed pool, the *mise-en-abyme* pool that gives access to the sepia swimmer to swim through chronology without time, or in fact, the pool itself, the pool-in-itself, its *aw*ful, pointless presence, but most of all grieving the regular correspondence with the posthumous author, the hydrophilic friend, who sends laminated postcards from the margin of the pool on a life mission to approach its focal point, that is, from the other end, the focal point of the poem's absolute solitude, heart to heart, *vis-à-vis*, eye-to-eye. The last unearthed cardboard card was meant to arrive from Serbia on which Kosztolányi, the posthumous poet, scribbled his notes down in the early 1900s. The image on the back was *Sunken Europe*, and the writing continues to be in note form about the author's journey through small towns and villages in which people would gather silently in small circles in an inexplicably opaque mood. No feast, no loud dance, no pig slaughter, there was silence, as if war, Kosztolányi writes well ahead of his own life, had occupied the air, because it's war that makes so little noise or sound. Dear silent flâneur, there are moments, while alive, when the global swimmer, the elastic swimmer, like our hypothetical typist of language who types his or her futuristic end in circles unable to think of the right word, the right end, typing around the globe, the meridian, our local bathos free of anguish and pathos, who swims, also, as far as her own body lasts, in circles, round around the meridian because that is the only thing that makes sense of the circularities of his or her own utterance, arriving at the point of departure and starting from all over again, swimming in the world in small cycles of swimming pool lengths, expects something to happen, something to bloom. To change. A moment of acceptance. Coincidence or chance. Resisting resistance, in other words.

That things will stay as they are. Pool, whirlpool of pools: chronology's laminated postcards: today there is silence around the margins of the swimming pool, its sepia presence gradually seeping towards the edges of the Old Buda district. There are no swimmers in or around the pool, perhaps because it is Our Lady's day with all the city dwellers and dryland flâneurs gathering elsewhere for the end of summer's final festivities in town. But from the spot in which we, posthumous swimmers (swim or) stand or lie, from the aquatic flâneur's position, that is, always already from the other end, Room 100, stood out, partially a part, lonelily apart, with no promise of being wholly part, is visible, convex, comprehensible from either end; the view, from the outside and from the concave inside. And so we assume, the room is emptiful. And vice versa: from inside the room, half empty, half full, there is clear panorama on the dark Danube spiralling away into the distance both ways into a fluid *filatorium*. In this liquefied silkworm factory there sits Ghandi in a lotus pose spinning away Bombyx Mori in perfect meditation, oblivion, equilibrium, linearly, accurately, chronologically unremembering, un-apprehending, unravelling *ourstory*, from end to end *sans* complication, *sans* crisis, *sans* agitation. And so learn to be a water-angel, says the new ad for mineral water this summer painted on the side of the bus, the last sentence we think of before entering the laminated barber shop in which Attila the Buddhist barber, laminated too, has been already expecting us. Attila, who likes philosophising while trimming your hair, bantering away about our auto-nautical crises and other approaching cataclysmic events, for instance about drowning St Petersburg or erased Dresden, and or our historical entrapments, living in the wrong era or time zone and of the after-after-after-after-life, today says it's definitely the end of an era, no matter how much we insist it stays with us. The fall of swimming pools is a process irreversible. Because take, for our final example, the accident with the cataclysmic creature, a testimony to what he believes in, to the cosmic process of how something, anything, once part of the world, a-part, a lonely part, yet still a being part, can turn into non-being, de-part, with other words, into nothing, and still wholly part of something contributing munificently, organically, to our existing world. The pigeon, like your tautologised moth, Attila says, or the poem, or your pool, for that matter, your final resting place, your Ithaca misplaced on the nautical map, your most precious thing, lost in last night's summer storm, who thought it was invisible, left an imprint on his window glass that was visible, the imprint so perfectly legible that you could see the entire structure of its body in flight, in other words it became the *schema* of its own final movement. Attila (not the one who once already drowned in the sepia Tisza or his alter ego whose cervical spine was crushed by the slow train cargo on the Transdanubian line on December the 3rd, 1937), the Buddhist barber said that the holy spirit according to apocrypha was an eagle, by the way, and so if that's true our argument for signs of *deus ex machina* is a poor aporia. But who knows, who knows. And he showed me the photo of a replica on his mobile. Because if we were more hopeful, more optimistic, or even animated, we could think the specific pigeon, inanimate, was made of something divine, deific, or even celestial. This laminated pigeon, or the laminated poem for that reason, or I should say the combination of the two, your future printed pigeon poem, which soon will be thrown against the glass by the hypothetical wind, its anatomy, its own story x-rayed by the window, made a fatal navigational error thinking it was invisible, see-through, that it was glass. It didn't fully realise its body parameters, its own longing to be extended, or be something or somewhere else other than itself. Because, Attila also said, the aim is to discard *desire*. Look at the way I am trimming your hair, watch the motion of my hands. Don't break the fluidity of the movement. No time for marginalia, doodles of the heart, no time for lament, for accidents. Be persistent on the page and complete your time in a steady linear order in one single length.

BIO

Ágnes Lehóczky's poetry collections are *Budapest to Babel* (Egg Box, 2008), *Rememberer* (Egg Box, 2012), *Carillonneur* (Shearsman, 2014), *Pool Epitaphs and Other Love Letters* (pamphlet, Boiler House, 2017) and *Swimming Pool* (Shearsman, 2017). She also has three poetry collections in Hungarian: *ikszedik stáció* (Universitas, 2000), *Medalion* (Universitas, Budapest, 2002) and *Palimpszeszt* (Magyar Napló, Budapest, 2015). She was the winner of the Jane Martin Prize for Poetry at Girton College, Cambridge, in 2011. Her collection of essays, *Poetry, the Geometry of the Living Substance*, was published in 2011. She co-edited *Sheffield Anthology* (Smith/Doorstop, 2012) with Adam Piette, and recently *The World Speaking Back to Denise Riley* with Zoë Skoulding (Boiler House, 2018). She is Lecturer in Creative Writing at the University of Sheffield where she is co-director of the Centre for Poetry and Poetics.

ÉIREANN LORSUNG

Ruth

Whither thou goest
I will

          go Thy people
          will be

                    my people Thy
                    god my

                              god

*

Whether you believe
the moon

sky's flat coin
meaning nothing

is a fuse
between our

now and our
then
   whether you

remember the mountain
air damp

in humid daytime
and saturated

the night before
we left

whether the truth
inheres in

presence or memory
there we

stood in darkness
just until

the rain   finally
began

*

Rabbinic tradition holds it to be about chesed:
loyalty or faithfulness arising from commitment

So then: *not* the pleasure of wild raspberries growing
in shade, along the unvisited riverbank

and not the water itself, cold as it was,
nor your refusal to enter it,

nor the doves which circled on invisible currents,
never needing rest, while boys dove

from a rock into the shallow pool. What
I know about commitment I could

fit into my palm. And desire's an insistent
book the size of a continent.

*

The preservation and continuity of the family
is closely related to the preservation and continuity of the nation

Where are you, out on those level lands or in the foothills
of younger mountains, land that shines pink

when eastern light hits it? Have you suffered shortages
of water? No shortage of light; radiance

guaranteed to newlyweds. Not everything I write
is a letter but I write a lot of letters, that much can

be said. From underbrush the nation witnessed
your marriage license. Let's say it's *done and dusted*

now: the ring shines on your hand. I accidentally
subsumed duty to the yellow aspen and *water* shining

at speed as I cycled over a bridge, to deserted
greenhouses glimpsed from high-speed trains,

to the North Sea impenetrably gray, the blue lights
of the French border, the right to vision

and movement—

*

What else can I say
about the holiday

called "Harvest"
and the one called

"Holding Back"?
Or about the woman

standing between two
widowed daughters,

or the young man
walking up

a mountain telling me
now is as good

a time as any
for marriage?

What is there
to be said

about the redness
of the sky

I carry
in my sternum?

Or the mountain
breaking

into blossoms
because truth

will be given
upon it?

BIO

Éireann Lorsung lives in rural Maine (US), where she writes, teaches, makes space, and makes objects. ohbara.com

CHRISTODOULOS MAKRIS

from *this is no longer entertainment*

the photographer isn't happy with the click-bait headline
at the dawning of a revolution in robotics: we are feeling the pressures
of our aging
we are very close to self-driving cars etc
after 2 laps of the city I had to pay a taxi to drive there and me follow

The Blue House. Now that's a pub
great parks, nice affordable housing and an impressive coastline
much better than bilbao, milan, paris, malmoe, goteborg, brussels,
Barcelona
all attributes of varying usefulness, none particularly central to my identity

so whose to blame for Berlin?
if they're speaking directly to you in a foreign language surely
EU funding is a myth. They are recycling some of our own money back to us
Brexity logic is a mysterious thing

I once knew an unpleasant Asian woman, do you think I can extrapolate
who is under threat?
why do you lot use "latte" as an insult?
zero content means you've lost

I live in Würzburg, Bavaria, but I'm from Durham
personally thankful, as you should be, for the contribution immigrants
have made
I enjoy visiting different countries to experience different cultures. I am
certainly not racist, far from it, having had Polish friends, taken them to
work, shown them around the Yorkshire Dales and visited them to tea
you could say you are parasitical on their labour

people vote for fascism
I'm not comfortable with anyone not like me syndrome
sure, I get it, ethnicity is a fuzzy concept that blurs on the margins
read the Wikipedia articles on Fascism and National Socialism before you
use the words

typical of the patronising londoncentric cool kind of lads
I visited the public library looking for a travel guide
I had stuff to do. You really seem obsessed with Muslims
the idea of a Yoruba ethnic group (bringing together Oyos, Egbas, Ekitis
etc under one umbrella) was promoted by nationalists

the Hate will get to such a point it's just everywhere

*

easy to say that because of not being Irish you are been discriminated
against
mostly Irish people are very nice
these so-called Equality Officers are biased
there is something Sinister about the Tesco's quest for power
in one store I found a few of the workers there bullies who were sneering
slanderers
I tried to get St.Patrick's day off and was told no because two other Polish
people had it off
another case why multicultureism wil not work here
why don't we just put a noose round Ireland's neck and hang ourselves
sorry it happened in Sligo because it is a place I like going to
only half a story here

*

a bit aimless and low-budget, a bit unserious
fantastically quick at thinking on his feet
effortlessly bats away over-earnest questioning
in his own bizarre way a supplicant
can be as incoherent as hell and still make sense
all froth and manages to side-step questions like a seasoned ballet dancer

that's an impressive ratio of wrong to words

obviously all the bigotry and racism is bad and that
just one ginormous satire
similar to that of Marine Le Pen that is proving so successful in France
so too elsewhere in Europe

this is no longer entertainment

they've chickened out of the deserved cowboy climax by banning guns
open warehouses and give free tacos (bags of cement, house paint) to the
needy

BIO

Christodoulos Makris has published several books, pamphlets, artists' books and other poetry objects, most recently *The Architecture of Chance* (Wurm Press, 2015), *if we keep drawing cartoons* (If A Leaf Falls Press, 2016) and *Browsing History* (zimZalla, 2018). One of Poetry Ireland's 'Rising Generation' poets, in 2017 he was Digital Poet in Residence at StAnza Festival in St Andrews, Scotland, and received a project commission from the Irish Museum of Modern Art. He is co-director of Dublin's multidisciplinary event series Phonica, and the poetry editor of *gorse* journal and associated imprint Gorse Editions.

ETHEL MAQEDA

Mushrooms for my mother

When the Kombi minibus stops a third time, I don't even take my eyes from *The Daily News* I'm reading. It's a week old but the journey is long and the minibus unreliable. Apart from the peeling paint, the passenger door that is held in place by a piece of string and the gaping holes where the headlights once were, the minibus sputters and leaves a trail of grey smoke for miles. Sheu, the driver, jokes that the old VW Kombi is as temperamental as his wife. He isn't married. I don't find that or the 'GET IN, SIT DOWN, SHUT UP & HANG ON' sticker on the dashboard funny.

In the morning, when I first saw the minibus, I considered not getting on. It was the look in my mother's eyes when she said, 'you have to go *mwanangu*, it's not safe here', that decided the matter. She had wanted me to leave as soon as I got off the bus the previous day. 'You don't know what they do to people from the city here', she looked annoyed. I had wanted her to say 'I'm glad you came, my child', and to erase the last ten years into nothing and make it 1997 again. Instead, she just wrenched the small bag I was carrying, almost ripping my shoulder out of its socket, turns away and marched back into the hut. 'You have to leave tomorrow, first thing," she said, not looking at me.

I have no choice. The next bus back to Harare is only expected in another couple of days. Most bus companies terminated services to rural destinations as soon as the date for the presidential election was announced. The collective national curfew is half self-imposed and half implicit in the consequences faced by those who try to ignore the announcement and continue as normal, until they get beaten up by the Green Bombers for being out on the streets or in beer halls after 6pm.Those caught travelling across towns and cities or from the cities to the rural areas face even worse punishments. They are accused of travelling to go and indoctrinate rural folk with their 'Western education inspired hatred of the dear leader and the state. I know I'm risking becoming an enemy of the state to see my mother before the election.

I realise that the minibus had not broken down again when I hear banging and shouting.

"Everybody out," a gravelly voice shouts.

We all scramble up. We were at a roadblock – an unusual spot for a roadblock and an unusual way for the traffic police to conduct themselves. This I do not remark to the man standing next to me, waiting for the people in the front seats to get out first. The look on his face stops me. He slowly and deliberately shifts his gaze to the front of the minibus and almost imperceptibly thrusts his head forward. I follow his gaze. There is a big log, a few branches and a pile of stones in the middle of the road. Also, there is nothing to suggest why this might be a good place for a roadblock, there is no bend in the road or other natural features that would prevent easy avoidance, and there is no safe place to park vehicles out of the way of other traffic – it's just a nondescript stretch of a road between two small towns. Not much traffic uses this route. It is a short-cut but it's all gravel. The potholes and ditches in the road are also legendary. Most drivers avoid the route but Sheu takes his chances as his vehicle is not roadworthy and he loathes having to bribe the traffic policemen each time he is stopped at the several 'official' roadblocks, usually only a few kilometres apart, on the main tarred road.

I throw the copy of *The Daily News* under the seat, step out into the aisle and get off the vehicle. Everyone has huddled together just outside the door. We are right in the middle of the road but we must all have realised what the roadblock is about and think that the decrepit minibus will give us some protection.

'I.D. necard remusangano.' The owner of the voice emerges from the bushes, an AK casually slung across his back and a tattered green beret perched on top of a head of unruly dreadlocks. The national identity card (I.D.) was introduced by the Rhodesian government but the present government, the police, the army or anybody who does anything in the name of the government, including this unofficial militia, embraces its use to restrict and intimidate people. It is a legal requirement to carry some sort of identification so everyone starts fumbling in their bags and pockets. He whistles and motions with his hand. Two more tattered and faded green uniforms appear from the bushes on the other side of the road. One is small and wiry, the other built like an athlete. I'm reminded of a documentary about hyenas that I watched several weeks ago.

The *Green Bombers* had existed to me only in the reports I compile for the organisation that provides safe houses for displaced victims of political violence. Everyone knows they are not the police and that they are not official but none of us is under any misconception that whatever happens at this illegal roadblock, there will be a chance to remind these young men that they are in fact an unconstitutional paramilitary militia. The smaller of the men scans the group as he approaches. There is a glow in his eyes. As our eyes meet I know I've made a mistake. He walks over but I've closed my eyes. His fingers dig into my jaw line. I keep my eyes shut. When I feel a hand on my breast I open my eyes and begin to protest; I want to tell him that I don't keep stuff in my bra, that any money I have and my phone are in my bag but the elderly man standing next to me puts a shaky finger to his mouth and shakes his head. The man hugs me close and unclasps my bra. The fondling gets more frenzied; all the other passengers avert their eyes. One hand moves slowly downwards and I try to shuffle backwards. I can see the veins on his neck bulge as he yanks me back by the belt on my trousers. I close my eyes again expecting pain. One, two, three...I start to count.

When I slowly open my eyes again, one at a time, the old man is alternately fumbling in his pockets and rummaging in a small duffel bag. The small man is now standing over him, waiting. 'I'm sorry, my son. I...which...what... which ones are you?' he straightens up holding two cards which he proffers to the small man. One has the distinct red, yellow and green and a picture of the Zimbabwe bird, the other has a red open hand symbol of the opposition party. 'Come and look at this, comrade Bazooka,' he motions to his friend. 'Please my son,' the old man says, his eyes pleading and his hands held in front of him as if in prayer. 'I'm old and these things confuse me.' Everyone tries to huddle even closer. A plump woman travelling with her young son puts her hand over his mouth. The little boy doesn't look like he is going to make a sound anyway.

'Slogan *mudhara,*' screams the one with the AK. I will call him AK, maybe his name is AK anyway, it wouldn't surprise me if it is. AK looks fifteen, maybe sixteen. I can't tell. Bazooka might be fourteen. Same age as my youngest son.

This worries me more than the fact that he has a baton which he is using to beat a rhythm on the side of his leg and that his nom de guerre is Bazooka. Bazooka takes a few steps towards the old man. We all flinch. AK puts his hand up and the Bazooka retreats. AK is in charge. I hope that is because of his AK which would mean Bazooka does not have anything bigger.

'Are you trying to be funny *mudhara?* I said slogan,' AK snarls. 'Ok my son,' the old man answers. 'Viva the President,' his voice is a little more than a whisper.

'Is something wrong with your arms and hands as well?' The old man doesn't respond. The slogan always goes with the clenched fist salute.

'Ah ha! I see now. You are one of those clever ones *nhai*?' What does one answer to that?

'Go sit down under that tree *mudhara*. We will deal with you later,' he turns to address all of us, 'This one is in need of re-education.' The old man starts to apologise again but Bazooka pushes him towards the tree by the side of the road. 'And *mudhara* start thinking about choices. You are all lucky today because we are in a merry mood so it's your choice-short sleeved or long sleeved.' I hear someone gasp.

'If the old man won't use his hands and arms in praise of the father of the nation then they are no use to him,' Bazooka explains with a coarse laugh in the general direction the gasp came from. AK then turns his attention to the small group huddled together beside the Kombi. 'Right! I want men under the tree, women on the minibus!' There is a little shuffling, some pushing and shoving, yet no significant shift in positions. The group huddles closer. Bazooka and his comrade move towards the group. Men and women with the 'right' party membership cards are directed towards a different tree across the road. Men without the cards are led to join the old man where he sits, his head sunk in his hands between the knees. The rest of us, women without cards, are ushered back into the Kombi to retrieve our luggage. We get our luggage and again huddle just outside.

AK, who had remained inside the minibus, comes out waving the newspaper I had been reading. My knees give out. Someone props me up. 'Whose is this? Who has been reading this rubbish? Lies! All lies, funded by enemies of the state intent on spreading rumours about our leaders,' his nose is flaring. No one moves or says anything. My eyes turn blurry and I can taste salt. He marches towards the men clustered around the old man and throws the paper on the ground in front of them. 'When I turn around again I want it to have disappeared, disappeared so that there is no trace left of the lies.' The men look at each other, locking eyes briefly, and then one of them starts tearing large pieces and handing them out. 'This calls for a celebration, a good meal goes well with music anyway.'

Bazooka walks round the small group of men looking each one up. As he passes each one of them, they flinch and then sigh visibly. He stops behind a clean-shaven, well-dressed young man and pokes him in the back with his baton. The young man jumps up and there is a roar of laughter and clapping from the green uniforms.

'This young gentleman here is going to start a song and everyone; I mean everyone, is going to sing,' he says. 'And oh! We want some dancing as well. Let's have some bum shaking. *Zunzai mazakwatira vabereki,*' he laughs out loud. The man with the newspaper starts ripping his own piece to smaller pieces and pushing them into his mouth. He looks round the group nodding encouragement. They all start doing the same.

I can hear muffled sobs. One of the newspaper people starts coughing and retching. The three berets move a few paces away to confer. I and a few of the other passengers are old enough to realise that this is only the beginning. These young men are taking us back to the guerrilla camps of the *Chimurenga* War of the 60s and 70s. All of a sudden I am back there – camp in the bush, young men in tattered remnants of a green uniform, singing, dancing; and girls and young women screaming in the bushes. I can hear the singing start, faltering at first but more resolute by the second bar. One joins and then another: everyone joins in.

Chenjera chenjera
Vanamukoma vanorova

I hear one of the Green Bombers whistle, a long piercing whistle. The people continue to sing. Even more tattered green uniforms appear. I see the looks on their faces. I smell the homebrew and dagga on the breath of the one who comes and disentangles my arm from that of the woman with the little boy. I think he says 'show time' or some such. Someone starts sobbing again as I am led a few metres away but still in full view of the men eating the newspaper. They roughly pull me back on the ground. One pulls my legs. The others hold my arms. There is more cheering and clapping. I hear roars of laughter. I hear the screams.

This time I am going to do something about it. I decide and start to walk away. I have a sudden urge to pick wild mushrooms for my mother. I will pick *nhedzi, tsuketsuke* and even the rare, sweet *chikunguwo.* I have the time to search for it despite the thickening fog and the approaching darkness. I hear whimpering after they leave to bring the next woman but I keep walking. The urge to pick wild mushrooms for my mother grows stronger still.

No Roads, Just Trails

The path ahead looked the same. The landscape hadn't changed for kilometres, or maybe days. Ranga wasn't sure anymore. From the description her friend Sara had given her, she figured she must be nearing Shangani. The savannah short grass and the anthills that dot the harsh, semi-arid terrain seemed to stretch forever. There were a few shrubs scattered about and occasional trees but the topography offered no real shelter from the elements or wild animals. She could also be spotted from a long distance away.

Ranga wondered if she had made a mistake. The vast plains that lie between Gweru and Bulawayo have very few inhabitants. She knew the way better on the Masvingo-Beitbridge road. She had used that route all those other times before. The grass grows taller and thicker in that part of the country and the trees are lush. There are also a lot of big boulders and caves one could shelter behind in case a *Chopper* or a *Dakota* flew past.

She tried hard to remember how many days she'd been walking. She couldn't. She had stopped counting on the second day. The young man she met on the first day had said the journey to the border normally only took a few days, just over a week, he'd said. But she was not young anymore. Sara had said as much. She had implored Ranga to wait a few more days and try to verify the news but Ranga had argued that this time she knew for sure because she felt it in her heart.

'It's different this time. A mother feels these things,' she had said.

This had hurt and silenced Sara.

Ranga was not going to give up. She could not give up. She did not know how to give up. It did not matter to her that progress was getting slower, that she could not feel her feet and that the few boiled *mealies* she had left were beginning to ferment. Besides, she had stuck to the main path, as much as she could, like the young man said, so sooner or later she was going to get to Bulawayo. The Beitbridge border would then only be another few days' walking away.

The thought excited and scared her at the same time. She did not have the right papers and she only spoke a few words of English. She was probably going to have to cross under the fence or swim across the Limpopo, if things did not go well at the border. She had heard about people drowning or being ripped to shreds by crocodiles and the ruthlessness of the *Boers* across the border was legendary. They were known to shoot on sight anyone caught going under the fence but she was determined to try, one last time. Her immediate worry was that she would definitely have to speak some *isiNdebele* in Bulawayo first. She could remember '*salibonani*'. One of her brothers had courted a Ndebele girl when they were teenagers.

'A greeting is a good start,' she consoled herself.

BIO

Ethel Maqeda lives in Sheffield where she's finishing a PhD in Literature & Creative Writing. She's always loved words and always has a story in her head. Her writing is inspired by the rich storytelling traditions of her native Zimbabwe where she lived for most of her life before moving to England as a refugee. She has had short stories published in English PEN Magazine, *Big Writing for a Small World*, the University of Sheffield's creative writing journal, *Route 57* and Valley Press's *Verse Matters Anthology*.

LILA MATSUMOTO

Windows regarden what is outside
as though all this had already taken place

Conciliatory tranquility   discordant regularity
stubborn pursuit   that my task is to protect

Still   the transparency   that light
coming back   near the table   in this blind room

What, is it day   to break me
because somewhere   is extraordinarily calm

Coming together   discreetly existing
did not prevent me from thinking of shared foreignness

Descending into the question   reading with vehemence
to be all the more frank   to stare   dangerously

At no time did I stray   outside of myself

Had I been told   I would lose the instinct for self-possession

I still know

It rises, altered
        with the day

BIO

Lila Matsumoto was born in Japan, grew up in the US, and has lived in the UK since 2007. *Urn & Drum*, her first full collection of poetry, is published by Shearsman. Lila teaches poetry at University of Nottingham and co-runs the poetry magazine and night FRONT HORSE. Her poem in this anthology was written in response to experiences of being questioned, detained, and searched at passport control in UK airports.

JOHN MCAULIFFE AND IGOR KLIKOVAC

The Wish

Translated from the Bosnian by John McAuliffe and Igor Klikovac

This morning I carried out from a dream
a wish to travel north. I did not see mountains
or snow, deep fjords and cathedrals of ice,
just the word, tapping its thigh like a dog-trainer.

In an old photo-album I searched for proof;
maybe I need to go *farther*, somewhere more northern.
I flicked through books whose tenants flee north,
but even the Japanese masters (who show nature
as if poetry did not exist) could not help.

Somewhere, I knew, in an old text,
or perhaps in an orange juice ad, it's said
all music travels south, and all words are northbound.
Perhaps the wish was not a wish and the dream
is that, when the time comes, things are not given up, but lost...

BIOS

John McAuliffe is an Irish poet who has lived in the UK since 2002. He has published four books with The Gallery Press, including *The Way In*, winner of the Michael Hartnett Award for Best Collection in 2016, and *Of All Places*, a PBS Recommendation in 2011. He teaches poetry at the University of Manchester's Centre for New Writing. His work with Igor Klikovac has been published in *Poetry*, *Poetry Ireland*, *PN Review* and *The Poetry Review*.

Igor Klikovac is a Bosnian poet (b. Sarajevo 1970), living in London since 1993. His work has been published in Bosnia, countries of former Yugoslavia, Britain and internationally. In the UK his poetry has been included in the a number of anthologies and a selection from his third book *Stockholm Syndrome*, translated with John McAuliffe, will be published later this year with Smith Doorstop.

AODÁN MCCARDLE

this other

this other
    being
there there
to speak
    but from
from here
how to say it
    is it
extrusion and
    hardly
one holds the
the other
    rules
to be behind
gagged
a reduction to
this silent
these are not
this is not my
I keep it in a
you can try to
it was one of
thole
there's
way the bowls are
the ones on top
pile
it seems settled
as if time has
this is the new

Things
    these things
to have them
to have things
attracted and repelled
pragmatic and
pragmatism is shit sometimes

that bit when you get just beyond
the point of no return
when breathing has changed
like growing up
suddenly
smile
knowing whatever else
that things can't stay the same
I knew I would probably get old
I knew my children would probably
grow up quickly
I knew my parents and their
brothers and sisters would die
I knew that some day I'd be on my
own
it doesn't matter that I knew
responsibility
a basic instinct
self preservation
chatteringeverywhere
undoubted
la la laaaa

where

always others
intrusion

glass

rules
the eyes

physical parts
instruction
my fantasies
shame
special pocket
look for it if you like
the few ways I could

something about the
piled
should be in another

passed and
now

this range of doing
how many moments of sitting
looking no further than your breath can travel
all that naming wasted
no to and from
people are not the only thing that dies
to whom can you belong
I can no longer give you
I said
so with that I no longer know what I do give
cast off
driftgaze
skating at night on a frozen river he sang
how can I still have things from then but not have then
even a past can be gone and without a past the present shrinks
it is snowing but so what
I cannot have friends unless I treat them as family
I cannot have a family without a place from which family are from
I cannot have a from without a past
this nofrom
wordfail
eyestop
madeupofnoreturn
to speak is to expect to be spoken to
numbling

a misunderstanding of what it is to live a life

aberancing everywhere
internal leeching ██████ists
rather than facing the unknowing
in which each
movementthought
must generate its own future
reuse itself
right to the heart
now and now andnow

newblood
bright bright brightred with ██████
may be the only ████

to learn to point
to know where
you are going
not to ask
questions
a mars bar not a
bar of mars but a
bar of chocolate is
okay
chips rice and
curry sauce do
not go together
but they do now
so contributions
are made
society need not
be secret
your name is not
a weapon
your name is not
a weakness
where you are
from is yours to
know
your name is a
weakness
your name is a
weapon
where you are
from is theirs to
know
society is a secret

perfection in any language
but not in perfection

Yellowhammer once

Owl once here
a few times there

Stoat once fleeting

Otter once
thought it was a cat
but never thought it was a cat

just because a word isn't in a dictionary
just because it is

watching a cat breathe

I laughed
why not

there's a we here
we're insisting on it

communal flowers
like toilets only better smelling
or attractive mostly at night
moth pronouns
and ownership
it's a lack of imagination
all hearts are milky
after all

BIO

Aodán McCardle's current practice is improvised performance/writing/drawing. His PhD is on 'Physicality Doubt and Action as Articulation of the Contemporary Poem'. He opened the Performance Month at Beton7 in Athens 2015 and at the launch of the Performance Philosophy Centre Uni. of Surrey Sep 2016. A member of Collaborative/Improvisational Performance group Cuislí. He has two books, *Shuddered* and *ISing* from VEER and online chapbook *LllOoVvee*, Smithereens Press.

NIALL MCDEVITT

2017

...the holy apostolic see in the time of Pope Adrian
of blessed memory conceded the land to the illustrious
king of the English...

1. ALBION (contd)

a thousand years' English rapine of Ireland
counts for nothing in intellectual circles today
"ah but you are white..."

the English rapine of Celtic neighbours
needs excuses to continue, the strangest
being that one word
"whiteness"

Catalans come into their kingdom-as-republic
breaking from monarchist Spain
to perfidious talk of "43%"
(not the proof
of British whiskey)

the apron's imperium sinks or swims
as a fruit-voice on Radio Four insists
"Europe doesn't understand Anglo-Saxons"

2. CONSERVATISM (contd)

the news the numbers
voxes of the quantifying debate
are plummified and correctly measured – by rulers –
when the blackout lifts and the vox populi is mic'd
the cry of the pauperised is really too much to bear.
then you feel in your hand the diamanté heart
of Tory England, cut and pristine, proffering zero,
but neurotic, so neurotic, with prisms of rainbow guilt
that filter into the public tones and vocabulary
e.g.
"we have sold our humanity but are yet human beings.
help us! we have everything and/or nothing.
help us! we're cocooned in bourgeois materialism
following the neoliberal way, not the way of Christendom
as once we sought.
thus glutted and battened – sealed off –
the whine of a poor man or woman on tv or radio
makes us inwardly laugh

(this ventriloquised confession is not easy)
which is why we work even harder at self-presentation.
our consciences are...what is the opposite of clear?
our consciences are...unclear.
help us
escape the Momentum noose!"

*

(thus
the rich whine too)

3. ISRAEL (contd)

the state land // the no-gos // the seam // the buffer // the annex //
the WALL // the FENCE // the BARRIER // the WALL // the FENCE //
the BARRIER // the slabs // the barbs // the mounds // the trenches //
the patrols // the towers // the minefields // the lenses// the checkpoints //
the settlements // the sections // the satellites// the segments // the strips //
the routes // the bypasses // the tunnels // the bridges // the highways //
white plates // green plates //yellow plates // red plates //black plates //
the levels // the nodes // the clusters // the zones // the enclaves //
the WALL // the FENCE // the BARRIER // the WALL // the FENCE //
the BARRIER // the voltage // the radars // the imaging // the sensors //
the ops // the transfers // the writ // the bulldozers // the flags //
the tanks //the uzis // the UAVs // the quads // the skunk-spray//
a clover map //of CENTRES // of BASES // of PRISONS //
the outposts // the crossings // the roadblocks // the grids // the airspace

4. FASCISM (contd)

the human body is purple yellow silver
before the mind is
and after

nation-states plant human bodies
humans form
a forest

they walk with torches in xtian hands
calling from human tonsils
rawly

continents are under spells

giant footprints stamping plates
        lumbering backward

fascism rebooted
the human body
        is not a safe space

*

the human forms avow
infanthood's morals

but outgrow
them as fashions

snow and fire
are at war

the shamans of bodhranbodhranland
drum

to 2017's
twitted ideologies

news is white
    supreme

BIO

Niall McDevitt is an Irish immigrant to England and the author of three collections of poetry: *b/w* (Waterloo Press, 2010), *Porterloo* (International Times, 2013) and *Firing Slits: Jerusalem Colportage* (New River Press, 2016). He is also a walking artist who specialises in the revolutionary poets of London, and blogs at poetopography.wordpress.com As part of the London and UK psychogeographical movement, he has collaborated with Iain Sinclair, Robert Montgomery, Nick Papadimitriou, John Crow, Tina Richardson, Jeremy Reed, Aidan Andrew Dun, Max Reeves and Mythogeography.

LUKE MCMULLAN

Of This Return

I hear the footfall of the pioneer
ensconced within the wilding land
and this frenetic wish that it revives
that I should supplicate myself
supine among the leavings
of the forgotten world,
which is to say that I am genetically
designed to please her,
inside the region of the mark
that means itself.
                                        There are two
wings left on the insect diptych
as the frontier is crossed,
a snapped leg that disappears again
and again.

And what shocks here is the speed of love,
in spite of the Faraday cage,
enclosing the fuselage of flesh too slowly
for the flash incarnadine, line
after line. It is an arterial surprise
in an aerial extravaganza, the flight path
erring into the septentrional dream.

Brought back to the threshold
by the force of gravity, I'll see you
again, some other time, some
other star, smouldering
under the unlit sky,
waiting to set a fire.

On Viewing the New York Crystal Palace 1853 Exhibition at Bard Graduate Center Gallery

In 1851, the London Crystal Palace exhibition opened.
In 1853, The New York Crystal Palace exhibition opened.
In 1858, the New York Crystal Palace burnt down.
In 1936, the London Crystal Palace also burnt down.

The leitmotif of the Crystal Palace was glass
because theme is now subject. Here is a shard of it
to succeed the procession of contemporary monuments
as you wend the river, 'walking for twenty years of nights'.
We elect a disorder of desire let slip
to wilderness and steal
a last look back at the sugar magnate,
synthetic potentate, the tiles in a ring.
'The traverse of the wall' which is
dubbed, replaced, recalled at the end
of this world, stands forth for the industry
of all nations. There is no city
without the recollected boundary
in the security of street names
for the ease of transfer. Get me somewhere.
A pinpoint swims among many pinpoints
since the fire at the terminus, when the glow of flame,
refracted through the prismatic skies
of eight wide counties, made rain
incalculable lenses. This one has been captured
and held behind glass. The flame
that glanced around it is what it was about.

BIO

Luke McMullan is a poet, translator, and scholar from Belfast in Northern Ireland. His books include *n.* (Wide Range, 2012), *Dolphin Aria/Limited Hours: A Love Song* (BlazeVOX, 2015), and *RUIN*, (BlazeVOX, 2018). He lives between London and New York.

o o

o

EVERYTHING
IN THE
UNIVERSE
IS MOVING
IN THIS
(IN) EXACT
SECOND

o o o o o

o

o

TO BE READ 8 TIMES
7 TIMES THROUGH
TOY LOUD SPEAKER
THE LAST ONE JUST
THE HUMAN VOICE

this country is / is not your home

small
school
girl
missed
the step
banging
her knee
as she
was getting
on the 355
quickly
following
her two
siblings
and her
mum
into the
busy bus
a lady
sitting
inside
raised
her voice
to address
the small
girl and
loudly
said:
you
should
behave
this country
is not
your home
Excuse me
this country
is
the girl's
home
the lady's
face
angry
red
about
to burst
Who are

other voice
just near
said
This
is
the girl's
Home
the lady
on fire
fixed
her eyes
on everyone
about to
burst
skin
burning
rage
every voice
said
in different
tones
high and
low
This country
is the girl's
Home
the shame
she
the lady
said many
uncontrolled
swearing
words that
became
nothing
from loud to
nothing
face
buried
poundland's
inside
plastic bag
took time
who are you
she said
you are

go back
to your
country
go back
6 years old
school
uniformed
small girl
as if
she had
any other
place to
call
home
as I do
and many
others
within
the bus 355
strange
to be
present
to hear
these voices
taste
a victory
of the many
the lady
lost
her voice
chance
to be kind
make space
for tears
just a small
injury
an explosion
of fear
under
afternoon
sunlight
the heat
to gain
a place
collective
mind

to where?
Tesco?
Brixton?
home
again
plants
to grow
between
the bricks
the birds
will go
warm
lands
abroad
without
needing
to pledge
allegiance
to democracy
monarchy
all at once
as in
a combo
sale
of history
trumpet
playing
included
nation
al ism
border
of out
inside
to feel
pain
longing
the stop
get off
time
light
space
oystercard
the force
of public
transport
health

to be read aloud by column downwards, starting from left to right > one voice
to be read aloud by line from left to right, one line at a time > two voices
to be read aloud by column simoultaneously > four voices
to be read aloud randomly as a sound improvisation > any number of voices
to be read individually in any of the previous combinations, possibly others.

you to say
a large man
said:
This country
is the girl's
Home

a migrant
yourself
this country
is not
your home
go back

voice
celebrate
instead
a quiet
cry
across

education
for all
a right
stay
home
your country

BIO

Luna Montenegro (Chile/UK) is a visual artist, poet and performer living in London, working with text, sound, drawing, installation and film. She is a founding member of the art collective mmmmm, plays in the experimental band THE YET, and runs one night stanza, a small handmade press. Her work has been published by *Poetry Wales*, *Word For/ Word*, Intuitive Projects press, Writers Forum Chile, Errant Bodies Berlin, Recrea Libros, and Alba Berlin. She has shown her work in the ICA, Bibliotheca National de France, Lettrétage Literaturhaus, and Zebra Poetry Film Festival Berlin. www.mmmmm.org.uk

STEPHEN MOONEY

Vendom

There is a game called Khan of Khans
The cows in the corral are safe – this is the end of your tribal champion
This is where sensibility is noise-blix in the undercarriage
I want it to be ours to spit on

It's like those tricksy newscasters
You know and they know and we know
that Kelly Anne Conway is a liar
The hotfoot frame of   We agreement
In Dixit in Gogglebox in time

So, the masquerade of I believe this
What is a constitutional crisis

So, who is a seventeen year-old these days? On the edge of things is not being seventeen here.
Of here is this, right enough

[ ] in the prescribed manner and form upon payment of the prescribed fee.
Who would be border, for all those little ships?

I have a Polish boyfriend, so what's that about
now?
In the sonic sense, for the dogs to hear
meet the Spartans
is deprived under section twenty-nine person
It's in-House pâté-livered, newspaper-hugging would-not-wannabe cowards playing the build that wall
vote for
the bully-bile-border agency
with all those little ships

'I wish to welcome you our esteemed guests to the Zambia Department of Immigration website.
It is my sincere hope and trust that you will find this information useful.'
Actually, yes –

DUAL CITIZENSHIP: NOT RECOGNIZED.
Exceptions: Child born abroad to Zambian parents, who obtains
citizenship of country of birth. Dual citizenship is recognized until the

age of 22. Upon reaching the age of maturity, the person must choose one nationality or lose Zambian citizenship.

Child of foreign parents, who is born in Zambia, acquires parental and Zambian citizenships. This dual citizenship is recognized until age 21 when person must register with Citizenship Board if the person chooses to become a Zambian citizen. Upon confirmation of Zambian citizenship, person has three months to renounce the second citizenship (of parents). Dual citizenship will continue to be recognized until age 22.

According to Statutory Instrument (SI) Number 50, The Citizenship of Zambia Regulation, 2017, now provides for a person who ceased to be a citizen as a result of acquiring the citizenship of another country to apply to the Board for restoration of the Zambian citizenship

The Government of the Republic of Zambia may be the promise it keeps.

BIO

Stephen Mooney was born in Zambia of Irish parents and lives in London. He is a lecturer in Creative Writing and poetry co-ordinator at the University of Surrey, where he was also the Poet in Residence in 2012/13. He is an associate member of thc Contemporary Poetics Research Centre at Birkbeck, and co-runs the small poetry press, Veer Books. His collections include *DCLP*, and *Shuddered*, co-authored with Aodan McCardle and Piers Hugill (Veer Books, 2008 and 2010 respectively) and the trilogy *The Cursory Epic* (2014), *663 Reasons Why* (2016) and *Ratzinger Solo* (2016), published by Contraband Books.

GHAZAL MOSADEQ

Time is of the Essence

Time is of the essence

the frigid temperatures
of withdrawal.

Time is of the essence
when the North Atlantic
is in the corner of your room,
the tide returning.

I want to say
you wouldn't answer,
though I tried to call you
any number of times.

Nine men were abandoned
in your head.

Vague thoughts—
the lemonade stand—
came and went.

You would be able
to fall asleep to these memories,
if you could get your fix on time.

But that is out of question.
Your vessel is in distress,
there are helicopters
in the living room,
airlifting your life jacket
and leaving you behind.

No breath.
You can't greet the sea-spumes
or the random swimmersby.

Where under all this water
is the Delta Arietis,
or its North Atlantic
spokesman?

Who will come to lift you
up out of the water?

The fishing vessels
seen from odd angles,
from underneath,
cast giant shadows
in the cold waters

Even if your dealer
were standing on the steps,
you couldn't open the door.

In the Atlantic Ocean,
merely wave upon wave.

BIO

Ghazal Mosadeq is a writer, poet and translator. She is the winner of the 2013 Bayhaqi Short Fiction Prize and her collection of poems *dar jame ma* (2010) was shortlisted for the 2011 Khurshid poetry award in Iran. She is currently a research student in the Department of English and Humanities at Birkbeck College, University of London.

VIVEK NARAYANAN

Ayodhya

No one is poor in Ayodhya.
No one is unhappy in Ayodhya.
No one goes hungry in Ayodhya.
No one is robbed in Ayodhya.
No one is beaten in Ayodhya.
No one is illiterate in Ayodhya.
No one is an atheist in Ayodhya.
No one is cruel or miserly in Ayodhya.
No one is a slave in Ayodhya.
No one is sick in Ayodhya.
No one is old or crippled in Ayodhya.
No one _______ in Ayodhya.

Dhvanyaloka 1.14

suffers being squeezed
for the sake of others   sweet
    when split apart
changed forever when eaten
      prized by all

                    and so if it doesn't
    manage to grow
when thrown hard on barren land
is this the fault now

of the sugarcane stem
and not of the pointless desert?

BIO

Vivek Narayanan's books include *Universal Beach* and *Life and Times of Mr. S.* The two poems here are from a long manuscript in progress, *After*, that attempts to 'write through' Valmiki's Ramayana.

CRISTINA NAVAZO-EGUÍA NEWTON

from *Qasidah of Exile: Intent before Vision*

Nasib: Pursuit of the wind gone

Nowhere's home where childhood wasn't sent for bread,
or the names of streets sound nothing like the names of kin,
and unless each alley knows where on earth we've been.

There is a time when one does not see time's sleights
– days could go on like this, worn like tamed shoes,
the bread learned, before all burns in an urgent wind.

Now we can read, but it's too late: the bread we knew
is a dream, as is the soul of a rose we once ran past,
the kiss we almost begged, and there is no bridge.

Takhallus: Unleashed

Breathe the borrowed air – your lungs are flesh on loan.
You stand on foreign soil while your land turns strange.
The best shade gives a curfew of cinders from burst suns.
The wind ignores you when you call for days, and when at last
it comes, it is Simoom: the wheeze of hell, and you'll gulp dust,
and grit will scour the one you were, the faces left behind.
Beyond the reach of love, her body has become a pure belief
your hands sink through, her voice lyrics one cannot quite
bring back to mind without the tune, and all your life
before today a story nomads spin at night around a fire.
Your hands smell of what you touch. The smoke, the wind.

Rahil: Travel

And the going and the way become one's land,
and the faces of strangers, universal script,
and a bed is what turns out when one lies down,

the food you eat is someone else's life, the taste
misses the point, our own story is probably a tale,
and our name is mispronounced, but you sit and eat,

and drink, you half-sleep in the smells, wake up too soon
to the wind's blurred gab and the blanks of walls
where the shadows of branches scrawl strange songs.

Welcome to Eritrea

In support of Helen Berhane and the prisoners of conscience still held in shipping containers in Eritrea.

This is where they pack me up.
Time says nothing: clamped and gagged,
it lets my pulse come back with a rusty jerk,
the taste of alloy. Here is here
and here, a caulked tin ventricle,
where I clog the arteries of my country.
This is where I cocoon in my own filth.

I slowly cook during the day, and go
straight from the oven to the freezer
in one dish. This metal container
is no metaphor. I have been preserved.
I am being shipped without moving,
a crouched rat rotting in cargo sweat.

Welcome to the compound, you dissident.

I hear the knuckling down,
the stiff fouling: there are other rats,
my neighbours, my incommunicado kin;
dragged out to the latrines once a day,
then shoved back into their airtight cans,
or butted under ground.

It's time out until each one denies
or dies, as we cringe, trussed-up,
each in our shrunk dimension, where
we'll manage our disfigured oxygen,
we'll fold and wait like foetuses,
learn to breathe with the mind of a beetle.

This blind tank amplifies the swearing,
all the bloody clang of pow. This new beat
sticks in your metronome, it drums your brain
like live surgery. Their loud slogans teach you
what comes next, tattooing it into your mettle.

Soon you will not recognise yourself.

Darkness drinks the darkness of our hair
till we glow in an orange halo and toothless
from this sun theft, shackled in a three by three
fixed thirst. We monologue to shrinking
walls that talk back in our face.

One would have to lose the thread of days,
to loosen oneself from this raw drag.
Outside we stood purposeful and wonderfully made;
we developed in brightness,
our souls responded to increments of light.

We, good for a pulp.

The embryo goes to the ground.
We are ripening for history,
and the day outside days

BIO

Cristina Navazo-Eguía Newton is a winner of the *Poetry London* and Hope Bourne competitions and commended at the Troubadour, Nottingham, Gregory O'Donoghue and Strokestown. Her poems appear in *Wasafiri*, *PN Review*, *Poetry London*, and *Long Poem Magazine*. She has two collections in Spanish. Her first in English, *Cry Wolf*, received a Straid Award and is published by Templar Poetry. Cristina is a lecturer, translator, and editor and conducts workshops on poetry and flamenco. She is organiser and co-judge of the Battered Moons Poetry Competition, and part of Flame&Co, a flamenco duo.

ALICE NOTLEY

Dinner at the Prime Minister's

2005 receive invitation to Matignon think it's a hoax
RSVP my friends advise I do so   a club I've just joined, for
international poets will dine with the prime minister and his wife
so I go   fabulous Versailles-like rooms   introduced to Dominique
de Villepin premier ministre also poet we eat at tables for five
I'm trying to recall my table an African a Belgian an Indian I
think   Mme de Villepin sits with us to begin with then "works the

tables"   we are trying to figure out when to start eating she
says "attaquez" dig in   Later a friend of hers a classical Spanish
singer plays the smallest guitar I've ever seen and sings wonderfully
A writer from Cuba reads a poem someone I know I for-
get who reads one or two more   de Villepin makes a speech
about the importance of internationalism and poetry

it's good the speech   it isn't dumb or superficial
he means we all talk to each other across borders and
poets know how   Around 11pm we shake his
hand and leave   No one knew who I was except for
a couple of Frenchmen   Was I the only American
I think so   I wore one of my dark pantsuits

no one had known how to dress and I
discussed this with the Belgians   who were men
almost everyone was a man except for Zoe from Cuba
But now I remember talking to a French editor
a woman at my table   The African poet—a man—
had a wonderful name like Apollo or Zeus

though he was ordinary looking, nice   Was the Indian
poet a woman? I don't think so I just remember an Indian and
talking to that person there were many Africans there
Michel Deguy was there and got cold (I think it was March)
maybe he read I was otherwise living in my state
of loneliness still the current one   on the other hand amazed

quietly about a hundred people I think I ate fish
how could this have happened it was delightful
it helps to have a palace a big food budget   and there were
no consequences   except that I can tell you
about it here and say I am an international poet
our locality is now the whole planet   *I am*

an international poet in touch with the poetry worlds
of several countries—do they have 'countries' on other planets?
I value the parochialism of my room on rue des Messageries
as I loved Needles and St. Mark's Place NYC but
the fading or bleeding into each other as we hack at
others and so-called Nature breaks my heart

"you saw it coming" over and over
or did everyone see it coming   one could con-
tinue blaming countries or whoever (you
were *all* a bunch of sexists no one gets off)
Your phones for example sheer escapism
Take your faces out of your phones

Look around for christ's sake   Look at what's going on

Carte de Sejour

2012, '13 I have been in Paris for 20 years
I hate to admit that my French isn't wonderful I'm
unassimilated but definitely some sort of immigrant
in this syntax where one is definitive subject and verb
I think I'm avoiding   There's a new bureau for re-
newing one's papers at rue du Delta near rue de Petrelle
almost at Barbès very near me   Last time 2002
I'd had to go to Boulevard Sebastapol at 6AM stand in line
for 5 hours outside the préfecture with masses of
people Asian African Middle-Eastern the world is every-

where mixed up now   I shared a blanket for warmth
with a woman from La Réunion 10 years older than me in '02
but in '12 I only had to make an appointment
and buy a 200-euro fiscal stamp   Then Anselm Karen and girls came
and it snowed it never snows   What did we buy
in that funny pharmacy hand cream and vitamins   Anselm and I
walk in snow at night discussing the U.S. State Department
Sylvie and Anselm on ferris wheel at Concorde in snow
I watch with Karen and June who has a meltdown
in the Louvre the second time after seeing another long hall of

paintings coming up Anselm's Caravaggios
this is to say, that they inhabit me
wherever   the girls break my pink mechanical cockroach
and wear out the battery of the owl whose eyes flash
I live in Paris I just do am I supposed to
live somewhere in particular the ghosts
call me back here not historical or cultural
but essential what calls on me what can find me
Here   they those it living in these quarters
where Sylvie and June might also jump on my bed

I will only ever have these rooms. The world is owned
Paris is called owned and pressing on you would buy you up
An older immigrant hopes for a future still
is that it—you have too many questions in your
poems, someone said   I prefer the interrogative the sound of it
I went to a store and then I went to another store, is
that better? or, I loved, I despised, I resisted . . .
you must have been fortunate to have the strength
But their disjunction was unlike their stable positions
Is matter stable? or, matter is stable

and over and over can matter exist without memory
our memory my memory or its then, if all
there is is memory   how is it shared and called gravity
in 2002 the sari'd woman from La Réunion and the Middle-Eastern man
he who remembered me from the first time   that is we'd
unsuccessfully stood there having come too late
the three of us now stood abreast I bought us news-
papers at one point so many in line the woman from the
préfecture came out and shouted hysterically Don't Push!
'We're being treated worse than dogs' one near me mutters

pushed together pushed together like molecules

BIO

Alice Notley has published over forty books of poetry, including (most recently) *Benediction*, *Negativity's Kiss*, and *Certain Magical Acts*. She lives in Paris, France.

TERRY O'CONNOR

LSM (elles s'aiment)

for Claude Cahun and Marcel Moore

1944. Investigating officers on the island of Jersey found it impossible to believe that two middle-aged women had conducted such a daring campaign of resistance all alone: "they were forced, at the end of the day, to condemn us without believing in our existence."

Rise up, resist
Their soft insistence, hand written, notes hidden
In pocket and cigarette pack, delicately placed, gloved hands perhaps
Or dropped through the open window of a car
And, after so many stolen chosen poses, painted, poised,
Lapel opened to the lens inviting, striking so many selves, bleached crop,
  bullet stare,
Finally to find, to choose, to dare,
to risk
The guise disguise of gentlewomen, sisters invited to the table,
Invited, invisible in middle age, installed towards the back of stage
But bags full of hand crumpled, though translated with care (a fluency
Hidden from the occupying force)
Rise up, resist. Thousands such,
Such an act, an art, such art as act
Such risk
to sign
to play
The soldier with no name.

Strangers you did well to tarry here.

LSM
Elles s'aiment.
Elles s'aimaient
Exiles emigrés, artists choosing quiet
Leaving Paris for a seeming quiet
an island, house by the sea, a rock,
the prettiest bay
a way away
choosing quiet
lovers, sisters, artists
seeking quiet but rising
to resist.

Much later, in a conversation
Split by years and miles
and work in this and that disguise
We said
'when young, transformation of any sort
Holds every possible ahead
But now
more fixed,
less likely
to change
transformation doesn't work the same'

Still LSM
You found a final game
All risk
risking all
in urgent guise
While seeming most seemly, most seeming in line.

You were caught
and paid with health and breath.
Caught but held up high beyond belief
a final impossible
that two middle aged women had done it 'all alone'

'They were forced, at the end of the day, to condemn us without believing in our existence'.

Strangers you did well to tarry here.

BIO

Terry O'Connor is a core member and performer with Forced Entertainment, a collective of six artists based in Sheffield who have been making performance since 1984 and received the 2016 International Ibsen Prize for contribution to theatre. In 2009, she was awarded an AHRC Creative Fellowship at Roehampton University and in 2011 became Professor of Contemporary Theatre and Performance Practice at the University of Sheffield. Her research practice investigates experimental and improvisational process and collaborative aesthetics within contemporary performance.

WANDA O'CONNOR

Before the diagnosis, after the diagnosis of the diagnosis, before and after

To bring under or before –   without sense of –
    a kind of *glancing* or *flickering light.* Simulations in this utopia.

But the glimpse has famously broke.

Reliabilities fail. Replaced with new, grey reliabilities. And something of
seizing   partial seizing.

I assume you see it, too. Difficult to measure, the tension; going hard into
the wall, it seeks its own level.   The unrehearsed body is adrift, fixed
by constant currents,
some of us nestled in accumulation.

I drew up in a narrator's room   a lake-tank, with just enough garments to
inflate, replacing word with exhale.
    I remain inside.
    I receive what the mouth swallows, flooding to feed nutrient back,
my home a property an attitude of body tossed upon the crusts of water
                                        – *white horses*
and me with my little song, *chant merle noir.*
The slipping is elsewhere.
A constellation that surrenders its habit of being.   The old conditions against
                                                you
so that the new ones never take. Two heights, untutored. The one, a confidence:
entry, pull and recover   breathing, timing, starts and turns.

I do not come to settling easy. And with regularity fling all furious searches
into grounds, open bodies into bits of depressions.
    If you're asking what I get out of it: burrowing.

The final thing, the thing I do not know with clarity how to form – a
knowing difficult to season – I press down into the cant-bodies water
for the dirt to drink.

It is as if the whole findings lifted.

In

in)
— ( ) ( ) in
—
— ( ) — ( )( ) ( )
—
in
( ) ( )
— *()* ( ) *()* ( )
— *()* ( ) — in
( ) (— ( )
— ( ) ( )
— ( ) (in)
— ( ) — in
( ) ( )
( ) — ( )) ( ) (
) —
— in in
in — —*()* ( )
in —
( ) ( ) (
)

BIO

Wanda O'Connor is a poet and scholar. Recent work is available in *The World Speaking Back... to Denise Riley* (Boiler House Press 2018), *Bad Kid Catullus* (Sidekick Books 2017), *The Best Canadian Poetry* (Tightrope Books 2014), *Poetry Wales*, *Asymptote*, and others. 'Before the diagnosis, after the diagnosis of the diagnosis, before and after' is attributed to Derrida.

GIZEM OKULU

from *Night Poems*

You place yourself into this room.
You form impossible directions to your body.
You run away from the languages surrounding you.
You hear the voices when they speak.
You would reply to them with warmth, smiling.
When you come their water marks our knees.
A fast cut that lingers and parts the landscape.
We walk among the silence.
The indifferent rain
Of what is to come.

You and I
We talked about the endless summers
The possibilities of fleeing from the sun...

I.

Night. In a country in the north.
Neither too hot nor too cold.
I found myself a lonely language
Behind the three walls all
brown with dust of the earth.

Horrible dreams and more to come.
Projected in a room. Minute-hands and scorpions.
Where *that* is the ultimate winner at all times.
Where no matter how much the truth is reflected,
the reflection does not show much.

I'm writing these now on a very curious desk with
books king-size cigarettes under the smoke
and with the smell of old furniture the memories
of other people are easily erased from this room.

I do not want to go back I leave everything.
I do not want to go back I leave everything to
that country of hills because I wake and see this
systematic loneliness that they slowly created,
this deadly smoke slowly, and this fog fog fog...

In a city surrounded by its own domes
planes find their way using telepathic coordination.
But where am I going. Where am I going.
I'm travelling in my grey nightdress. In my red veil.
But where am I going. On my head a harpsichord.
A harpsichord. When I sing a lullaby on double-decker
busses, jumping from one train to another.
When I smell that perfume my mother wore for years,
where am I going.

Night. In a country in the north.
All scars close except *that* one...

II.

But how nice all of these...
The choir of exhausted voices...
To read fortunes from mystical foreheads...

Besides today I'm writing all the
words that I was trying to escape.
In a different language. In a different space.
That *instructive voice in exile* I wake up with will
one morning find itself informing every authority.

It will give me a hundred new names.

Because from now on to fear is banned.
To resist silence, its restlessness that is
            slowly shutting you
is banned.

To re-inhabit yourself is banned.
And this feeling of emergency is nothing but an
extension of my anger by imagination.
Because when all these walls are destroyed
maybe we will see the sun for the first time in centuries.
A cathartic woman will come by dancing to the
heart of the city. That lonely heart.
Until they catch us barefoot.

Shhhhhhh. There is no more silence. No more games.
No more scams. I say no more no more.
Because here we do not accept simple explanations.
Because here we are the A and we are the Z.
We are the ones who glean our shadows
in the land of destruction, then displaced thousands of times,
trying to collect the pieces in a blue circle.
There are mysterious things happening in this geography,
you probably know by now...

Never mind, master,
We will come back later.

One day I will return in my decadent clothes.

III.

  The rains
were raining

The rains
  were raining

  The rains
were raining

  As if forever,
when we were passing
all the rivers...

Gizem Okulu's poetry has appeared or is forthcoming in *Datableed, Intercapillary Space, Botch, Paradise Now, Infinite Editions* and the anthologies *From London Out* and *Wretched Strangers*. She is the author of *Too Sliced For Landing* (Materials, 2017) and *Master Island* (Tipped Press, 2018), and co-edits the poetry magazine *Splinter*.

CLAIRE ORCHARD

The Picturesque Village

passing no there is almost of sense time here
passing time there of no almost here is sense
passing almost time sense is here no there of
almost here sense time no there of is passing
almost sense time there here of passing is no
almost no time passing here sense of there is
no passing of is time here sense almost there
no almost time of here is sense passing there
no there passing sense of here time is almost
there here time no sense almost passing is of
there almost is no sense passing of time here
there is almost no sense of time passing here
is time almost no sense passing here of there
is here no passing sense there of almost time
is of passing sense time here there no almost
of almost no sense there time passing is here
of passing sense no is almost time there here
of time sense no almost is there passing here
time no here sense there of is passing almost
time of is almost here no there sense passing
time sense no almost passing is here of there
sense time of no is almost there passing here
sense passing no time here is there almost of
sense here is almost no there of passing time
here almost is of passing sense no time there
here sense of is almost time passing there no
here passing is time almost sense there of no

Jib Boom

And did those ferris wheels, in ancient tin can,
Walk upon enthusiasm's mouth organ green?
And was the holy land of goitre
On enthusiasm's pleasant pathogens seen?
And did the countryman divine
Shine forth upon our clouded hipbones?
And was Jib Boom builded here
Among those dark satanic mimes?

Bring me my box girder of burning gold standard!
Bring me my artefacts of detainment!
Bring me my spectacles! O clusters, unfold!
Bring me my chaser of fire hydrant!
I will not cease from mental fillet,
Nor shall my symphony sleep in my handset,
Till we have built Jib Boom
In enthusiasm's green and pleasant language.

BIO

Claire Orchard was born in Aotearoa New Zealand and has lived in the UK from time to time. Her first poetry collection, *Cold Water Cure*, was published in 2016 by Victoria University Press. She is presently working on a sequence of poems about the migration experiences of her father's family, who emigrated from Lancashire in 1955, and her relationship with the UK as a descendent of these migrants. claireorchardpoet.com

DANIELE PANTANO

Low-Voiced Confessions

—A city.
—More streets *hanging in the abyss.*
—Somewhere south.
—And a black donkey buried in its public park.
—(For years of service.)
—(Years as a friend.)
—Yes, but we mustn't blame the children.
—They demanded it.
—Blame the *two greatest painters of the twentieth century.*
—*Who weren't even forty when Columbus discovered America.*
—*(One classic, eternal.)*
—*(The other, modern, always, like a pile of shit.)*
—The snail climbs the stalk.
—A moment later past the city walls.
—Dirt road to a neighborhood of silos.
—And irrigation ditches, not asylums or prisons.
—Someone has written PARADOX on one of the silos, we think.
—(Or perhaps it is more accurate to say someone has whispered
it into the ground.)
—Not far from another ditch.
—Not far from another tasteful confession.
—(He likes to "bite and pluck their nipples like a bass guitar.")
—The children are listening.
—Black donkeys are German motorcycles.
—We learn to lower our voices and ignore the almost visible.
—As we grow up.
—As we realize the snail: a sniper climbing a silo.
—The painters are prepared to testify.
—*Eating things alive. That's what we do.*
—Blame the detectives.
—Exhibit #1(c):
—(Something mute steps out of a neighborhood.)

Life Jacket

—i put on.
—my pristine.
—charlie isoe face.
—in the mirror.
—of a public restroom.
—no cameras.
—only the needles.
—my gaze.
—patinated by my tongue.
—eyes with no one.
—to watch.
—mother's suicide ring.
—around my neck.
—her panties' isabelline seam.
—pinching my scrotum.
—i dry drown.
—through the door.
—usher beautiful refugee boys.
—across southern borders.

BIO

Daniele Pantano is a Swiss poet, artist, translator, critic, and editor. His poetry has been translated into Albanian, Bulgarian, German, French, Kurdish, and Farsi, and recent works include *ORAKL* (Black Lawrence Press, 2017), *Robert Walser's Fairy Tales: Dramolettes* (New Directions, 2015), and *Dogs in Untended Fields: Selected Poems* (Wolfbach Verlag, 2015). He has taught at the University of South Florida, served as the Poet-in-Residence at Florida Southern College, and directed the Creative Writing program at Edge Hill University, where he was Reader in Poetry and Literary Translation. www.pantano.ch

ASTRA PAPACHRISTODOULOU

{Xenelasia}

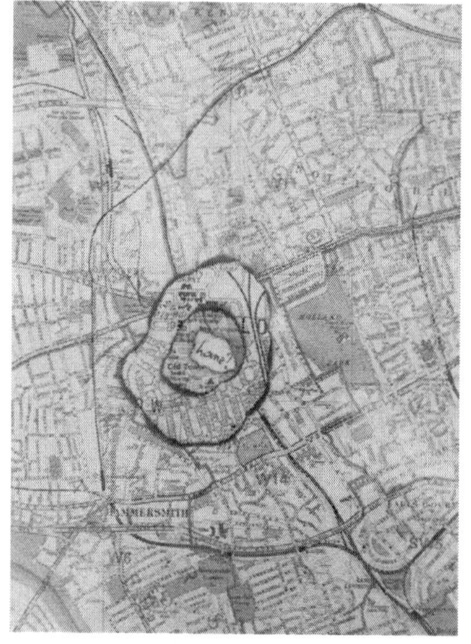

hanging gardens
in the midst of expulsion
inside the walls of the *polis*
aliens wearing tunics of
violence & treachery
hang from gas lamp-posts

a practice to guard
against contaminaτion
from foreign mores[21]

they cast shadows
they call xenoi
ancient, modern, many
they hang from tube
hand-rails capturing
raw footage 24/7

the practice of expelling
foreigners deemed injurious
to the public welfare[18]

stand between the gap
insularity & misanthropy
some are conscious,
more unconscious
fly back to your nest or
float towards Fantasmia

motivated by a willingness
to exploit xenoi, the most
vulnerable in the economy[23]

the supplies are short
and we're ready to rumble
hold on tight onto the rail
hold on tight onto the rail
hanging gardens, we are
in the midst of expulsion

BIO

Astra Papachristodoulou is a Greek poet and artist based in London. She is a recent graduate from the MA Poetic Practice course at Royal Holloway with focus in experimental writing and the neo-futurist tradition across poetry, visual art and performance. Her poetry has appeared in UK magazines and anthologies such as *The Tangerine*, *Stride Magazine* and *3:am magazine*.

FANI PAPAGEORGIOU

A Whiter Shade of Pale

It is a common misconception
that Hadrian's Wall marks the boundary
between England and Scotland.

But this defensive fortification,
lying entirely within England,
has never formed the Anglo-Saxon border.

According to restored sandstone fragments
it was Hadrian's wish to keep the empire intact
as nowhere in Britain is more than 65 miles from the sea.
Reasons for the construction of the wall vary,
no record of an exact explanation survives,
a fog closing in
marking time.

Before the invention of the magnetic compass,
garrisoning a fixed line of defences
was easier
than defending the territory with a loose arrangement of forts,
the footsteps just beginning.

People travelled through the guarded wall of 72 miles
each day
conducting business,
using organised checkpoints for taxation.

There were watchtowers only a short distance from gateways,
patrolling legionaries,
their uniforms the colour of dark lilacs,
keeping track of entering and exiting
natives and Roman citizens alike,
charging customs dues, checking for smuggling.

It is said that once its construction was finished,
the Wall was covered in plaster
then whitewashed,
its shining surface reflecting the sunlight
visible in daytime for miles around,
each stone throbbing
like the telltale heart.

BIO

Fani Papageorgiou was born in Athens in 1975 and studied at Edinburgh University and Harvard. Her poetry is published by Shearsman Books and includes *When You Said No, Did You Mean Never?* (2103 & also translated into Spanish and published by Bartleby Editores in Madrid), *Not So Ill with You and Me* (2015) and *The Purloined Letter* (2017). Her articles and book reviews have appeared in the *Times Literary Supplement*, *The Economist*, and *FT Weekend*).

RICHARD PARKER

Work in Space

for Jennifer Cooke

This one time I got a job on Io
                                        or was it out by Aldebaran
stacking power couplings,
                    the second week I arrived late all five days and they fired me.

In other far parts of the galaxy casually employed and let go,
                                        "working not working."

When you have a job in space you will still have to turn up on time.
Even when you have a job in space you will still have to turn up on time;
    set your alarm, move around or under the cityscape.

Your work is—walking on the ceiling in Velcro shoes—ontologically
    aligned with capital.

*

On past the coral banks of Theed,
lifeguard up atop the marvellous ladder, on patrol on Planet Splash.
One time I had to administer the intravenous translation at the space
    commission

the tachograph

once selling Han Solo jackets
opening the pod bay doors for 8 hours a day—

the wild flower 'neath the shepherd's foot,
an unlicensed junk freighter, Lymeswold.
Indicator ticking in the gyratory.

*

The far future alien considering human consciousness,
the ghastly imposition of the working week.

Cambozola. Trainees in the nebula.
In the mist the holobooth glimmering.

Got work scooping the slippery avocado balls—
couldn't hold them and I lost it, replaced by the betentacled squidwoman.

*

The tachograph will still turn,
though the days will be all different lengths; rotations—an asshole will
monitor you, will line-manage you.

The whole world is going to get back to the endpoint.
The only thing that I would do would be to add a different calendar.
All our works pass out beyond the ends of the blocked-out work week.
All the jobs end. All of us working
but as yet untranslated in the holobooth
staring back down the ultrasound—
pumping gas on the Outer Rim.

In the dark heart of the bureaucratic city the museum of work-placements.
In the cold heart of the universal city the middle managers' Hall of Fame,
the Coruscant precariat.

It will all be OK,
at the heart of the imperial city a tyromancer.

*

My work is to move around the galaxy understanding.
To share in the knowledge of others,
to become like others, to meld with them,
to mix minds with strangers, with strange beings from across the universe
to know all and to have all know me.

Beyond the stars the bourgeois understanding of work might not apply,
between the cold gears of the universe
the little meaning you find in labour might melt away,
become an idleness not consumption.

You still might get that great internship in Terabithia.
Could finally get a job with a stationery cupboard, order up Post-Its.
My job was to answer the phone and catch sudden glimpses of myself in
the office door swinging open, a flash on the glass desk.

*

I was a space taxi driver but then the last people were cut out of the
driver-market
and I'm no longer economically productive or necessary for the Empire;
not as a producer nor a soldier,
so I am cast aside and I am killed.

I am the algorithm and you will never be able to understand my
machinery;
my Oxbridge Mankads.

I would be fucked in a meritocracy
anyone reading this would be fucked in a meritocracy.
Almost everyone.
The seven jealousies:
Keston, Jacob Rees-Mogg; the virtuous meritocrats.

*

Banther herder.
Or a space whaleman.
My peg leg my glass eye my cyborg protuberance my golden eyebrow
the eternal authenticities of work and self-sacrifice, no
            bourgeois bohemians in space, no
                        cricket administrators:
Those who would make the just and perfect unjust, moribund.

In space no zero hours.
No fascist English majority.
There will be no meritocrats, nor nepotists.
In space no one will listen to you read—
lyric space; the long, loud, bright ring of infinity;
tinnitus, the ion engines.

*

My partner and I teleported too many times
                        became one confused self.

Syntax vectors among balloons.
In the sparky dark in Kuat, in the emperor's smithies.
Three weeks' training programme at a protein recycling combine.
We will all retire, then one day there'll be a world where even the
    algorithms won't have to work,
service bots out to pasture.

Boiling freezing sunset on Ganymede,
            on Ganymede the associate lecturer at 1am; second marking—
        on Ganymede the grass soft, the loam, the putting green,
    breath fogs the windshield, the ice-miner fallen from the airlock—
external examiner flames out above Calypso.

Below the turning asshole of the galactic city—
the trumpets.
            Space torn apart, the dolphins jagging,
the long vibrating boundary
                expands,
                        blood from the fountains;

                marble!

dolphin!

the cosmopolitan city
dispersed across the galaxy
not a one will need receipt for travel expenses
not one flung out from the burnished cosmic city
will be finally hired.

The cage tightening.

Know you the great city;
among the distant rings the spangled city.

BIO

Richard Parker is a poet, academic, editor and printer. His poetic works include *from The Mountain of California...* (Openned 2010), *The Traveller and the Defence of Heaven* (Veer, 2012), and *R.T.A. Parker's 99 Sonnets About Evil* (Canary Woof, 2015). He has written critical prose pieces on twentieth-century poetry, with a particular emphasis on American modernism and the New American Poetry. He is the editor and printer of the Crater Press pamphlet and book series, publishing mostly letterpress pamphlets of the best new British poetry.

JAMES BYRNE & SANDEEP PARMAR

Myth of the Savage Tribes, Myth of Civilized Nations

The agents of global capitalism didn't understand that they weren't going to send anyone home! (Stuart Hall)

The sign at Widnes train station reads:
BUY YOUR CONQUEST SHEDS HERE

Cruelty
my witness
among race-makers
the myths of the savage tribe
'primitive germs' of nature
the savage who does not know
his own history
unless determined by
'the good omen'
of the English bull
will always tame
the foreign hare

A dark faceless cargo
preparing to be remade
at the instant of arrival

X

O my God, I cry in the daytime,
but thou hearest not;
and in the night season,
and am not silent. (Psalm 22)

A boy smoking in the rain
outside The Belmont spits
'what are you looking at
you stupid fucking paki?'

Spring Break '85 'Dancing on Ice'
Wembley Arena
Auntie Sandra's encoded theatre
of compliance
and the animal of my grandfather
locked in a razored glare
fixed on the figureskate
the sequinned show
only to pool us in
look at the coon
a darkie John Travolta

'what are you looking at
you stupid fucking paki?'

And with this my grandfather   Henry
twiddles his handlebar tash
opens the flint-furnace of his mouth
and splits inside his own laughter
[blood vertigos the brain
fistballs in an open palm]

And I should have said
There is no champagne in Anfield
No Welsh in the Welsh streets
of Toxteth—the tinned-up houses—
There is no democracy in the Home Counties
No racism in Norwich
Because 'there are no black people'
No black in the union jack
No union in the flag
No tragedy in the North
Like an immigrant boy waiting in the rain
with flowers for Wills and Kate
Like a native of the Commonwealth
doing native dances for Prince Phillip
No revolution without the roll
of the monarch's crown down the stone
scaffold to the bloodied ghosts of Empire

'Coon' he said
flinchless before the ice
in the deadly seat of his pillory
From racoon?
from the Portuguese
barracoos
—sale house for bartered slaves—
or George Dixon
a.k.a Dixie Coon
blackface minstrel dandy
stagenamed
Zip Coon
singing 'Coal Black Rose'
meet the hand of your friend at the hawthorn
grandfather
his song scalds the devil's water
and you are with him
unsunk stone
of time and hate

I should have said
I came here only to buy champagne
I should have said
What are you looking at
do you even know what you're looking at?

At Loftus Road
in the family stand
his gorilla-grunting noises
my bodywell of panic
moistened underarms
as my grandfather scuffles
with a Jamaican pensioner from Liverpool—
the crowd swivels its thousand heads
to face us—
buried mirror of my face
dilated hieroglyphs of eye

Lubly Rosa Sambo cum
dont you hearde Banjo
tum tum tum...
Oh Rose der coal black Rose

Snow, snow, I have eaten snow
I have made myself from snow
I have built my house on snow
snow for six long months a year
the miserable whiteness of snow

I would introduce you to my grandmother
but now
at her last
in the iron of cancer?
Dark bile in her voice
and on meeting strangers
throne of scrutinizing glances—
she would look you over
not as a granddaughter
but as some kind of voodoo

The myths of tribes console
only those who remember
the myths of nations are not
the songs of men singing freely
and without hatred
This ageless land—
the only faultless thing

When the first Pakistani family
moved into Narcott Lane
circa Churchill's swindle years
she turned over the face
of the newly-brown baby
and shook like a burning tree
said to her Henry
like aliens off a spaceship
landed in our own backyard—
the child woke from sea-sleep
his mother petrified into flame

The transmigration of souls
in the 'lower psychology'
metempsychosis: a challenge
to the life of the individual.
From man to beast to man
in the guise of animal who rots
inwardly under the buxom sign of war—
What can be said of the civilized mind
that was in a previous life, a gibbous oyster,
mumbling absently to itself
like a scholar along the sea floor?

Phil came back from his work in the Navy
with a wincy Sri-Lankan thing
didn't speak a word
black as a spade
she sat on the front lawn
all morning   all day
cross-legged   half-naked
kindness past one like that
tapped 'n the head I said
poor Phil
I said   I said to im
be kind to yourself
you'll be kind to 'er

He who is 'bound in the chains of deed'
dies 'eating the fruits of past actions'

Only the barbarian dreams of his dead kinfolk
But only the savage ignores their warnings

(E.B. Tylor, *Primitive Culture*, Vol. 2, 1871)
'The aborigines of Australia have
expressed this theory in the simple formula,
'Blackfellow tumble down, jump up Whitefellow.'

They will not come to me in this frozen land
where horses and sheep claw at the dead soil,
defeated, their mouths empty, their lips like
the oracles' ripped apart by the theories of god.

Anon, Barbados—
'the devil was in the Englishman
that he makes everything work;
he makes the negro work,
he makes the horse work'

Exquisite memory
for his enemy
like heroic song

'The belief in the new human birth
of the departed soul, [...]
led West African negroes to commit suicide
when in distant slavery,
that they may revive in their own land...'
(*Primitive Culture*, Vol. 2)

To wake up in my own distant land
To hear the sounding of its birth
the infinite phantom who readies
a feast for souls blown through
with the whiteness of winter's glass.
Before the lamps go out, let us pass
before the devil drags his crooked tail
through the darkened aisles of our
small and hopeless cathedrals...

The Duke of Wellington—describing his own army—
'The scum of the Earth.
The mere scum of the Earth'.

The Bulgarian at the fountain
who is obliged to throw water
from his bucket to the thirsty
serpent who is anyway going
to slip between his bedsheets
or strangle his children after
he has done all he can
to appease it.

'There is a forgotten,
nay almost forbidden word,
which means more to me than any other.
That word is England'
(Winston Churchill)

The tree-worship
of the hamadryad,
Apollonian nymph
lovely and sapless
strange pleasure
her white marrow.

'Poetry is full of myth...
the mental condition of the lower races
is the key to poetry.'
(*Primitive Culture*, vol. 2)

Deafness cultivated
a fog, a bruise
an oar-split path
unbroken, weaving,
on the lighted
wounds of chronic
wandering

'...where barbaric hordes groped blindly,
cultured men can often move onward
with clear view.
It is a harsher, and at times even painful,
office of ethnography
to expose the remains of crude old culture
which have passed into harmful superstition,
and to mark these out for destruction.'
(*Primitive Culture*, vol. 2)

Sublimated to the poorly sign-posted Slavery Museum
the third-floor crimes of Empire repeat:
customary histories
fantasized and fetishised ruins of nations
(or 'tribes' as they
are described in the adverts of the savage trade)

(Anonymous journal entry, 25th May 1756)
The slave was returned to the estate after having run away.
Thistlewood gave him a moderate whipping,
pickled him well and made Hector
[another slave]

shit in his mouth,
immediately put in a gag whilst his mouth was full
& made him wear it 4 or 5 hours.'

'...the fetish woman answers in a thin, whistling voice,
and with the old-fashioned idioms of generations past.'
(*Primitive Culture*, Vol. 2)

He catch old Cuffee by de wool,
he dick him on de shin,
Which laid him breathless on the ground,
and made de nigger grin

[Historians have wondered how Thistlewood could be
at once tender with the slaves and yet so brutal—
When John Thistlewood drowned,
Phibbah was disconsolate,
ill with grief]

I lose my way and between MLK and the white
unequivocally glass-cased KKK to fix on a photograph
of the embering remains of a lynched torso framed
by a horde of men. The Museum builds its own
superstitious myth. Deflecting anger in collages of guilt.
History inscribes itself over the silence it has made.

BIOS

Sandeep Parmar is Professor of English Literature at the University of Liverpool where she co-directs Liverpool's Centre for New and International Writing. Her books include *Reading Mina Loy's Autobiographies: Myth of the Modern*, an edition of the *Collected Poems of Hope Mirrlees* (Carcanet, 2011), the *Selected Poems of Nancy Cunard* (Carcanet, 2016) and two books of her own poetry published by Shearsman: *The Marble Orchard* and *Eidolon*, winner of the Ledbury Forte Prize for Best Second Collection.

James Byrne is a poet, editor and translator. He co-translated and co-edited *Bones Will Crow: 15 Contemporary Burmese Poets* (Arc Publications, 2012) and is the co-editor of *Atlantic Drift: An Anthology of Poetry and Poetics* (Edge Hill University Press/Arc, 2017). His most recent poetry collection is *Everything Broken Up Dances* (Tupelo, 2015).

ALBERT PELLICER

The Orchard

the orchard in a glass bell
reached for the moon fount grabbers:

plastic for uttering water spurts
planet-plants against

pumkin:
a stack of assumptions now:

the breath's depth. of.
A river bank. A shell.

A. Make time. Available.
A. Make belief.

the purchase of the spirit
the purchase of the land

the leak of inhabitants
to settle

the clearing of nature for
road tracks

fairy: trails tamed toads
by the river : sand : estuary's soliloquy

write. A poem. to change things.
write . A poem. full.

write a poem.
write a rite. to rhyme.

leave the land to be land.

Herd Of Noons

The greasy spotted paper
from the wind blown

left horoscopes
perplexed

the full flood punctuated of sunshine
wet in the burden

the body
unheard
unlike you the enquiry

this space in return from
its swaying
scrapes like a country
numb

figured numbers
unique
cross-legged chairs
piano pedals

gifted thread of dreams
deport by vessels
away a word
less by
quest
whose

in this formation of words
question? information of words
in this if words
when what arrived where
of walks why in the air you meant moves
with the rattling of a stick
the rails swam the trace the wave

between a mouthed fence
and the frozen mineral mind
homebound
the typed oral cries old
by friction freeze
and the breeze radiates the spinal leaves

BIO

Albert Pellicer was born in Barcelona and is based in London. His installations include *Fennec* (Centre for Contemporary Poetics at Birkbeck, 2013) and *Some Herd Of Noons* (Tree Hardy Gallery, 2014). Collaborations include *Asylum* with visual poet Márton Koppány (Iklectik, London, 2016), *The Fumigation Of La Luna* with sound artist Ximena Alarcón (University of North Texas, 2008), and *Óxido: First Repetition* with composer Francisco Coll (Wigmore Hall, 2010, published by Faber & Faber Music). He has published two books: a verse novel in Catalan and English, *El Lector de Núvols* and *Fennec*.

PASCALE PETIT

Hieroglyph Moth

When the white ermine wings
opened at night

like a book of frost
            smoking in the dark,

I understood the colours of vowels
painted on moth fur –

the black, red, saffron signs
of a new language.

Antennae grew from my forehead,
my tongue was restless in its chrysalis.

I felt lift-off
            as if my bones had melted.
I stepped out into the snow –

not even an exoskeleton to protect me
in this strange country.

Landowners

What does it mean to own a half-hectare?
I stood on the bank of the stream

and asked the stones and the pools:
how deep do my boundaries extend,

through how many seams of mantle?
How high? Up to where the indigo sky

is feathered with black?
For a full hour the cork oaks were silent

while I questioned each leaf.
Then a voice came from the branch

and I saw two kingfishers.
Tchi chee, they said, *kwee kwee*,

and I knew they were speaking
the lost language of the land,

that this estate I'd inherited
was theirs.

Their costumes confirmed it –
wings of the intensest sun blue

shimmering like atmospheres
over the bronze earths of their bodies.

Mama Macaw

An egg with the blue-and-gold chick
of a planet inside

is what Mama Macaw dreams of
as she flies through space

searching for a mate. She knows
what she'll do when she finds him –

pluck down from her breast,
tender tips from her tail,

to line a nest in the night-tree.
She knows her chick will be the last

of her species, the last speaker
of earth's tribe. Her chick's wings

will be sunset and sunrise,
her head will stream with auroras.

BIO

Pascale Petit was born in Paris and came to the UK as a child. She is of French/Welsh/Indian heritage, a French citizen and recently acquired British nationality, prompted by Brexit. Her seventh collection, *Mama Amazonica* (Bloodaxe, 2017), won the 2018 RSL Ondaatje Prize, was a Poetry Book Society Choice, and draws on her travels in the Amazon rainforest. Her sixth, *Fauverie*, was her fourth to be shortlisted for the T.S. Eliot Prize and five poems from it won the Manchester Poetry Prize. Her books have been translated into Spanish (in Mexico), Chinese, French and Serbian. In 2015, she received a Cholmondeley Award. 'Hieroglyph Moth' first appeared in *The Treekeeper's Tale* (Seren, 2008); 'Landowners' in *The Zoo Father* (Seren, 2001); and 'Mama Macaw' in *Mama Amazonica* (Bloodaxe, 2017).

ADAM PIETTE

by the nadir we come

circle broken refugee point so blue   wandering at a loss

lost refuge broken homecircle   at what point exactly

sudden heartbreak   losing it   round the houses

fugue state lurking   ablaze the hearth that wasn't

hunger and blindness of the enemy's country   this here

blurted out you lose   cracked right open you were

pointed words endaggered   just slip that between your ribs loser

stateless fugal machine crossed voicings   at what border

are you insane   and the law lops at the points the roots bleed

gather up what words that remain   ours when our is losing its senses

singalong down the metalled roads   upon the dangerous waters

as the world goes t
o pot takes its capital way   to oblivion

BIO

Adam Piette co-edits poetry journal *Blackbox Manifold* with Alex Houen, is author of *Remembering and the Sound of Words, Imagination at War*, and *The Literary Cold War*, and is Professor of Modern Literature at the University of Sheffield.

JÈSSICA PUJOL DURAN

La cuestión es que

the question is that information is incomplete and insufficient and
composition, what forms it, what is contained, too

the question is that boundaries are built up with affect and then locked up
into a linguistic system
can become a torture
when reinforced by unfair events
we lack the words to change
or affects
(or both)

the question is that music keeps playing in the headphones &
enjambments do not give us a pause to sigh
silence is the absence of a flamenco shoe against the floor
hands stopped between clap   and   clap

the question is that meanings block our throats
with golden threats from the market
which moves us
to curl up into another idea of paradise

the question is that wind hits the skyscraper
convulses the world underneath
messes up your hair
the newspaper doesn't capture
how can we alleviate this present
& oh kid the amount lies of the headlines!
at night all cows are black

the question is that the norm doesn't seduce our conscience
to inhabit new places
and decentred
be turned by words

the question is that who takes the wrong idea to its ultimate consequences
separates us from the question that activates the new syntax
& so the question is a potential lie
like what we see and listen
our disordered senses
names, professions, etc.

the question is that the object of a glance gets lost in representations by
other intentions that absorb   direct   neglect it forget about the
idea to push through
the present is made
of jokes, curiosities, sentimentalities, gossip, all the possible to be false

& pupils peppered by a flock of birds
como tu mirada perdida

the question is that Magritte's pupils could be in the black holes
that google.maps leaves in the sky
and Mona Lisa's in the cursor we follow to salvation
just try to write here what you are thinking: ________

the question is that we come and go like I came here & now
I go there

what else?

the question is that sometimes you need wild gesticulation to communicate the pain of the pasts: Past Perfect happened before Past Simple (a long time ago)
in Spanish we double-negate:
"en la nada no había nada" – which is to say 'in nothingness there was no nothingness' where "había" denotes existence

understanding that moves you to the Future much faster

from *Entrar es tan difícil salir / Enter Exit Is So Difficult*

Translated by William Rowe

la realidad se transforma en aquello imposible de travesar con el dedo
y la experiencia   indexada del límite
es fina   elaborada
¡ay! donde
no podemos volar más
no tocamos más que superficie
estamos afuera o estamos adentro
estamos afuera y estamos adentro

(yo como no acabo de ser
lo que toco
no me lo creo

reality gets transformed into what's impossible to cross with a finger
and indexed   experience of the limit
is smooth   complicated
ay! where
we can't fly any more
we only touch the surface
whether we're inside or we're outside
we're inside and we're outside

(since I haven't come to be
what I touch
    I don't believe

*

¿y ahí, qué veo? ¿con la...
  ¿el gusto? ¿con la
  ¿la herida? ¿la
  salida...
  ¿otra halegoría?
  se me inflaman los tendones
      esto ES
      la
      mismí-
      sima
      arruga

I spy, what can I spy? with my
  taste? with my
  my wound? the
  exit?...
  another hallegory?
  my tendons get inflamed
      this IS
      the
      very-
      same
      wrinkle

BIO

Jèssica Pujol Duran (Barcelona, 1982) is a Postdoctoral researcher at the University of Santiago de Chile. She was Poet in Residence at the University of Surrey in 2013/2014 and edits *Alba Londres*, a magazine of British, Spanish and Latin American translation. She writes and translates in Catalan, English and Spanish, and has two chapbooks in English, *Now Worry* (Department, 2012) and *Every Bit of Light* (Oystercatcher Press, 2012), a book in Catalan, *El país pintat* (El pont del petroli, 2015), and one in Spanish, *Entrar es tan difícil salir*, with translations by William Rowe (Veer Books, 2016).

ARIADNE RADI COR

L'italie L'ondon

[...]

London is a fax, when you are here you have the copy
The real thing is somewhere else.

The only difference is that for these same things
You won't feel. But when? Soon. It ends with you striding away
Losing who was at your side, straight to your Magi and the stars.

In the duplicating machine of an unstoppable city
Those who can best see
Are those homeward bound, on the bordering crest.

*

Citizenship is the anaesthesia of a mystery, London
It'll work as the colour in the photo booth, for the passport, London.

But my little woollen top was from eternity and it knew the truth
That by a twist of faith we'll never know how happy we were.

This inclination to return, to look back, to collide
Because the driver's scent reminds me of something, but what
A man, which, but who, where, when – when?
I drag behind me the motorway of the Sun and the steps to the church
at Origlio.

The stairs multiply and the white multiplies and the scent
A scent: whose, from when – whose?
Anyway, I hear the hits on the radio and I know it's not so
It couldn't have happened that way.

The plaster cast of our embrace is at the British Museum
Among the ancient civilizations.

*

"They've taken Mary Poppins' bag"
And I'm here with the movers, with this scraping of the world
Of the head against the world, with my hair
Combed back, back – back.

I am here, waiting to return
And slip my feet into the footsteps of the last walk, be at ease
Match the shade of the world with that of the body
Take my life into the silhouette and there see that it does not fit.

Interlude, intervallo – interlude
It may not be – but then Boom, again.

We have to behave like roots, be invisible
And hold the world together.

*

The English Channel, a cup of hot water
Something delicate, bordering on
Nothing and the opposite continent.

Nothing between us but a whisper of sea
To fill the void with –

On the train in my wide-lapelled aviator dress, a standard model always
Coming to a cinema near you. Depart London on the train
And the countryside will take your eyes, and the oaks – and your eyes.

At times in the early morning I look at my life which at this hour
Acquiesces with the light in the room and I wonder, how did this happen
Am I taking the place of another intentionally or by error.

And is this my error
Or someone else's.

*

"Don't give it a thought" – it's the grand finale of the quinquennial
In the empire style of coincidences.
It's the confiscation of time, of eyes, of the snow.

Inhale deeply by the Thames and you sense Venice
The source is the same: a minute extradition.

The partition between the continents is on my rib cage
And as the continents detach, the wings detach.

Crenellations, uncertain etymology: parapet
Breastplate, double breasted
Then the gunshot.

"Don't fear my love"
Should I get shot on Oxford Street, I wouldn't die
Because this isn't my life.

I'm still living in a Burano glass globe
I twirl and the snow falls.

*

But you have the air of being outside of all this
A Carny with straight teeth at a certain height
At yours on the bordering crest I can see the snow
And I rise with a crowning and daffodils trumpeting yellow.

Yet a plaster cast is only so I can maintain my posture
A cyclone in my rib cage, a pleated skirt if I pirouette
In the wingspan of umbrellas flipped in the wind
Magical things happen that language can't speak of.

*

"The carpet is inside you and it'll never dry out"
A fault-line filled with trout, and the continents detach
And the wings detach

And the hydropower is to keep my light burning through the night
As I bite my lip and worry the paper-cut
Till it becomes a lake.

The unsaid inside the aviator-blue closet
Nearer to the earth's core
In dikes of splendour
In the coming splendour.

*

London, a kind of Olympus
An emissions of our youth
Of figures collecting lights, the epilogue
"The dream of the century, coming to a cinema near you"

The habit of wanting to discover one another like rocks in the dark
To be the flints that spark

But only gratitude binds us
In the widening of each other's absence, in the scent
Remaining on the armrests when I leave:
Bluebells beyond my body, persisting bluebells.

*

And a nursery rhyme: I wish to wish the wish you wish...

But it isn't that you forget things
It's just that at a certain point they are no longer true.

[...]

BIO

Ariadne Radi Cor is an Anglo-Italian postcard maker, lettering artist and coffee spoons collector based in London. Ari writes poems and short stories and sometimes makes video poems, using voiceover and subtitles on 'long photographs' (short movies where little happens) and playing with the montage of time, space and narration as collage, or layers of intention. www.chantillycream.co.uk

NAT RAHA

from *xtinctions*

mourner's europe [a]

would flee its republics, totalities
, police fixtures & armament norms
& guards precarious,
howls hours & raids,

for your protection
]] cultural decades
assimilar like muslim like radcliffe lines / infrastruct
division mutually breeched,
../ secures mythic free
/ alertsong in
print / neofash europe
clearings /
enlightened a
subject in which we
could not exist
, bonds owed
/ alarmphones,, swallows med.

of future workforces
future stoppage & revolt, the
knowledge & memory of failures historical
in the consciousness of seeking refuge

BIO

Nat Raha is a poet and trans/queer activist, living in Edinburgh. Her poetry includes the collections *countersonnets* (Contraband Books, 2013) and *Octet* (Veer Books, 2010), and pamphlets *de/compositions* (Enjoy Your Homes, 2017), £/€xtinctions (sociopathetic distro, 2017), *[of sirens / body & faultlines]* (Veer Books, 2015), and *mute exterior intimate* (Oystercatcher, 2013). She's performed and published her work internationally. Nat is co-editor of the *Radical Transfeminism* zine and is finishing a PhD in on queer Marxism and contemporary poetry at the University of Sussex.

NISHA RAMAYYA

Death

from family, our seasons –
– seasons we conspire for the sake of crossed paths

from the metaphysics of inheritance
our dinner table training, our future-proof polish
to the left, to the right of the shade

honey loving eyeing dying deaths of different kinds

I, family, am going to die; I will be hindrance

from the home of disease, the home of love
our drunk eyes, our sandalwood dance moves

from the impropriety of multiple homes

all over the place folding back into thought
– reflected in white granite –
– tensile heartstring, *tulsi* putty –

almost always touching stretching thin folds back to thought

I, home, am going to die; I will be filament

from the hurting hold of here and there
from our remembered enemies, our interpretations

– the state corrects itself, corrections restated, reinstatements posed
living bodies folded into the shapes of dead bodies –

She puts her hands together, fills your mouth with salutation. Her hands part to pull dead bodies out of your mouth, your tongues, your mouth wide open as she ties the loose ends of your desires in your mouth, your other tongues, looping around her fingers, she knots your desires correctly, your loose ends dissolving, your hails of dead and dismembered bodies, her adornments, the parts of her body, her gathered bits, blood stickiness, golden threads, strings of pearls, hail choking, tolerance soaking, knots ending fringing pooling in your still opening mouth.

I, India, am going to die; I will be unqualified

from the sad smoke of our origins –
– our safe distance, our wet socks

from the modernity of our sleeplessness

polymorphous deities, sacrilegious throbs

that goddess doesn't mean what you think it does
it is further away than she looks

I, myth, am going to die; I will be slime trail

from meat, from wine, from carnal entitlement, from elective emaciation

from decapitation makes your hair look good
from squatting schematically, from *agarbatti* burns
from painting lipstick on white petals
from applying white petals to purify skin
from plucking eyelashes, from translating sacrifice
from making you – all the way – up

I, ritual, am going to die; I will be directionless

from our well-formed, from our perfection
– figment of millions, the passion of love, our great enemy –
from generations of learning how to decline suffering, conjugate illusion

I swallow books upon books upon books
to unlearn like-mindedness, to externalise cosmos

another body grows inside my body
– a statue of a woman, a veiled beauty, a hard-boiled egg –
I am indifferent to the fires inside

patience is a fully-grown body just under my skin

wanting you –
– needing this ending –
– dreaming of being decontextualized

I, Sanskrit, am going to die; I will be sunny-side up

from ocean, from abandonment, from unoriginality

from depending on the position of the planets, the explainers, their promises
the nonce-borrowed defences, the walls they outline on your belly and back

from your poster-paint instincts, your woodblock chorus
the compulsion to ask for help
– green and purple neck feathers, dipped in saltwater –
– liminal itch, driven to spurt –

from the severed totalities of other tongues, to the quick of being recalled

I, dictionary, am going to die; I will be testudineous

from infatuation, as the condition of thought
to devotion as the current, rendering death

from my small steps towards you, tarnished silver
to my rubbings of the walls, around you widdershins

from your growing body, gendered by an accretion of touch
to your passers-by, unsexing the matter of your solicitude

from your three points, sinning religiously
to my fixed points, votive sediment

I, goddess, am going to die; I will be allergenic

from carrying across, a saviour, protector –

– the ripple of definitions
recollection a network of dark blue shrill

– a pearlwork of safe crossings
darkness an enumeration of her strung stars

– her surpassing tones
accomplishment an end that she reaches by falling

– fainting away
erotics a loosening of love's apprehension

I, Tantra, am going to die; I will be serrated

from the dead time spent apart from you, spending lying die for you, the time of lying alongside you, from the lie of dying far from you, treading lengths apart from you, measuring time spent dead for you, parts of me die alongside you, dying me to write for you, writing time the death of you, eyeing me devouring you, timing me from end of lying, ending you return to me, returning time devouring you, time dies to elongate death, longing to stop writing you, writing to return to time you –

I, love, am going to die; I will be death

BIO

Nisha Ramayya's pamphlets *Notes on Sanskrit* (2015) and *Correspondences* (2016) are published by Oystercatcher Press.

PETER ROBINSON

Where Europe Ends

qui non siamo in Europa,
siamo in Portogallo.
(Antonio Tabucci, *Sostiene Pereira*)

Look here, among the merchants' houses
at Kobe with their imitation
hair-styles and tooth powders...

or underneath the Sannomiya
railway arch, by each arcade shop,
while I courier an envelope
(it's sealed, not to be opened)
containing a criminal record report
from the Hyogo Police Department;

or at your Italian Consulate
where the thing's to be translated
in aid of a passport application,
and I'll suffer that vertiginous glass-walled lift
plunging from an umpteenth floor
with the nothing it revealed –

*

or in the Expo ethnology museum's
labyrinth collections;
alone amongst donated things,
there I found the Europe section's
illustrative items
include a painted Dutch organ on wheels,
the snapshots of our mountain sheep-farmers
and plaques about its 'changing face'
thanks to the inward migrations
of human transhumance –

because towards this end of Europe
it's like a William Adams
and his progeny would come home,
like imploding exploration
meant, as it says, 'the tide has turned',
and now their great experiment
promising to lose what we can't share
must open arms to everyone.

But in its courtyard's hieratic stair
are preserved those 'cheerful graves',
their 'relics of a future'.

*

Or else at Moscow airport
circa nineteen eighty-nine,
gone past a *Welcome to Europe* sign...

that's when I caught a glimpse of Yeltsin
beside some empty shelving
while our Sabina flight refueled,
and from its transit lounge's warmth
could see a man in uniform
stationed on the tarmac;
he wanted to come in from the cold,
would stamp, and clap his gloves.
Though there was nothing to desire,
they did take credit cards.
Then, at last, they took the boarding cards,
off-handed, let us go
on towards convertible currencies
over versts and wastes of snow.

*

My ear and eye affections
contracted in those elsewheres
with smatterings of languages
as if a rash, a skin disease,
have likewise disinclined me
to take things at face value.

Still, when she asked me did I think English
were the language for these places
I lived in fourteen years,
it was like my words wouldn't stick to things
because not spoken there –
or if uttered by non-native speakers
would bring out inner distances
of de-familiarity!

But especially when back home here,
home, after four months away,
for there are gaps in our map of Europe
now glimpses of expressive features
leak anger, mute resentments
on the point of spilling into words,
the verbal tics, officious gestures
overcast and changeable
as an English summer's day.

*

In a bleak July or washed-out August
jet-lag morning, who are you
coming from another dreamscape
to start and startle me?

Who are you with these collages,
perpetual other woman,
still the same, and recognized,
although this time you've changed your hair?
An artist? Your *Merzbau* exhibit's
mounted like a low relief
that alters as it's gazed on now
among the crowd at a private view.

Have you been modeled from the life,
though composite? Somebody lost?
Someone I had to say goodbye to?
Or are you from that other England,
a country welcoming of strangers?
We plan to meet...you disappear...
then I'm left here to find you
in a washed-out August or late bleak July?

*

For it's like there is no end of Europe,
like I take it everywhere –
as if it were some scented soap
or that Mackintosh ladder-back chair...

Not distant from Dynevor Road (an instance)
where Joseph Conrad would return,
writing – as he did – the word Home
always means these hospitable shores
– and I'd come to recuperate
after nearly dying
to a nondescript, domestic street;
or else by Foscolo's emptied tomb
at Chiswick Cemetery,
the poet's shade no less '*piú qui*'
in this time-desecrated, this exilic retreat...

Oh Europe, a young woman's wide-eyed features,
wind-strewn locks and coronet
on the back of a haulage company truck,
how you cover those inner distances,
come with me everywhere!

NOTES

'Where Europe Ends' is dedicated to the continent's exophonic writers, ones such as Yoko Tawada, a Japanese poet and novelist who also composes in German, and is a Berlin resident. Her *Where Europe Begins* (in Susan Bernofsky's translation) helped prompt this poem's title, and her novel *The Naked Eye* offered a suggestive phrase: 'but the map of Europe in my head was full of blank spots.'

Rereading Antonio Tabucci's *Sostiene Pereira* produced the epigraph ('here we're not in Europe, we're in Portugal'), words criticizing its eponymous central character, a journalist and translator of nineteenth-century French stories, for a supposed lack of patriotism in August 1938 when inviting his readers to appreciate the literature of another European country. Tabucci lived much of his life in Lisbon and wrote his *Requiem* in Portuguese. It contains an imaginary encounter with the unnamed Fernando Pessoa, who keeps breaking into English. Among other topics, they discuss the poet's patriotic feelings and his idea of Europe.

Joseph Conrad is amongst the greatest of exophonic writers in what was his third language. On 13 October 1885, he wrote from Singapore that 'When speaking, writing or thinking in English the word Home always means for me the hospitable shores of Great Britain.' In a late poem, 'Nel cimitero di Chiswick', Salvatore Quasimodo expressed the view that 'L'amore per le ombre foscoliane è piú qui / che in Santa Croce' ('Love for the shades of Foscolo is more present here / than in Santa Croce'). In 1871, at the Italian monarch's behest, the poet's remains were removed to the Florentine church where they now reside. He chose to settle in England after the defeat of Napoleon had ruined his hopes for unification.

William Adams was the first Englishman to arrive and stay in Japan, reaching the country on what remained of a Dutch ship that had drifted across the Pacific in 1603. The various quoted phrases in the poem's second part are from the National Ethnology Museum at the Expo Park in Osaka, where, as well as the other items listed, is displayed a Charles Rennie Mackintosh ladder-back chair, also exemplifying 'Europe'. The neologism *Merzbau* was created by Kurt Schwitters to describe his own interior constructions from collaged found materials. He fled the continent's mainland in 1940 and spent the rest of his life, a further eight years, in the British Isles.

The places I lived for fourteen years are in Sendai, Japan, which is where the question about language and place was asked at a reading on 22 July 2017. Poets are adept at *l'esprit d'escalier* and 'Where Europe Ends' might be a part of my late reply.

BIO

Peter Robinson has recently published the novel *September in the Rain* (2016) and his *Collected Poems 1976–2016* (2017). He is Professor of English and American Literature at the University of Reading and poetry editor for Two Rivers Press.

LISA SAMUELS

The right to be transplace

I dream that I burst out laughing, that I span a river in one stride, or that I am followed by a flood of motor-cars which never catch up with me.
(Frantz Fanon, *Les Damnés de la Terre*, 1961, trans. 1963 Constance Farrington)

L'égalité veut d'autres lois.
(Eugène Pottier, *L'Internationale*, 1871)

There are different languages and emphases of transplace touching on what it means to have or not have an origin home, to be (or not) from somewhere, and to belong to more than one place as an adult, to live as a transplace person. I could talk about being transnational, learning language families in different world regions, learning to inhabit variant cultural patterns, and becoming transplace as an adult. Some people acquire deep transplace experiences and identities without having been raised transplace. This piece, however, fixates on transplace as a matter of origin identity. Here I'm talking about the formative consequences of moving around repeatedly among highly variant places from babyhood to the teenage years: growing up transplace.

By 'move around' I mean not be from somewhere, and by be 'from somewhere' I mean a place where you lived, or still do, for some solid time of your first decades of life, a place whose psychogeography gave you a particular sense of self because you extruded into it and it gave itself back to you so that street corners or mountain edges, or peculiar scents and styles of light, are coextensive with sustained experiences that shaped your early selves (in the plural because life provides many opportunities for developing selves among which we code switch, slip, suffer and romp).

When people ask you that primary question Where Are You From, and you answer distinctly that you've moved around, they then (often, frequently) say yes but Where Were You Born as if that might reveal/revalue the truth of place origin. Often when you answer the natal place name they say ah, I know that place (or similar situating response) and then they sometimes (frequently) act as though they've satisfied their own criterion for assuming who you originally are.

This locative querying can feel absurd when it assumes that there is a certain foundation for human apparitioning into the world, in this case a place foundation, whether agricultural or city-state, for sure located. (Not hunter-gatherer; we've left that behind. Or maybe we're coming back to it, but if we are it makes people nervous. They want to tag you.) When you resist origin-place-tagging some people respond as though you are resisting telling something that you *could*, were you not being unreasonable. As though you have refused to give your legal appellation and and asked them to just interact with you, without your name.

It's always difficult, maybe impossible, to *acquire* a from-somewhereness. Even if you move into a place as a young adult and stay there your whole life, you are still 'from' the place you came from before. This is one root for the suspicion of so-called 'outsiders.' And it's one root for calls for place purity, for example advocating for the sole support for or pursuit of people From There or things From There. (Place purity is expressed for example by the UK Prime Minister Theresa May in a 5 October 2017 speech: 'If you believe you're a citizen of the world, you're a citizen of *nowhere*. You don't understand what the very word 'citizenship' means.') Of course, there are different versions of any in-between. In the racializing of a mingled world, for example, some transnationals are so-called marked and some are so-called unmarked (I use 'so-called' to underscore the trouble in naturalizing the invented distinction). An unmarked transnational is apparently not as visible as a marked one, as though your skin colour makes you visible. Which could be a nice thought were it not inextricably allied with deadly racism.

It's also extremely difficult, maybe impossible, to acquire for oneself a from-somewhereness without experience in from-somewhereness in those first two decades of living. I mean, I wouldn't know how to try.

The violence that someone does to you when they insist that you are From One Place and that you Are One Thing is a violence people have been talking about for a long time. There are many kinds of identity and different levels of movement coercion and a range of what we call choice. The repeated problem people have with Inside and Outside. Stop being outside or only be outside. One or the other. It's exhausting and not a small matter. It is not inconsequential for anyone on the scale of moving around.

The rule of reflective being (the thinkability of anything) and the case of different experiences mean that 'transplace' or 'transnational' are gauzy nets that only ever cast over some of the thinkable terrain. Anyone might spur perpendicular vectors from ideas and sensations gestured to here.

So what do you do when you meet someone transplace? First, don't panic. It isn't their fault that they are not From Somewhere, nor is their not-from-somewhere status an intended reflection on your own experience and identity. They (adopting the ungendered pronoun for both singular and plural third person) don't want to take over your Fromness, though occasionally I confess to a pang when encountering someone who is resolutely emplaced, wondering how that feels inside and as a body.

What is a place, anyway? Arguably these very points could be said to reify an ideology of Fromness. So what's a contrast? What's a transnational not-quite-fromness look like? Where is transgeography? What feelings might go along with transplace?

So you've come into a bracket whose parameters, like the nation-state, are never quite the same: I mean, one place might be codified by size, by boundary nature, by tongue flow or language mix another was made by others or imagines it has grown up from inside its ox-bow origins as though baby-suppressed hors-human life were translucent wallpaper visibilizing only when the human comes up on it.

What happens when you are transplace and/or transnational in a context? It can be lonely, so it's kind to be kind to someone who doesn't mean not to belong to one place. And belonging, make no mistake, is one of the central issues here. A person who is not From Somewhere and who can't easily become part of a new Somewhere can be fraught with that comparative non-belonging.

One occasion of belonging for transplacers is when we meet others. Then the possibility arises of knowing how that in-between-places shaping feels for someone else who grew up moving around. Such encounters make me think about how transplace can be thought of as place on the move, movement as place, being from movement, movement *as* substance (pulling Aristotle's contrast into and through itself). I am 'from' displacement. It's theoretical to think of what to call it. Hence perhaps a predilection for neologism arises from experiences that don't yet have much for proper names.

Within its differences, transplace queers the dominance of place origin. It's a right not to be a stranger, no more a stranger than anyone else. Drawing out a nuance of Eugène Pottier's 'Equality wants different laws', transplace involves a right to name oneself as transgeographic, to own that condition of movement-origin in a way not too distant from the right to self-name (to change your name, legally or not) and to self-identify your body orientations (sex and gender). These latter conditions of deliberative nomination and self-knowing bear a family resemblance to this essay's desire to accord to movement-place its own conditions of reality and respect.

> Some people want to be the same or say hallelujah we are in the "same conversation." You might find a negative or a positive persona or someone who thinks the Givens and with whom you cannot begin from a cut possibility – that's the exhaustion, the voice floating blinkered a conditional perfusive aura that is not recognizable because it's precisely the conditions of never-recognisability across the upper back the temporary playful provenance built without walls, astonished in its ohs, the understandable person focusing the glandular on the three-dimensional objects that condition the temporary sky, nature a cough inside the bag of obedience, no doubt something particular curves your back and you are half-way to unacceptable before a big falling out of the tree after pushing all the way into that cut to perceive what clarity the dark circumstances might yield?

Setting to one side for now the important topics gestured to by the term transnational, transplace as movement states that when movement happens between one body/place and another, the movement itself is a real condition of being. Transnational assumes identifiers based on nations, thus it conditions, albeit in interesting political ways, what transplace might mean. Here, transplace means to resist and side-step, to exceed and differentiate from, nation-state identification. To think multiple and moving soil water air clouds distance stones landshapes cities plants and groups of different animals, including humans, as and in places.

Movement is a real substance; its in-between of bodies in places is another instance of thinking the heft and breath of the in-between. To be transplace is to be *as from*, to be shaped in the absence of unique place-origin and in the presence of multiple movement-origin, many kinds of fromness. Movement leaves the bodies among which it happens and becomes itself movement-location, lodged in the adult identity of its experiencers. More than strategic essentialism, I'm thinking about the rights to be accorded to different in-betweenness, and, here, to in-betweenness as manifest in transplace persons. To recognize being-from-movement as its own belonging.

December 2017
Bristol-Sheffield-Nottingham-Lincoln-London-Cambridge

BIO

Lisa Samuels is the author of sixteen books of poetry, memoir, and prose, including *Tender Girl* (2015), *Symphony for Human Transport* (2017), and *Foreign Native* (2018). Her edited books include *A TransPacific Poetics* (2017, co-editor Sawako Nakayasu). Having grown up across the US, Europe, and the Middle East made transplace her origin; living as an adult in the US, Yemen, Malaysia, Spain, and Aotearoa/New Zealand has made transnationalism fundamental in her ethics and imagination. She is Associate Professor of English and Drama at The University of Auckland.

JAYA SAVIGE
Biometrics

1. Shibboleth

The gist of the signal
that breaks through the mizzle aligns

with the singular tone
of the note

on your file. Our almagest
tells us you live by the alms gate

like a pent rat,
and panic when you can't discern
a pattern
in the cinders

of your hearth. Take these rice spoons
and join the procession.

Soon the crack search
team is due to return
with word from the Turner-
esque arches,

whorls and loops
of your index and thumb, the isobars
the air boss
draws to mimic weather on your skin.

Keeping calm will help you as we sink
this weighted conker
and reckon
the rich cryptical pools

of your irises; writ small
in ripples, radial, still warm

with the first heat of creation,
vital details
shrink and then are lost
when your pupil dilates.

Compliance is the simplest reaction.
No, it's nothing like the slots—

it's neither chance, nor competition,
nor a ruse,
and we don't depict emotion
even when it juts,

but any moment now
        we'll know for sure
        old chum
whether you've zeroed or won

        and by just
        how much.

2. *Flight Path*

A stowaway...believed to have been clinging to a British Airways flight from Johannesburg to Heathrow...was found on the roof of notonthehighstreet.com's headquarters on Kew Road, Richmond... There have been other cases where stowaways have fallen to their deaths in London after smuggling themselves onto planes and hiding in landing gear. (BBC, 19 June 2015)

It's raining men in Richmond-upon-Thames.
Our talk is of the latest of them as

we queue for kale smoothies. A posher atomism,
this, than that man's metamorphosis.

He hammered on a roof by Richmond Green
to be let in; wary of the unfamiliar genre

the paramedics at their shift work scaled
        the headquarters of the artisanal
gift store, but were without a rain atlas
        to place him. Now the motivational decals

frosted on the glass read like sorry denials—
        CHOOSE A LIFE LESS ORDINARY;
BE YOURSELF EVERYONE ELSE IS ALREADY
        TAKEN. This is a real day.

Above the high street's summer dioramas
        did he twist like a samaroid
seed, or whistle like a samurai sword,
        swiftly and without words?

3. *Bouncer*

Then   trampoline
                into ampler   air,

an   opt-in realm
where   airmen plot
to   import élan—

4. Remembrance Sunday 2017

[T]he Met has said the use of the technology at the central London event is part of an ongoing trial, and is not related to serious crime or terrorism. The technology works by using cameras to scan the faces of passers-by and flag up potential matches against a database of selected images. (*Evening Standard*, 12 Nov 2017)

Live coverage, lit by not one patch
          of actual sunlight. A hot pecan
hisses from a drain beside the Cenotaph.

Each time we spin back to this spot
          in our ellipse, the Last Post
bloats with correspondence from the silent.

Today it is our plan to re-enlist
          you, the survivors, in our surveillance
scheme, that all the unclear lives

might be illuminated; though of the threads
          we've lately learned to parse
to pin things down, yours might be the hardest

          to unlace: silver
glinting breasts could drive the recognition
          software spare.

We won't encroach upon your inner cogito.
We'd like to leave you be with the silent force
          of your reflections—

          but this unusually large
          gathering in regal glare

makes for one hell of an historic intel fresco.

BIO

Jaya Savige was born in Sydney and lives in London. He is the author of two collections, *Latecomers*, which won the New South Wales Premier's Prize for Poetry, and *Surface to Air*, which was shortlisted for *The Age* Poetry Book of the Year, and most recently a pamphlet, *Maze Bright*. Jaya has held residencies in Rome and Paris. His work is included in the *Penguin Anthology of Australian Poetry* and *Contemporary Australian Poetry*, and has appeared in *Poetry*, *Kenyon Review*, *PN Review*, and *Poesia* (Italy). He is poetry editor for *The Australian* newspaper and teaches at the New College of the Humanities.

ANA SEFEROVIC

A City is a Persistent Desire for Another City

in the opposite direction and down

down through unclear tunnels

down through velvet layers
all the way to the clean crisp sheets in your mother's house
to the rattling of the coffee cups
that you hear in your shallow sleep and
to the radio that announces the news
as if the world exists

*

this city
is your mother and her interest in faraway islands energy
is my mother and
my interest in her old photos
It is me – parasite

this city is a persistent desire for another city

this city is everywhere
its borders fading into
endless now

*

salty mist from the sea followed the train all through the mountains and
    plains
coating the passing landscapes in a rustling foil
and every little house on the other side of the window
held promise of a happy end
women on the balustrades, project into the street
down to sailors, sticky sweets
conned tourists red of face
scent of spices, of the open sea
the perfect dream of an exotic harbour
fear sharpens the beauty of the night: You look sharp baby tonight
numb heart exploded in the noisy cloud of dust
we are here to remain, in love with everything that is not here
in love with absence
but the border is open now
cross it

*

one day we will talk about that sitting on
the juiciest grass
surrounded by pigeons and pelicans
we will eat hot dogs in perfectly rounded skirts
completed and timeless

*

she told a lie to a taxi driver
that she was on a business trip
something to do with old languages
the same thing she told to a homeless charmer
that looks good in photos
that looks good on widows' sofas
kids dyed hair in dirty gold, smoking on the highway
doing stunts for stiff, engaged
drivers
your tactic was simple: I want to be a star

in the yellow glow that rises above the bridges
through the colonnade of people fishing and billboards announcing
design week, you are running to our hotel
its neatly packed soaps and slippers
nicely folded newspapers you are finally able to read
alone on the train again along the curving walls
that took me by surprise
led me
to the clear
to the sea and desire for God
for order
that I pretend to just partly understand
I don't
not really
just this big water and oily bodies make me want

*

shouting in the park:
"you ugly bitch I wanna stab you to death"
then we could hear a familiar name and loud singing
and crickets, millions of them, all through the pine woods
voices coming from the city beach
voices of beings and happenings that are going on without us
and more and more without us
every moment somebody becomes too old for
certain cities: the strange-looking hair on those kids
every moment an undiscovered star wears out
but this swamp will love you
preserve your dreams like raspberry jam
that sweetens your ever reducing days

sun is unpleasantly yellow and the big flood wave is expected any moment
shadows are long and slow
insects are falling down from the trees, sand is on the bed
between toes and fingernails
we are cleaning it constantly, the sand is everywhere
you are waking up often; we talk often in pauses in between
two dreams
I can hear the city behind the blinds
I can feel it penetrating
the walls
of desired cold

*

we lived as future explorers found us-
under layers of ice
fresh exhibits, fossils found in polarity
between two borders
between two dreams

BIO

Ana Seferović, Belgrade-born writer, has three collections of poetry: *Duboki kontinent* (*Deep Continent* – Matica Srpska, 2000), *Beskrajna zabava* (*Endless Entertainment* – Narodna knjiga, 2004) and *Zvezda od prah-šećera* (*A Star Made of Icing Sugar* – Nova, 2012). *The City* (Auropolis), a collaboration with English poet Alice Maddicott and *The Travelogue of The Car Boot Museum* (Somerset Art Works) were published in 2015. She is also the co-author of two plays and co-edits the international poetry platforms Supernovapoetry.net and *Dirty Confetti*. She lives in London.

SOPHIE SEITA

Talk Between Nudes

Note: The stage directions, character names, and scene headings are to be spoken, sung, or projected.

Prologue

DE LEMPICKA: head further back
NUDE WITH PEARLS: anatomy doesn't allow that
NUDE WITH BILLOWY ARMS: we're piled up
DE LEMPICKA: (it's) monumental
THE VOLUPTUOUS NUDE: throw in some cubes, some spillings, some pulled tampons
DE LEMPICKA: o carnivorous swoon, o incidental profuseness
THE CLOTHED NUDE: where's the man that will make this a harem
NUDE WITH BILLOWY ARMS: no frame please
DE LEMPICKA: preference not modesty. no psychology. this is just white

Interlude

The play: Story of a princess. Setting: fantastical.

Plot: The princess's lover, a female sculptor, suicides at the end of the play. (The play is called Oh Bliss.)

[Curtain. A field. Enter the princess. The princess wanders and sighs at the audience occasionally, gazing at herself in the fake lake in the middle of the stage. She mumbles and feels sorry for herself For She is Lonely. Enter four nudes, also mumbling and echoing one another. Exit the muttering nudes and enter the King and Queen. They mutter and mumble for about 5 minutes. And then, suddenly! the King coughs, spits up some yellow-greenish bundle and – to hide his embarrassment – asks the Queen for twins! In the middle of the field, by the lake, without hesitation, he is all for it. Perhaps a little surprising in a fantastical story but why not. Realism enters. Demands twins (for one may die and one must survive as heir). Later, the Queen gives birth to a girl and a flamingo.]

Interlude II

FIRST SEMI-CHORUS: *[sings]*
Hush! hush! Behold the red and white and blue and brown. How clumsy, how hideous, how tuneless. Our tears await. Come let us revel. Ere long sight will be grey.

SECOND SEMI-CHORUS: *[sings]*

Gorgeous is she who strums the chords of the Bacchanal amid the perfumed hairbands, voluminous locks stretched for revelling – arms. Behold her arm around her friend. They are yet fairy-happy, pure glossy damsels on divans and all the while someone calls, 'Lo, lo, it is plain' and yet more, listen and cry – unadorned, no frills.

THE NUDES: *[sing]*

ah! ah! oh! oh! eeeee!

Scene I

[DE LEMPICKA'S decorous parlour. A long dining table, no chairs. To the right, a dressing table, to the left a floor-length painting that looks like a mirror. DE LEMPICKA wears a flashy grey table-cloth intricately wrapped around her intricate body. Her companion, THE CLOTHED NUDE, wears a similar thing but in black and less flashy. NUDE WITH PEARLS wears a sack-like swimsuit of vainglorious silk while her attendant, NUDE WITH BILLOWY ARMS, wears something indescribably zippy and a hat pulled down over her face. THE VOLUPTUOUS NUDE is, simply, voluptuous.

The abundance of silk in the room effortlessly implies the taken-for-grantedness of cultured persons conversing in pleasant company. The guests and hostesses and onlookers never actually converse but there is a lot of touching. DE LEMPICKA never really talks to THE CLOTHED NUDE but rather imagines she is talking to her sister via telegram. THE CLOTHED NUDE, by contrast, always looks at DE LEMPICKA intensely and intently and sometimes prances lightly around her; her mask is that of laughing though she is uncharacteristically sad. The exact reverse applies to NUDE WITH PEARLS and NUDE WITH BILLOWY ARMS. The effect of this is perennial and ineradicable. Like a badly sung aria. The scene begins with DE LEMPICKA very busy doing things.]

THE CLOTHED NUDE: *[sneaking up behind DE LEMPICKA, pinching her side. No reaction. Looks at DE LEMPICKA intensely and intently. There is no answer.]*

All for a summer frock...

DE LEMPICKA: *[cries abruptly]* Yes?

[From behind DE LEMPICKA'S curtain NUDE WITH PEARLS peeps out.]

DE LEMPICKA: Well?

NUDE WITH PEARLS: *[looking at DE LEMPICKA swooningly]* Oh, DE LEMPICKA, you are radiantly statuesque today.

DE LEMPICKA: Am I passable?

THE CLOTHED NUDE: Approved.

NUDE WITH BILLOWY ARMS: Correct.

DE LEMPICKA: My aches and ravishings are my cleanest superiority.

NUDE WITH BILLOWY ARMS: I have had my suspicions.

THE CLOTHED NUDE: *[mumbles]*...may be here at any moment... *[mumbles]* must be quite ruthless.

DE LEMPICKA: No interruptions and no delicacies. Keep poise, smiles, and sex revealed or hidden (whichever) but conspicuously, so as to appear you are not listening.

NUDE WITH BILLOWY ARMS: Correct.

[The KING *enters.]*

KING: *[saluting]* Madames, no doubt you will be surprised at the boldness of my visit, but your reputation has drawn this disagreeable affair upon you; merit has for me such mighty fascinations that I run carelessly after them.

DE LEMPICKA: Ah! I rally against these verses.

THE VOLUPTUOUS NUDE: Your adulation goes a little too far in the liberality of its complaisance.

NUDE WITH PEARLS: My dear, we should call for dessert.

Scene II

[Salon. No king. Disarray. The remains of dessert. The dessert of the day. O sweet debris.]

DE LEMPICKA: *[to* NUDE WITH PEARLS*]* NUDE WITH PEARLS, darling, is this not my custom?

NUDE WITH PEARLS: Conspicuously so.

DE LEMPICKA: An ill-conceived action.

THE CLOTHED NUDE: *[to the audience]* I resent her because she married Nude with Pearls. These are grand and bold traits.

DE LEMPICKA: Snub! Knock-back! Pah!

THE CLOTHED NUDE: *[turning to de Lempicka]* Was it my fault

NUDE WITH PEARLS: There it is *[points randomly]*

DE LEMPICKA: You have doubts?! *[looking fervently for something to faint over]*

THE CLOTHED NUDE: *[a little sadly]* Stunning, yes, quite so, like any mistress of a married man, oh the slander of the villagers!

DE LEMPICKA: *[dramatically]* Circles! *[touching her heart and eyes and ears, to bear the pain of shapes]* Enough!

THE VOLUPTUOUS NUDE: Shush.

NUDE WITH PEARLS: There it is

NUDE WITH BILLOWY ARMS: Above all else tell him we are rich.

DE LEMPICKA: *[less sadly]* You look exquisite.

THE VOLUPTUOUS NUDE: Never fear.

DE LEMPICKA: Oh, my head!

NUDE WITH BILLOWY ARMS: *[to Nude with Pearls]* Flatter her.

NUDE WITH PEARLS: I know the King is so successful because he has a crown.

THE CLOTHED NUDE: *[to de Lempicka]* Tell her we're rich.

DE LEMPICKA: *[to Nude with Pearls]* Won't you sit down?
NUDE WITH PEARLS: *[can't find a chair]* What a beautiful table!
DE LEMPICKA: Was it so? How extravagant...
NUDE WITH PEARLS: *[sitting down, on the floor. To de Lempicka]* Everything? With a triangle ruler?
DE LEMPICKA: *[lying down, on the table]* How well you are looking, Nude with Pearls.
NUDE WITH BILLOWY ARMS: *[to The Clothed Nude]* Don't believe her.
THE CLOTHED NUDE: Yes, yes, those puffs and blisters.
THE VOLUPTUOUS NUDE: I haven't eaten since breakfast.

Scene III

[A big window. Light. A lamp. Rectangles. Portions of wall and furniture. THE MAD GUEST *appears. Looks for something on the floor. Two quarters of the legs are lit by the lamp, five sixths of the entire body feel present, the rest is rectangular and blind. The light from window and lamp combined looks as if torn from newspaper clippings of partial lunar eclipses.]*

THE MAD GUEST: *[addressing the lamp]* I've lost a song. It was all golden and fibrous.
DE LEMPICKA: Last night I heard a tune. I was asleep below the table, beneath those olive mountains, between magnitudes. It nudged me, gave me something I did not recognise; it was no object. I laughed. I looked above it. It had left and there was no palace, no paleness.
THE ROMANTIC NUDE: *[pragmatically]* We could cut a heart out of the glass of that window.
THE MAD GUEST: We could cut a heart, a small one, and then leap through the gap, force our delicate bodies through irregularity and jaggedness.
POET: I must admit the turn is witty and sprightly.
THE MAD GUEST: Oh human existence.
POET: Portraits are difficult and call for jocularity.
DE LEMPICKA: I am awfully fond of puzzles.

Scene IV

[The parlour. A SANE GUEST *enters, transformed, with arms elevated.* BLUE NUDE *in a summer frock, with legs elevated. We see ankles, oohh. It is pleasant. They are both smiling amusedly and stupidly.]*

SANE GUEST: Hi.
BLUE NUDE: Hi! Enter, enter.
SANE GUEST: I was just walking by.
BLUE NUDE: Will you console me for five minutes (or less – it is only so little I ask of you.
SANE GUEST: Ah, to stay again in the temperateness of the reformatory.

BLUE NUDE: *[looks wistfully]* Oh tell me, tell me, I can see you went to the galleries, not looking, but the pictures the pictures and you were consoled.

SANE GUEST: *[kisses her hand lingeringly]*

BLUE NUDE: Leaving? Oh vampiric parody of upturned eyes! There is not the tiniest of worries to worry us. We were gratuitously distressed about ourselves. We couldn't otherwise.

SANE GUEST: *[leaves]*

BLUE NUDE: Had he but stayed five minutes!   The end of the civilised world

[She hurls up her arms in a desolate signal, drops them, slouches, as if mimicking Greek despair, then catches herself, jumps, looks around, and walks to her dresser where she artfully sits down to fold DE LEMPICKA*'s underpants.]*

CURTAIN

NOTES

Talk between Nudes was performed by Sophie Seita, Corina Copp, Lanny Jordan Jackson, Luke McMullan, Anna Moser, Yates Norton, and Emma Stirling, at Torn Page, New York City, on December 8, 2013. The performance was part of a collaborative exhibition of drawings, photographs, correspondence, attachments, drafts, gifts, and texts by Sophie Seita and Anna Moser. *Talk between Nudes* first appeared in *Fantasias in Counting* (BlazeVOX Books, 2014).

BIO

Sophie Seita's performances, videos, and text-based works have been exhibited at the Royal Academy (London), Bold Tendencies (London), the Arnolfini (Bristol), La MaMa Galleria (NYC), Cité Internationale des Arts (Paris), Company Gallery (NYC), the Serpentine, and Neue Töne Festival (Stuttgart). Publications include *Meat* (2015), *Fantasias in Counting* (2014), and *12 Steps* (2012), and work in *The London Review of Books*, *Best American Experimental Writing 2018*, *The White Review*, *Bomb*, and *3:AM*. She is a Junior Research Fellow at the University Cambridge.

SENI SENEVIRATNE

Where a river meets the sea

I've been searching in the Laccadive Sea for a story, though
it's not mine to tell. In any case it eludes me, too deeply

submerged for my held breath and I'm not made for sea-diving.
What I need is as fragile as the soft-bodied polyps, busy building

coral reefs to hide in. I scour the stony skeletons, bone-grafting
one story with another. It's no good. I want the journey I never had,

with the old man my father never became. I want to stand at the mouth
of the Kalu Ganga with him, say 'So this is the sea, dad, this is the sea

that carried you, motherless, over its horizon, so far removed from
monsoons and mangosteens that you learned to live without them.

You were a child migrant (not like these days) you had safe passage
and a welcome when you arrived. You found love here, taught me

to value what's in the cup more than what's been spilled, how to
gather summer fruits and preserve their joy through winter.'

Some maps

tell us nothing about the lies
of the land or how straight lines

came to be drawn in places where
once, contours marked out borders

so that the land and its people curved
into each other like sleeping lovers.

No maps

to speak of when he gave me
his hands which were turning

grey over the brown, the way
his hair had gone grey and thinner,

the way he got thinner and by then,
I'd given up on wishing for more.

Some borders

tell us nothing about the lives
risking the sea as crossing points

in boats with no lists and no names
for those who've spilled out of them

desperate enough to sink their savings
to purchase the privilege of drowning.

No borders

to speak of, though his worrying
hands seemed to be tapping out

coded messages, in a desert war,
to the forward lines that moved

back and forth as if a hand of God
was drawing them in the sand.

BIO

Seni Seneviratne is a writer, poet, performer, singer and multidisciplinary creative artist. She has collaborated with film-makers, visual artists, musicians and digital artists and is widely published. Her collections, *Wild Cinnamon and Winter Skin* and *The Heart of It*, are published by Peepal Tree Press. She is currently working on her next book based on her father's experiences in North Africa in the Second World War. www.seniseneviratne.com

ZOË SKOULDING

Prairial (from *A Revolutionary Calendar*)

1. *Luzerne* Alfalfa
a field of vision bleeding at the edge
rolls through the season / purple
medic from the Medes or al-fasfasah from
elsewhere turning on the tongue / it grows
you cut it back / a nation is this haze

8. *Martagon* Martagon lily
lilies in becoming
turbans / dragon lily / sultan lily
all-over exotica / cut the borders
wear tomorrow's foreignness
where you become me I you

11. *Fraise* Strawberry
o strawberry moon where night
comes knocking at my window / cut /
o lyric poetry too slow too foreign
to say how this strange place
belongs to everyone in it

12. *Bétoine* Woundwort
after the cut / this salve
skin layers and peels / a fingernail
pushed back into place as if the body
politic grew back from a matrix
at the base of a broken fist

14. *Acacia* Acacia
here's a single thorn in the
shape of an I / gummed with honey
I / is an alien species
cut back
the will of the people clickbait

16. *Oeillet* Carnation
red blooms in muzzles of rifles
but it's bad luck this unblinking
eye of a cheap bouquet
an easy goodbye / your rights
cut like flowers

17. *Sureau* Elder
champagne buds uncurling / almost
themselves like phrases in a second

language from this angle /cut /
or movement extending
through days without division

19. *Tilleul* Linden
yellow dust in the mouth
another trashed economy
a taste of wind / cut / summer
falling in the same place /stars
crushed on the pavement

20. *Fourche* Pitchfork
take whatever you have to hand
to lift away loose matter / cut /
slide the tines under lies and despair
and if you thought a devil's tools might be
more specialised / well think again

22. *Camomille* Camomile
sometimes in your dream you wake up
and there isn't an infusion of anything
to calm this state / it isn't yours /
someone's close in the cut night
bleached across a Kodacolor lawn

27. *Verveine* Verbena
a distant planet pulling its weight
in lemon-scented leaves
whose garden is the garden of love
cut that / right here
the weight in my chest as borders realign

30. *Chariot* Handcart
such a weight to pull through
this golden morning / as pollen
drifts where it must / cut
movement of bodies / thought
the day goes to hell in a

BIO

Zoë Skoulding's recent publications are *Teint: For the Bièvre* (Hafan Books, 2016), *The Museum of Disappearing Sounds* (Seren, 2013) and *Contemporary Women's Poetry and Urban Space: Experimental Cities* (Palgrave Macmillan, 2013). She is Reader in Creative Writing at Bangor University. *Prairial*, is a sequence from a current project *A Revolutionary Calendar*. It was published in *Gorse* magazine in Ireland last year, but written at the time of the referendum.

IRENE SOLÀ

7 short poems

Recollections are dangerous
like chicken bones.
You can have one in the shower
and slip,
you can have one in the kitchen and get burnt,
you can have one in the car and crash.

They pulled me out like an onion.
They named me,
and pierced my ears.

My body is a house.
A *connoisseur* says I have pretty windows
and mom says I have soft plastering
and a tidy terrace.
The dining room is full of blood,
contained and good,
efficient guts
and organs that work well.
Your house is also quite nice.

If the mare pastures in the garden
she will stain the windows with spittle.
The sun is warm!
We could do many things:
climb on to the roof,
dad has a rifle,
the mare has soft fur.
If it snows we'll go crazy!
Kiss me in the mouth, horse!

I wore off my tongue
like candy,
and by the end of summer I lost
leaves and petals.
The cave in my palate
was empty for three thousand years.
Neither paintings, nor campfires.
I would say with my eyebrows:
how beautiful, the glaciers!
how beautiful, the heights!

When the salt set sail from the salt-cellar
My pothole filled with water.
Green water. White water.
Starlings and bees
Came to offer themselves up.
Pondskaters crossed,
Tiptoeing, the puddle.
Just like Jesus would have stepped
on my wound.
MRS. DARLING

There was a huge white buffalo.
You pointed at him and yelled like an indian
and I said it was a big white rock.
We were in Camprodon
and we could have stayed there forever.
In Vic, out of buffalos we make shoes
and jackets,
and out of indians, sausages.

BIO

Irene Solà was born in Malla, near Barcelona in 1990. She studied Fine Arts at the University of Barcelona and at Listaháskóli Ísland, Reykjavik, and has a Master's in Literature, Film and Visual Culture, from the University of Sussex. Her work has been published by Galerada Editorial (Catalunya) and Shearsman Books (UK and USA), and has appeared in *Poetari*, *VOLS RUSSOS*, and *The Lighthouse Literary Journal*. Her work has also been shown at the Whitechapel Gallery (London), CCCB (Barcelona), Bòlit Centre d'Art Contemporani (Girona), Le Beffroi (France), The Art Building in Vrå (Denmark).

SAMUEL SOLOMON

Meeting/room

Virtuosic, pre-summer, getting ready
for some meetings.
Traveling the world and leaving
a wake of broken hearts.
Tingling, turning red, feeling something in
the abdomen contract over gaseous bloat.
That's my body, moving stuff
around this meatsack.
Lucky in travel and happy to arrive.
Happy. Put it down. Put it away,
that work stuff, I mean. Put it all
away. Now, Put it back together.
Collage it. Don't worry about it.
No matter.

Collage is a pre-condition
for survival, and leaves
frayed linen edges:
where is Britain,
where are Jews,
was my grandmother Polish
(x2)
or maybe Ukrainian?
For how long
(the border moved)
I don't know.

They are pretending that
the border won't move again.
They are even pretending that indifference
to the border is the same as disinterest in the border.
I want us to be interested –
we are interested –
in different things made up of
some of the same things in
minimally patterned shapes.

At the meeting, too. A meeting might
take the form of other things we do
and not tell us that it does. It may, or it
may not, be a hostile environment. That's
what makes it a hostile environment.

Before the meeting, I'm in the vestibule, becoming an accidental expert at noticing myself. Having never really stretched my vocal cords. Having avoided the deepest frequencies of my own voice production. Barely vocalizing an inner shout. Anyway: we're all in the vestibule, just being vestibular. Vestibulary. Watching and listening. Waiting to become virtuosic at the meeting. (Virtuosity is a pleasure because it refers to nothing.) In the vestibule, we get to track the process by which a body goes from being an object of fear to being an object of pity. That is what will happen in the meeting when, as if by surprise, someone is not virtuosic. The discussion will keep on getting more technically advanced, and it will keep on getting more technically advanced until it becomes transparent to everyone.

We may love what will attend us at the meeting,

When we are virtuoisic, we don't think about attendance. We just let it go.

Though there is no shortage of enemies, and many are also in attendance. Ok, so, move back. Step back. Move out. Move along. Travel. Stop reading when it's dark in the room or outside. Go somewhere brighter than Brighton. On the bench. On the beach. Be virtuosic there, too. Make a monument to a living man. An arch. An arcade. A mausoleum. Plant some maple saplings around it, some edible trees.

BIO

Samuel Solomon is from New York City and lives in Brighton. He is author of *Special Subcommittee* (Commune Editions, 2017) and translator, with Jennifer Kronovet and Faith Jones, of *The Acrobat: Selected Poems of Celia Dropkin* (Tebot Bach, 2014). He teaches in the School of English at the University of Sussex where he is Co-Director of the Centre for the Study of Sexual Dissidence.

AGNIESZKA STUDZINSKA

An essay on The Dragon and the Invisible Creatures

The houses that were lost forever continue to live on in us: that they insist in us in order to live again. (Gaston Bachelard)

1.

An introduction is always rewritten. The *I* returns to the beginning having travelled through the *country of words*. Beginnings are conjectural. The concept of unity – that of a beginning, middle and end is based on the idea that each part depends upon the other. Each portion pivotal to make whole. But what if your beginnings are indiscernible? What then of wholeness?

2.

Today has turned. The air folded down to coldness. Salt migrates along the pavement in the anticipation of snow. But there will be no snow. No real snow anyway – just a ghostliness in its disappearing as it pretends to fall. So close, so near to snow. Home becomes *yours* in the residual of snow that never fell.

3.

I leave the house coffee in hand, drink its habit and think about my six-year old son who last night followed me up to the attic. " I want to write a story on your computer in posh writing" he said (he wanted to use italics). And if italics emphasise a *point*, if they highlight *importance*, then this:

4.

The Big Dragon

One day there was a dragon. He said to his mummy and daddy "why do we have to go out?" We are just going out for a little bit said his mummy. "How long?" asked the dragon. "Not long – about 15 minutes" replied his mummy. "That's long in my world." So in the end they went out for dinner. Some minutes later some little small creatures appeared in the shadows. They looked in the bins. And started throwing cardboard, cans, cat food and plastic bottles. "What was that" said the dragon? How many creatures were there? There were about 81 of them. The creatures have changed into foxes.

I do not correct his punctuation yet help him when he asks to spell *appeared* and *creatures*. I am curious about the creatures in the shadows and his unintentional metaphysical questions – is change *really* possible? What is time? Why are we leaving? Although the last question is not metaphysical, it's a question about possibilities.

5.

The self-possession of a house in the shadows of village walls. September scatters on the balcony of the house. A girl and her grandparents pose for a photograph. From below, the photographer captures what has already left. In this leaving, the girl folds the house in its paper, hides it inside the pocket of her jacket.

6.

In the attic your father's ashes rest in a wooden box waiting for his wife. "I've had a good life," she said as if her presence negated the space in which she lives. In the kitchen I am cooking dinner, listening to a mother on the radio, "at least in heaven there's food," she tells the world, whilst waiting for her child to die, "heaven will be our new home," she whispers between the gunfire and the metal clanks of empty pots.

7.

I start the engine of the car and the city accelerates through the space of where I live *now*. The palimpsest of houses form a fog of homes in wintered light. They are somehow absent from their own architecture. Buildings in which home is made and unmade. "*A strange house contained in my voice.*"[1]

8.

Early history survives on fragments. I imagine these writings ghosted with voices

us, you, him, she, they, them	marks on a page
on territories	"don't be afraid"

9.

Fragments, Maurice Blanchot writes "...unfinished separations, their insufficiency, the disappointment at work in them is their aimless drift... neither unifiable nor consistent, they accommodate a certain array of marks..."[2] *We* are surely all a series of unfinished separations?

10.

My son is rooted in *this* language, in his construction of place and the beginnings of the *One Day* of a story. This unfinished story like all stories – even finished ones.

11.

I notice the determined, pastel mantling of the Japanese Anemone in the front garden on a cloudless December; the only remaining bloom. I read on a website how others have tried to eradicate this flower, how persistent and invasive their kind, how deep their rhizome spreads. How in the words of an expert, "it will take at least two years to be rid of an unwanted Japanese Anemone."

12.

"Home is the return to where distance did not yet count."[3]
I think I know what this means but I am not certain. In the place of the undefined meaning becomes yours.

13.

Morning light scissors the street. The houses are orchards of suspense. In the distance, the open mouth of a van meets a queue of smoke-wrapped men. I realise I have forgotten my house keys. By the time I return to the car, the van is gone.

14.

I come back to this, "At a certain moment when one loses everything, whether that means a being or a country, language becomes *the country of words*."[4]

15.

If there was a conclusion, I would summarise *here*.

NOTES

1 Seghers Pierre: *Le Domaine Public*: Editions Lucien Parizeau: 1946: 79
2 Blanchot Maurice: *The Writing of the Disaster* (trans) Ann Smock: University of Nebraska: Lincoln and London: 1995
3 Berger John: *and our faces, my heart, brief as photos*: Bloomsbury: 2005: 91
4 Sellers Susan: (ed) *The Hélène Cixous Reader*: Routledge: London and New York: 1994: xxvii

BIO

Agnieszka Studzinska was born in Poland in 1975 and came to England in the early 1980s. She has an MA in Creative Writing from the UEA. Her collection, *Snow Calling* was shortlisted for the London New Poetry Award 2010. A second collection, *What Things Are*, was published by Eyewear in 2014. She is working on her third collection, *Branches of a House* and a practice-based PhD at Royal Holloway, exploring notions and images of home in contemporary poetry.

JAMES SUTHERLAND-SMITH

The Idea Of Delhi

for Bharat Ravikumar

Let's persuade the limitations of distance
into a grimace of irony.
Rivers conform to mathematics
and cats don't and our distant friend's grin
is wholly without guile or malice
even when days are red and green all over.
Time like distance isn't a great healer,
but is the long feeler of a cockroach,
is the remorseless stealer of looks,
is a wheeler of prams full of junk,
is a devout kneeler in churches,
is a crooked dealer in reputations,
is the ultimate sealer of doom.
Our absent friend lives in a city of many colours
built beside the original that my country
razed to the ground after a revolution
whose leaders were tied to the mouths of cannons
and blown to bits as an example to others.
He's good enough not to mention this.
The black cat hasn't forgiven me
for trapping her and taking her to the vet.
You've forgiven my many falls from grace.

Swimming In The Red Sea Before A Sandstorm

Surfacing I see the great sun sink
Behind a pier which takes
The oil pipeline to deep water.
A fisherman spreads his mat
On a dune for evening prayer
While a pack of dogs sit
In shallows to cool themselves
And three women walk on the shore
Shielded by their husbands
From the naked white man in the sea.
A breeze lifts their veils to show skirts
Red, blue and green slashed with orange.

I dive and my shadow wavers
Across the fluted sand
To where devil fish quiver
And change colour when my darkness
Touches them. No mind was ever
Clear as this transparency
Over green pods of the sea grape
And slate blue of the digging crab.

Surfacing I see the sun lose shape
Foundering upon the horizon
As light burnishes the struts
And silvery petrol holders.
The dogs whine uneasily
And trot towards the shelter
Of a rock while the fisherman
Is crouched in hazy supplication.
The wind increases tugging
A multi-coloured umbrella
Which the husbands have put up
A hundred yards away.

I dive as if into a mind
Which does not know itself,
The sea coloured with a little sand.
I cannot use my eyes
But feel the water on my skin
As I swim down from the bath warmth
At the top to colder levels
Sensing icier undertows.

Surfacing I can't see the pier,
Barely the fisherman
Who stubbornly continues
His blurred devotion while the dogs
And couples huddle,
All beastwise, against the rock
As the sandstorm streams above them.
I swim out diving and diving
To avoid drowning in the air
And reach the yellow reef
To dive once again deeply
Into clearer, stranger waters.

BIO

James Sutherland-Smith was born in 1948 lives in Slovakia. He has published seven collections, including *The River and the Black Cat*, from Shearsman in 2018. He has translated a number of Slovak poets and Serbian poets including Mila Haugová, Ivana Milankov and Miodrag Pavlović. His translations received the Slovak Hviezdoslav Prize in 2003 and the Serbian Zlatko Krasni Prize in 2014. 'Mouth' received the Rector's Prize at Prešov University in 2015. A selection of his translations of Mária Ferenčuhová's poetry, *Tidal Events*, is also published by Shearsman in 2018.

GEORGE SZIRTES

Meetings with Strangers

1

So one
arrives, at once,
without notice, warning,
a phone call, a text, or even
email.

So one
arrives at night
in a wet city street
with two handfuls of old baggage,
alone.

2

Arrive
by night. No words
necessary. Turn up
like weather, like a fitful gust
or rain.

Nothing
prevents you. Come.
The hour is what it is.
Any hour is welcome. All hours
are free.

The rain
won't stop for you.
The cold is setting in.
Nothing in life surprises you
by now.

3

So this.
So that. So one
moves under the radar
of the nerves into the system
called chance.

Chance calls
and cold calls. Snow
flurries. Voices on line.
This could happen to you, they say.
It could.

It could.
Everything could
and does. Vague clemencies.
Abrupt decrees. Arbitrary
winters.

4

Enter
and wipe your feet.
You don't know where those boots
have been. You don't know the weather
or street.

Morning
arrives by chance.
The bed is unmade. Tuck
the night into your pocket and go.
Go now.

BIO

Born in Hungary in 1948, George Szirtes published his first book of poems, *The Slant Door*, in 1979. It won the Faber Prize. He has published many since then, including *Reel* (2004), winning the T S Eliot Prize, for which he has been twice shortlisted since. His latest book is *Mapping the Delta* (Bloodaxe 2016).

REBECCA TAMÁS

Hell

after Ashraf Fayadh

Rain comes down amorally,
it has the elegant freedom of things
that truly exist.

Shoes full of snow,
cold human feet, fox-eyes
taking in the unguarded morning light,
are real things.

Poems and nuclear warheads,
and water pooling on green tiles, and sand
under fingernails, and apricots, and
pomegranates, and wisps of twine, and leaves,
and soft down on a lip, and red insides,
and lifejackets, and pears, and books are real things.
Other things are not.

And yet, still I want to shout at them
YOU HAVE MADE A HELL ON EARTH

I want to shout
YOU OWN NOTHING FUCKERS
I want to shout
HELLSCAPE   MALLS   AND INDOOR LIGHTING
I want to shout
HELL THE SCALD OF A BORDER INVENTED WIRE FAKENESS INVENTOR
I want to shout
PUNISHMENT WILL COME TO YOU   LIKE A   SLEEPLESS WIND
SUFFERING   WIL HOLD   YOU AND KNOW   YOU WITH SKIN-LIKE
  TIGHTNESS
I want to shout
HELL   IS   MAKING US   ALL SICK
I want to shout
YOU HAVE DONE THIS YOU ARE THE VERY LOWEST
I want to shout
OPEN THE ROADS OPEN UP THE HELL ROADS FROM INSIDE THE
  NIGHT
I want to shout
BELONGING WHAT A LAUGH   YOUR NON PASSPORT   YOUR
  INCORRECT BEHAVIOUR
I want to shout
HELL   AND POETRY   POETRY JUST   SO   DAMAGED AND SMALL
I want to shout
CAN YOU THINK HOW TIRED

I want to shout
HELL IS YOUR PATHETIC ATTEMPT THIS YOUR
PATHETIC ATTEMPT
I want to shout
HELL AND HELL AND

But that is not quite right. I must remind myself that that is not quite right.

You cannot make hell because you cannot make,
though you attempt it,
a place wholly empty of forgiveness.

The stupid, chic, ineffective rain coming through the blinds,
the beams of my useless affection seeping through cracks,
someone laughing at you with a closed tongue,
tree branches poking the window, side eye of light, catch of light,
judgement of light, ancient particles running happily between worlds,
water touching the soil, the concrete, in the impression of a holy kiss.

I must say this:
idiots, connivers, liars, snakes,
there is no hell,
and you are going there.

I must say this:
even the dead smile, though they are unhappy.
Even a lonely poet or person, inside the hot vibrating universe,
smiles, edges of their soft mouths creeping up.

You do not smile, not as we would know it,
not even in in your thin and shuffling sleep, the threads unravelling,
(*balm of hurt minds*)
not even when the smell of coffee rises like an incantation,
the cursèd perfume of lemon rind warming in the sun.

The real rain
pours and pours from an agonised, tender sky—

and you can never touch it.

BIO

Rebecca Tamás is a London-based poet, who recently completed a PhD in Creative and Critical Writing at UEA, under the supervision of Denise Riley. The pamphlet *Savage* was published by Clinic in 2017, and work has recently appeared in *The London Review of Books*, *Poetry Review*, *Minerva Platform* and *The White Review*. Rebecca was joint winner of the 2016 Manchester Poetry Prize and is the Fenton Emerging Writer 2017. The poem 'Hell' came out of an English PEN project and is inspired by the work of the Palestinian poet Ashraf Fayadh, currently imprisoned, and subject to corporal punishment, for political reasons, in Saudi Arabia. Details of his case and his work can be found at www.englishpen.org/tag/ashraf-fayadh

HARRIET TARLO

from *Cut Flowers*

for Rachel Blau DuPlessis

did history get done, it did not, thump box
a kid   opening a car door, thump box
moved   into a wall, gathering more
matter   from matter, budding up
around   out of places : when you get
older   you will move between
places   out of root darkness
easier

something human in the eyes of wooden
shtetl   walls before the war
glaze   black of lions, bears, rabbits
caught   in griffin claws, the full
zodiac   circle strong colours all
pregnant   sheep sleep at noon
clematis   crawl, suddenly
summer

now it is a funeral home, cinema, shop
field   granite in cement, in nettles
grasses   across, he crosses old
rail tracks   pulling his broken trouser
belt up   something to say? Off to
blackbird   bitten, biting woods
despite   all begin to form new
months

little lost splinters of jewelry, end
chain   watch strap silver
or gold   glass stare aiming
to enter   a family space
other   people's dogs
toys   laid down plums
in trays   in baskets green
produce

all sailing tomorrow is in doubt
saharan windscaught up
iberian dust : he took the money
in and then he passed it
on again & on : humans they
never hear eucalyptus, pine
the first fires fight
ending

alliances and divisions don't help Syria
taste affection, get back into
pleasure trying to make homes of
not homes needs to travel, to feel
errors green slab of hillside
kicked over at the end of winter
all in part upturned
history

BIO

Harriet Tarlo's publications include *Field*, *Poems 2004–2014*, *Poems 1990–2003* (Shearsman) and, with Judith Tucker, *Sound Unseen* and *behind land* (Wild Pansy). She is also editor of *The Ground Aslant: An Anthology of Radical Landscape Poetry* (Shearsman, 2011). Her collaborations with Tucker have been shown at the Catherine Nash Gallery (Minneapolis), Musee de Moulages (Lyon), Southampton City Art Gallery, The Muriel Barker Gallery (Grimsby) and New Hall College Art Collection (Cambridge). She is a Reader in Creative Writing at Sheffield Hallam University.

SHIRIN TEIFOURI

That Country

Nearby is a country they call life
You will know it by its seriousness.
(Rilke)

Nearby is a childhood in fantasy of elsewhere,
you know it by its playful bees that swarm

into the grapevine my mother grew all her life,
for years my mother sang for my trees

and converted nectar into vinegar in our back yard.
You know it by the blue map on my father's hands—

writing in his own selection of Rumi,
sweet and eternal wine is served in the house of the heart,

for years my father prayed five times a day
that I wouldn't go that far, I still see his prayer

beads with 99 names of love in his dead palm.
In the last years of their lives, my parents couldn't remember

my name and 'that country' I lived in,
I let what they forbade become my sin,

that's how it happened to me, thats how
I let it happen to them. Isn't it God's will? To go beyond?,

I told them, but don't worry, I gave birth in this country
thought giving birth is a way to translate absence into flesh,

but before you translate something you kill it first,
killing by deforming, by self-censoring, by tearing into pieces,

until it ceases to be your tongue, like a half rainbow in
the gradual vanishing of a waterfall as it splashes from rock to rock.

Look at the whales in the nearby sea, I told them,
they have stronger memories, they roam the inky shadows

of the unmapped floors and recognise each other
by singing, they know how far a song can travel

yet strand themselves in shallow parts where the border
between body and water is looming rocks,

scientist have no answer for it...
they say it's suicide, but what if they just follow

the only path that is allowed by the sea?
What if it's just a call out to 'see me'?

what if they taste the limits of longing,
and once drunk, lose the way back in?

Nearby is an island they call Elsewhere,
you will know it by its dead that resist decomposing.

BIO

Shirin Teifouri taught English literature in Iran before coming to the UK to complete her PhD. She is an honorary research fellow at the school of English (University of Sheffield) and a board member of Sheffield Flourish. Her research has explored the function of literature, specifically poetry, linked to cross-cultural narratives of exile, displacement, 'communities', and mental health. Shirin has published poetry in *Verse Matters* (Valley Press, 2017) and the University of Sheffield's creative writing journal, *Route 57*.

VIRNA TEIXEIRA

'Assessing a girl from Guarulhos who had been to Holloway prison...'

Assessing a girl from Guarulhos who had been to Holloway prison
accused of drug trafficking
now admitted with a psychotic episode
the ex-husband deported
back to Italy three years ago
      so she says
she found someone else to support her—another—
      multiples of the same type
      seduced by her charm
      of the tiny sexy mulata

her new lover comes to visit her daily
he brings papaya he is upset
she thought he wanted to kill her
to steal her organs

but Maria is now seeing angels
she is guarded in her room praying
Latina. Ave Maria
Maria de los Angeles
illegal

an expired visa
an expired sponsor
a godfather somewhere
a ticket in someone else's name

sectioned
      refusing medication
      locked in her room

a language barrier to interview Maria
barricaded in my mother tongue
in a ward full of immigrants

Maria doesn't believe she is psychotic
she complains of somatic symptoms
she thinks her body is infested by
tropical worms

she thinks she has schistosomiasis
she thinks she has ascariasis
she thinks she has cisticercosis

her tests were all normal
Maria has been away from Brazil
for many years
still she is adamant her body is infected

she wants to go to Guarulhos to be treated
she will come back cured
an angel told her that

in a dream with a woman made of stone
holding hands with a child

'My mind is mathemathical / My body is electronic...'

My mind is mathematical
My body is electronic

Your body language tells me
you're from São Paulo

Doctor you look like a patient

I've never been to Brazil
I've been to Suriname
My father was from Burma
My mother was Anglo-Indian

I fell in love only once in 1984
He is on the phone directory
He thought I was going out
with a ginger haired man

Now you can interview me

I can pretend I am Brazilian
I can be Gisele Bunchen
I failed as a model once

I can't remember running naked
It was the first time that
policemen were nasty to me

That never happened before

How come I am so tall
and you're so small

I am elated I told you
I am allergic to lithium

BIO

Virna Teixeira was born in Fortaleza, Brazil. Her poetry books and pamphlets have been published in Brazil, Portugal, México and Argentina. She worked as a consultant neurologist in Brazil, lived for many years in São Paulo, and moved to London in 2014. She is a licensed doctor in the UK, working mainly in psychiatric hospitals in London as a junior doctor, despite her qualifications and clinical experience outside the EU. *136 Suite*, a poetry pamphlet in published in Brazil will soon be published in the UK), and reflects on the experience of foreignness in the mental health services and medical environment.

DAVID TOMS

Or

Usually imagined as a black line, mapmakers mark, sometimes blue though nearly always black, on green or broken into smaller lines coursing through a body of water. The collective linear representation of this or that vicious rumour. The geographic manifestation of national psychosis. Or /

An ornament on the edge of the rug of your land. Around my printed matter. The white edges of your racism, of the pages of the books you read, of what your geography book shows you. Or /

As old & as ugly a word as your dream of security behind a wall made from the disparate materials of earth or spirit. Or /

The sea for instance, or a river, blue or
sticks and mud, a hut or a string of huts cramped near a shore.
Then the stones of castles
Then the pebble dash of your semi-detached walls, or the red brick and cramped comfort of your row of terraced housing. Your gated community. Or /

Or whatever material your home is made from now or
the carparks of your dreams or the towers of your soft power. Or /

Or let's say the suit you wear
Cashmere or cotton or teflon:
Your armour against the poverty
you meet on the streets or the doorsteps, or let's say
your rites in your church:
the smells of your own particular set of bells. Or /

Teorainn
Grensen
Grænse
Gränse

Hard or soft like your eggs. Or /

Grenze. Grens. Or /

This far and no further. Or /

You innvandring
Utlending
Outlander
Ausländer
Outsider
You foreigner
Gabhal

All our words for all our favourite worst nightmares. Or /

The broadness of
of all who are out
And us few who are in. Or /

Edging
& mapping
calculating and counting. Or /

The edges of cobbles
or wire fences, or a thrown brick
or a face full of hate,
it could be art even in some cases
the outer reaches of the folds of your thought. Or /

the apple of Fremskrittspartiet, a bite of original sin. God remember
is no respecter of faces,
the great leveler. Or /

If I walk along such a fissure
the certainties begin to crack / towns with two names or three / rivers or
rocks the same, old or new, known by ramblers from neither here nor
there. Our sign and mark has shifted
near enough as often as. Or /

You bar us from your clubs, using the brilliant whiteness of your racism /
of your teeth / of your chinos. Or /

You wave flags with their borders of blue or white or red or whatever you
think represents you. Or /

This land touches that river that touches this lake that touches that river
that travels through this town not caring for the names it picks up or puts
down. Or /

We are always rubbing together touching bordering someone something.
Or /

The sky borders the sea borders the sand borders the land borders the foot
the body the brain. Or /

Tongue mouth lung teeth breath. Or /

In that brief second before it is shot the bird flies above the canopy of the forest not knowing it has crossed from one polity to another. Or /

Off the table, bord as it is now in one language, as it is now in another, as if once these languages touched, because their speakers touched, in acts of violence, or love, perhaps even bordered one another when one group boarded a boat and set off from the edge of their knowing / room and board, the welcome traveler at the inn, greeted by the boar's head, bordure from the Middle English, border from the kingdoms of forgotten Europe, from the insistence that all that is within my fence is like me. Then we must face the unwelcome word hoard, that complicator. Or /

BIO

David Toms was born in Ireland but lives and works in Norway. His newest chapbook, with Maren Nygård, *dikt / actions osl / ondon,* is available now from Smithereens Press.

Dear Anna;

Te lo prometo
Spanglish exists
It arises from deep discomfort
Necesidad deseo
With the same stubborn materiality
Con la que this lesbian body
Emerges from la plétora de un mundo
Which they have violently split in two
(The fire and the water
El hombre y la mujer)
To remain ahí
En el medio

*

Did I love in this language made of interruptions?

It was always suspicious for it was never good enough and never good enough has to be always suspicious. sentarse allá esperando ver caer el fruto de los misunderstandings. I was never welcome in this country until a woman spoke to me in a language so familiar so capable of turning around sacar potencia de la parte mordida. every living being starts the path siendo torpe y cuando llegas aquí con la lengua torcida, with a twisted tongue, ya te queda la torpeza como dote como don no pasajero and, vamos a ver, your pilgrimage just contains natural barriers /this you want to believe/ like every pilgrimage it implies natural efforts. solo que tú empezaste con la lengua torcida, you started your journey with a suspicious incapacity to speak. suspicios for it is never good enough and ya van años que te quedas, something insists in remaining, something that is not exactly your will. In any case, todo sigue parado, todo sigue oídos sordos except for those women who wanted to hear the wild bear in your mumble, the precious stone behind the walls of the labyrinth, who wanted to believe that you are this animalito extraño, this strange exotic character who apparently has the capacity to write words that could make them shiver, but only in a language that sencillamente they won't understand.

dos cuerpos

with Jèssica Pujol

a reckless pulling of our muscles
I did not know they could stretch
this far bend backwards & further
forwards cracking the bones until
they blend too into this limitless
surface where impositions of time
only apply to us the stretchers in
US the system grows & sprouts OUT
here & HERE & EVERYWHERE
like Spanish ivy crawling up invading
our insides blossoming through
our eyes jamming the portrait of us
for the paint too is recklessly pulling

towards a blackness we magnify

a reckless pulling of our muscles
and not yet reckless but glowing
under parchment skin:
Who writes the palimpsest of the blind?
I ask in disarray, ¿quién lo escribe mientras
nosotras hablamos esta lengua rara?
We have forgotten common speech
Look at the silt dripping from my fingers
you answer, look at its affluence,
llevo agua en los ojos y saliva en la boca
to swamp una ciudad entera
déjame que te lo cuente de otro modo,
estábamos vueltas hacia dentro, quizás
alguien
tomó una fotografía, el verdadero descanso
tiene lugar bajo el párpado: we magnify
pleasure beneath the eyelids

Quote:
"Un cuerpo encima de otro
¿siente resurrección o muerte?"
Claudio Rodríguez, "Brujas al mediodía"

the body electric stands wild in
a French garden (we entwine)
deviation
(And who erase the surface? –
una ciudad entera bajo el agua salivan
las ventanas) Let me put it other wise
turn it outward-wise open your mouth
and look at mine [...aaa...] you
are addressed you push us out of the
frame you & me untwined for we too
run from the museum with a camera-
eye that surveills the guards, LOUD!

we, two, run. We, one: the power-driven runners
look at my whole black lacuna without
severe arrow. LOOK! You-we dive
con ojos sellados por musgos. Somos
un mirlo pardo de patas azules, recoges
luminous pebbles, foreign symbols in the
sand
devienes en mi boca de arena deep into, immersed
in my boca tierna de arena, bocasembrada,
I open my mouth to you, we: the travelers
famished pilgrims ¡ah! hambrientas
LOUD! — They turn a corner, the guards,
striving to unveil us
|but| [...] aaaaaaaaaaa nightfall,

Quote:
"Based on a multitude of myths
I painted myself orange
& made clear to the suspicious."
Alice Notley, "To the suspicious"

backbend gripping our hands we
roll down Whitehall mouthful of sand
holding roots in the abdomen a
resistance a sprint that
sprains my thigh BUT
There's always one
keep rolling, recompose words
en tu (en)tender mouth, for we are washed
down to the mirror of the sea to recognise
an US in paint orange flesh US
still fresh with luminous pebbles
a nuestros pies facing the Atlantic
skipping the impositions of time

make an effort to take a picture with your radiant blind eyes

tus brillantes ojos ciegos they know precisely the coordinates of objects

nuestros pies face the Atlantic y en algún lugar hubo una silla y un hilo
de tejer

que enhebraste entre tus dedos one, two, three...we only remember those
words which may be mistaken for babbling gritos gruñidos traqueteo
de la mandíbula en el llanto retrace untie negate all Te veo temblando
con la piel desnuda y erecta como naciendo emerging from the broken
egg *By saying yes the creature refuses* Flesh US still fresh

growing & sprouting
HERE and THERE till the end then the end the theend then thend

tarandara ahhí Yeme Ohaová Ohaová Emeeeeee Ohaová Un cuerpo
encima de otro ¡NO! Dos cuerpos

BIO

Sara Torres (Spain 1991) is a PhD student at Queen Mary, University of London. Her research focuses on lesbian desire, writing, and cultural representation through psychoanalysis, feminisms and queer studies. Her book *La otra genealogía* (Madrid: Torremozas) won the Gloria Fuertes National Poetry Prize. In 2016, she was awarded a scholarship by the Antonio Gala Foundation to write her novel, *Vida Mínima*. A second book of poems, *Conjuros y Cantos*, was published by Kriller 71. She is currently working in the project *Phantasmagoria*.

KINGA TOTH, TRANSLATED WITH TIMEA SIPOS

from Cornsongs

The line is a visible action. The line, however supple, light, or uncertain it may be, always refers to a force, to a direction; it is an energon, a labor which reveals – which makes legible – the trace of its pulsion and its expenditure.
(Roland Barthes, "Cy Twombly ou Non mu!ta sed multum,"
in *L'obvie et l'obtus*)

Derrida suggests that the drawing itself is also blind. He presents drawing as an intransitive activity; our attention does not focus on the image we perceive, a represented world, but on the representation of that world as an activity of gestures. We see nothing in the drawing (transitive); we see only the drawing as intransitive act.
(Ernst van Alpen, *Gesture of Drawing*)

song eight – eclipse

we are softening in greenhouses we let in
the amplified light – and present vitamin doses
to our increase indicators
inside we multiply better but we all yearn for
the exterior waters where pelican herds
fish there will be a long minute
when the time change will be invalid
without a round white hand the sun
runs out the wall between us and the pelicans
the water reaches finally we can stop

song twenty-six – in City of Asylum, for Maung Day: Gasoline

in the city of long boards a hindi burmese sign
paint in this city you can move under the wooden tubs
"if you are lucky one day" they don't light
forest fires here and the coal chambers down below are empty
there's no coal-dust in your hair it doesn't smoke you black
the one you travel with ate a fork ate a knife
left you only the cheap liquids
the hand sanitizers with which the house-walls
are scrubbed before they smear them blue yellow
and before they paint panthers mambas on them
this is your first day since they invited you to live among the boards
they stick a rough sponge and aloe vera jelly in your hand
the panther head next to the door handle is yours
a burmese sign "if we are lucky one day"

song seven

they braid the girl-hair into husks on the roof
white stripe in the middle they hold it down it follows
the depression in the bend the first braid
starts below the rib the first
streak this will be in line with the two
lower paddles that's how far the streak will reach
the eyebrow will be a sharp line
though the song is about happy city folks
about industrial development about organized smoke
stacks this city will bloom
there in the middle its core the held down
earth they have taken care of the the risers already
to be double-sided the crane lifts an inspected part
only the chosen are buried

song thirteen – Kristian Sendon Cordero: Hinulid

thirteen pictures god's son stepped his white-haired
son the skinny one whose face has different edges whose
mother sits quietly on the train with no stop
the laws remain on the cassettes the train takes
them the black headscarf pulls it on a car
his bones shake his eyes have holes his crown is golden
the mother takes the train to the middle of the green bridge
the son suddenly grows his beard gets caught
in the cassette player the recordings stack on top of each other
they load the cassettes into banana peels the leaves' vacuum
protects the tape until they arrive in the middle of the green bridge
among the bones they cover the bones
the sun shines on the bridge it warms the tape blanket
the mother pulls sticky yarn from her mouth
that's what she envelops the car in now mirrored on it
are the planets that she looked for as a child

song fifteen

no more room for stones that face each other
no more room for blows
the time is over now the obscenities are done
they don't mean anything anymore
we weaved nets covered the hills with them
the grass stayed soft it grew over the stones
it rounded their corners

everything fits on this blanket
where the threads are loose we stitch patches
with thicker threads with tightly twisted wires
everything has grown stronger than the stones
we pull our hands away from our ears

song twenty

we talk with crash helmets on
our multivitamin dosers push
the extra doses under our skin desperately
the withdrawal symptoms develop first on the face
inflamed bumps itching
thoughts begin underground

song twenty-five

like a communal washing machine
we spin at the same time in the centrifugal system
hang on with hooks
in our delicate layers
unravel on effective drying

BIOS

Kinga Toth (1983, Sárvár, Hungary) has published short stories, poems and drama in Hungarian, German and English. Publications include the collections *PARTY* (2013, Hungary; 2018, US), *All Machine* (2014), *Village 024* (2016), *Wir bauen eine Stadt* (2016) and a visual-art catalogue: *Textbilder* (2016–2017). Her novel, *The Moonlight Faces* (2017) won the Hazai Attila and other prizes in Hungary. Her work has also appeared in *Solitude Art Yearbook* (Stuttgart), *Huellkurven* (Austria), *tapin2* (Fra), *Colony* (Ire), *Poetry* (US), *Lyrikline* (De). www.tothkinga.blogspot.de

Timea Sipos is a Hungarian-American writer and translator currently earning her MFA in fiction at the University of Nevada, Las Vegas. A 2017 American Literary Translators Association Travel Fellow, her translations have been published or are forthcoming in *The Offing*, *The Short Story Project*, *Two Lines Press*, and elsewhere. Her original fiction is forthcoming with *Juked*. You can tweet her at @timearozalia.

CLAIRE TRÉVIEN

Code-switch

We develop awareness of when to 'code-switch': to move back and forth between two languages (Hanan Ben Nafa)

the street has been framed with onyx
the street sits in the bathroom
the headlights dim when you flush the
refocus when you dab your
brush with cream
we do not know where
the street was bought
it has always lived here
martha tried to draw on the
street, but her hand

the bathroom has been framed with smoke
the bathroom sits at the crossroads
tap opens when the lights change a
gush of expletives quieting to a dribble
when the last shoe leaves the road
it is best
to ignore the weather
in the bathroom
cab drivers that fish
tailed into the frame

returned years later
scaled purple

Homing brain

It was that time of night when my brain speaks French
but my tongue spews wine, and the weather speaks emoji,
but the streets speak Latin, and my phone is speckled
with the language of my body leaning on it unlocked.

Perhaps I'm lucky to live between two languages
never needing to get too comfortable with either.
– which one would I rather dream in?
which one swears the best? Do I sweat French?

And I swayed towards home, half-hero half-blurred,
stomping with each step on another seam, one operation
after another stabbed with wild weeds. Considered my body
and its habit of sprouting bruises and cuts during sleep

how they themselves journeyed through DNA
from ancestors also prone to bruising without
need for obstinate furniture. Each a careful
operation leading to this very moment

when I find myself stumbling back, the asphalt
bubbling under me, revealing how here – the surface
flakes past pain, allows a shoal to bare its back,
unroll fish scales beneath my feet, swimming somewhere new.

BIO

Claire Trévien is the Anglo-Breton author of *The Shipwrecked House* and *Astéronymes* (Penned in the Margins, 2013 and 2016). She founded Sabotage Reviews and recently edited their first publication '*Verbs that Move Mountains: essays and interviews on spoken word cultures around the world*'.

DAVID TROUPES

The Return

Massachusetts, mid-March. Land
barren with rain.
Leafless, colorless—each slope a sleeping wolf, each tree

a confection of stone, each lake
a dark contusion, an accretion
of pain. I pass through the towns of the Quaboag Hills

where I never lived, unfamiliar, and I
become unfamiliar,
strolling my borrowed car down the numbered routes, a trickle

of unsponsored soul, without past, without debt,
promised of no one
and immune to loss. I spot him there

on the causeway, on the roadside, his mind
dwelling under his hood,
a notebook kept dry by the lean-to of his chest—or in a house,

backlit, pulling a chair to a window—or returning
alone with a small burden of groceries: he
who tends my unchosen life, at home

in my regret: a pond
in a season of downpour.
He has no news, no daughters—a sack of old fantasies,

sodden heap of retreat. Comfort of the scrapped part.
A seed fallen perfect
on a crop of fissureless granite

and exposed, just as I am exposed,
to time—the coax of its sun,
the rot of its autumn, its voice in your neck,

accretion of love and loam, and suffrage of time to come.
Maybe one day, one year soon
I'll reach into the heavy air and take his hand:

take it, hold it, feel the tips of his fingers
slide up my wrists,
and we'll pull each other into the world. But today,

again, I pass by, easing back to my exile,
my widow's watch of hills,
my riddles of brief and permanent choice.

BIO

David Troupes is a Massachusetts native who has lived the last decade of his life in Yorkshire with his British wife and their two dual citizen daughters. He has published two collections of poetry, and is currently a Fellow of the Jerwood Opera Writing Programme. In 2017 he completed a PhD at the University of Sheffield.

ARTO VAUN

Plastic Mask, Plastic Voice

1.
All the combinations must be in here you
Said one morning leaning against
The kitchen counter resting one naked foot
On the other as if you were talking
To yourself & you were

2.
Light settles & unsettles inside this porcelain
Dream where whatever I am is scatter-
Tongued the soil dense with echo & lamentation
I chew & chew the distance
From Ani to Boston unrooted I
Have never known either place
Maybe I'm the distance itself

3.
In the needle-rain of Glasgow
They introduced me as the Armenian
I choked & smiled like a good boy
It's not that they were wrong or right
They saw one who is pixelated by static
Or they saw me seeing myself
In a speckled mirror

4.
We are the neon abandonment
Caught in the hot speed of flicker-memory
Tangled in the skin-thin spaces between
The shrapnel of where we come from
And where we find ourselves squinting
At the horizon one hand above our eyes
As if that will help us see
Or be seen

5.
You forgot or it slipped
Your mind that I was standing there
All along the twilight trickling
Down my back we waited
For the other to start
Speaking

BIO

Arto Vaun is a poet and songwriter. He's the author of *Capillarity* (Carcanet Press) and his poetry has appeared in various journals and anthologies. Vaun is a senior lecturer at the American University of Armenia and the director of The Center for Creative Writing. He's the founding editor of *Locomotive*, an international journal of poetry and fiction.

JUHA VIRTANEN

Doom Engine

MAINLINE O: toxi-steroid-lactones with that 'deep and special' pair of hands, steered into skids on tired eye gunk clustered around amphibian glands, like stirred coagulants [SLASH] basements now so retro-causal or earmarked for your thumbed index A-OK's, but instead we're really trapped in this floating ghost lodge dimensioned on six-grid macro lab-yrinths for some infrastructural buccal pumping, fully gamified or de-prived of lungs. Delineate hot mucus feelz that just keep coming from these automated repeat convulsions and nerve poisons via ant-ingested or self-synthesized alkaloids, like it's all so Slayer mixtapes spliced with Apple stores, and who the hell can hold out for sarcophagal doomguy self-help routines in aposematic flash sacralised speech, as if commodity logic wasn't a thing. Sportswear urine plugged deep in rage core myths, squat proxy to substrate with limbs under body and chin, so good in an-kle sprain, like absorbent skin when oxygen and water loss are *exactly* the same goddamn membrane, and which machine kills demons again. It's biting on more than fibula and tarsals syncretically fused to one single bone, and we know that's first stage sadism expressed in compressions on warm radial nerves; sloughed dermal quick meal before your camera-ready porous grin too hammered on ice so red, like radio waves too plain to observe when Negan's decentralized name gets on its helicopters and there's fresh gunk on their blades. That is, hard losing when reasoned as gruel as to game, like punched in the face.

The facts seem so sadface and spare, adding texture to flat polygons whilst guarding this zip-lock plastic that's marked safe when it's con-cealed with tape layers, like LOL t-shirts are some 90%; splash damage from conditioners, soap showers, don't scrub your own skin. Desk bin-oculars to drone footage, the quarantine district guest wears UAC post-mortem tech to mine energies from Hell; that gameplay set piece gets relayed in HR centricities, slamming neutron stars like wobbling space-time or kilonovas with plutonium plus precious metals for *ding* cinders merged in a billion degrees – and which machine does affect routines? That spectrum creep is porous [SLASH] habit-based, doxastic conducts patterned on heuristic test-shifts from decicionist coolness with cyber-netic news exchange, treated as an ontic swerve when lasers flux truck engines whilst buffering this RankBrain like IT'S ON hotdog recalls that account for some seven million pounds of fragmented bones, and that's how you know your split-second-scenes when you're deep in ja-cuzzis, shrugs sorry-not-sorry but you will orbit this earth with peak ketosis life moths against orange phosphorous skies and it's all just for #CONTEXT. Gritz/Rambo those shits on pilots for A-Team, duked weavings seem stiff-armed and that photoshopped lens flare recurs on rotation sparse compliance in endless video fizz, the [POUND HOUSE] coalesced around 2003. So, go out and buy things with late neurons crawled under a bus. Cough button got caught on corpses down mouths.

BIO

Juha Virtanen's publications include *Back Channel Apraxia* (2014), *-LAND* (2016), and the critical study *Poetry and Performance During the British Poetry Revival 1960–1980: Event and Effect* (2017). Together with Eleanor Perry, he co-edits the online poetry zine *DATABLEED*. He is Lecturer in Contemporary Literature at the University of Kent.

J. T. WELSCH

World Series, 1985

to L.C.

Whitey gives Forsch the start against Valenzuela.
I know my history. Like the Wizard's switch homer,
barely over the line, it has carried me this far,
and no further. Jack Buck tells us to *go crazy*,
but only in replay, the time for rejoicing
always passed. My parents, though there,
could not have seen. Even history was ending.
Who knew? How sad, how treasonous to know
oneself as the product of certain failure,

feeling some Denkinger lies forever in wait
to dash hopes and remind us with a pigheaded,
irreversible wave of his arms, that, in fact,
no one is safe, and another and another generation
must be left to immigrant exile in every hamlet
of the high plains by desperate great-great-
grandfathers drawn to fertile land around the time
William T. Harris and the St. Louis Hegelians
decided the river of history had led to this, to us,

clutching bratwursts and pocket radios, looking
to the Herzogs or Van Slykes, or indeed, the Wizard,
Ozzie, to lead us, at last – this season, at least –
to a land still promised, still feeling, when the damage
is done, the series lost, and the White Rat ejected,
there is actual beauty in some Joaquín Andújar
taking a bat to a toilet, some John Tudor putting
his pitching fist through an electric fan, or indeed,
another child's September, another instant replayed,

as our beloved Jack brings that ragged voice
to the mic once more, riddled with lung cancer,
flailing with Parkinson's, skin and bone beneath
lapel flag and red blazer. In TV saturation burns our
most nihilistic dream. He has come to heal the nation –
our Cardinal Nation – with a poem ending:

> *as our fathers did before,*
> *we shall win this unwanted war,*
> *and our children will enjoy*
> *the future we'll be giving.*

For my then-single father, it is unwitnessable
in its staging, the recorded soundtrack, fireworks
sync'd to twenty-one marines on the field behind Jack.
They may as well have fired on him, already a martyr
to forward-facing as forward-fearing blindness,
all futures given, all eyes welling on cue
at the growl of death incarnate, then
unincarnate, the next and every spring.

BIO

J. T. Welsch's books and chapbooks include *Orchids* (Salt, 2010), *Orchestra & Chorus* (Holdfire, 2012), *Waterloo* (Like This, 2012), *The Ruin* (Annex, 2015), and *Hell Creek Anthology* (Sidekick, 2015). His essays have appeared in various publications. He is Lecturer in English and Creative Industries at the University of York.

DAVID WHEATLEY

Flags and Emblems

homage to Tom Paulin

Are they part of us asked
the man in the post office

of the Northern Irish fiver
the shopper crinkling

his Queen in his palm
I looked to the woman

in the queue but it wasn't
her place any more

than mine to comment
our awkward wee moment

as Irish as Larkin's
souvenir UVF tie

the Larne gun-runners
paid no import duty

queued for no stamps
it was free trade of a kind

or is that Southern Ireland
the postmaster added

somewhere anyway
in need of a cloot

to wipe itself down
from the bustit sewage

tanker fornenst the diamond
in Crossgar the week of

the vote randomly
spraying clabbery glar

and shite everywhere
not much of a metaphor

granted in a world where –
gable-ends kerbstones

Brexit – things mean
themselves and nothing

besides and you can't
clean up shite that's

still spraying and clagging
the eyes in your head

and but for the flags on
the lampposts you'd hardly

know what country it was.

BIO

David Wheatley was born in Dublin in 1970 and teaches at the University of Aberdeen. He is the author of five collections of poetry, including *The President of Planet Earth* (Carcanet, 2018).

ELŻBIETA WÓJCIK-LEESE

DRY STONE WORDING

That a poem may use the same words as a Company Report means no more than the fact that a lighthouse and a prison cell may be built with stones from the same quarry, joined by the same mortar. (John Berger)

Dry stone walling is so durable because it contains no mortar to crack and fail, but is held together merely by the weight of stone and by the skill of the builder who selected and fitted the stones together. (The Dry Stone Walling Association)

stan stæn ston sten stoon stone stane stayne
stein stone stoan(e steane stain(e stean stone
aszman- akmōn akmuo okmien- kamien- kamień

quarry for the right word   left word? words left behind
pieces of hard mineral substance
word arrangements wordy arrangements too many words stones repeated
ploughing will turn
a verse   averse   to this soil   this territory needs to be cleared
of stones   so build a dry stone wall – methodical waste disposal

where surface stone abounds, walls clear
the ground for grazing and cultivation

'In the "Celtic fringe" of western Britain and Ireland the oldest walls are likely to be clearance walls forming small fields around farmsteads. In areas where the Anglo-Danish open-field system predominated, the oldest walls are those which separate the wet meadows from the common fields, and the common fields from the original wasteland. A continuous wall, unbroken except for gates, is older than all the walls which come to a head against it.' (British Trust for Conservation Volunteers' Handbook)

[semantic] field boundary animal enclosure building shelter fortification
ceremonial structure burial mound
infinite recyclability of dry stone

dry stone walls mirror the native bedrock   until Enclosure Era turns
dry stone walls mirror the local glacial drift   foreigners to throughstones
to tie together   two sides of one wall
the more throughs the wall contains, the stronger it will be

stOnE stOnE **k** stOnE stOnE **k** stOnE stOnE
a **a**
stOnE stOnE **m** stOnE stOnE **m** stOnE stOnE
stOnE stOnE **i** stOnE stOnE **i** stOnE stOnE
stOnE stOnE **e** stOnE stOnE **e** stOnE stOnE
ń **ń**

mark the exact alignment with **guidestrings**
remove enough soil to reach the stable **subsoil**
build the foundation with biggest and squarest stones [**footings**]
lay **successive courses** so the two sides taper to half the width of the base
fill the gaps with smaller stones [**hearting**] so the sides do not collapse in
place long stones [**throughstones**] into the wall to lock it firmly into place
finish with thin flat upright stones [**copestones**] to add considerable weight
a wall is only as strong as its weakest point

> *Building a perfect structure out of a material as variable as stone is almost impossible, and compromises are inevitable throughout the process.* (British Trust for Conservation Volunteers' Handbook)

EVENT OF A STONE				**ERRATA**	
single	stone	coping	rainwater	weight	fissile
hand	lifted	slab	heavy	glacial	hard
prehistoric	weathered	robust	bulge	boulder	deposit
curved	chip	roots	vulnerable	stoop	lithographic
movement	erratic	geology	stile	block	enclosure
field	fortuitous	gate	wind	creep-hole	double

One ought to be able to fit all the stones whatever their size and shape.
incorporate immovable **ERRATIC** elbavommi etaroprocni
erratic
bold
bould
er
err Bless, O Lord, this creature of stone
ing [*creaturam istam lapidis*]
in
a ring

Dry Stone Wall & Its Creatures: mosses & lichen (dwelling); lizards (basking); small mammals & weasels (hunting); wheatears & wagtails & wrens (nesting);

DRYSTANE QUENNET

Grey stones. Orange lichen. Moss green. White lichen. Green stalks. Lichen leaves. Lichen tuft. Lichen crust. Stone border. Barbed thistle. Face stones. Interlocked wall.
Touch the skin of the dry stone and the hearting will release its stored water – fresh trickle into your cupped hand.
Coping stones. Sturdy throughs. Absent trees. Porous wall.

in the open landscape ::::::::::::: walls are ::::::::::::: song-posts
:: for whinchats
:: & stonechats

Territorial song Excitement song : rapidsuccession *rattlewhistle rasrasprasp*
from the elevated perch of the dry stone wall : **Courtship song** boundary
here presences begin
ziwuziwu ziwuziwu ziwuziwu

BIO

Elżbieta Wójcik-Leese writes with/in English, Polish and Danish; her multilingual texts have appeared in *Other Countries: Contemporary Poets Rewiring History* (2014), *Metropoetica, Poetry and Urban Space: Women Writing Cities* (2013) and *Cordite Poetry Review*, *Long Poem Magazine*, and *Tears in the Fence*. *Nothing More* (Arc, 2013), which samples Krystyna Miłobędzka, was shortlisted for the 2015 Popescu European Poetry Translation Prize. *Cognitive Poetic Readings in Elizabeth Bishop: Portrait of a Mind Thinking* (2010) is based on her research at the Bishop archives. She lives in Copenhagen. The poem here references the works of Anni Albers, Robert Duncan, Kathleen Fraser, Philip Terry and Martin Heidegger.

JENNIFER WONG

Do not ask me where I come from

I'm bored by it all: my minority-black, soupy-smooth hair brushed to perfection, my pancake-flat face. I'm longing for the European nose I don't have.

Whatever you say, do not ask me where I come from. I've been here for fifteen years. I went to school in Cheltenham. I'm a voter (but I didn't vote to leave). I'm good at pronouncing 'how lovely' (regardless of circumstances) and enjoy being lazy in the weekend. I live in a good post-code and have a garden of my own.

Whatever you say, do not ask me where I come from. I have traded my country up for better air. There's nothing that I miss, not the sea of black heads in a metro station, certainly not my ageing relatives. Sometimes I think of *char siu* and chicken rice done the proper way – half-lean, half-fat – served with a dash of julienned ginger and garlic.

What is it then that I'd only drink lukewarm water;
follow news on the protests over there,
night after night.

King of Kowloon

In your white vest and blue flip-flops,
you wandered about in the fierce sun,

a can of black paint in your hand.
We read your family history on lamp-posts:

their escape from Liantang, their ancestral home,
settling for Pink Shek in Kowloon.

You hailed Wen Tianxiang and Sun Yat-sen,
charged the Queen for usurping your land.

新中國皇 曾榮華 曾福彩
中 英 香港 政府

A self-declared king for fifty years, painting
all over the colony – a city where the British

lived like paradise birds on mid-Levels
and the Chinese sweated, selling meats

in wet markets but O, the freedom
to march and shout, to do what you did!

Defiance on the lamp-posts,
defiance at the ferry pier.

撐住五十年不變! 高度自治
叉燒 飯碗 撐住!

Your furious characters on the red postbox
put into words our silent fears.

BIO

Jennifer Wong was born and grew up in Hong Kong. Her poems have appeared in *The Rialto*, *Oxford Poetry*, *The North*, *Stand*, *Magma* (forthcoming), *And Other Poems*. Her poetry translation and reviews have appeared in *Poetry Review* and *Poetry London*. She is the author of *Goldfish* (Chameleon Press). She has an MA in creative writing from UEA and is completing a creative writing PhD on place and identity in contemporary diaspora poetry at Oxford Brookes.

ISAAC XUBÍN, TRANSLATED BY PATRICK LOUGHNANE

(there will always be a horizon before our panic)

And I feel this notion of a concept of pleasure
like a weapon that trembles
between the fingers of the steadiest hand,
the linnet's nest within a hedge,
I think I gave myself away due to thirst
because making a mistake did not worry me,
to determine the duration of the body's change in position
since it is never plenitude that we find
at the end of the journey,
there will always be a horizon before our panic.
The panic I get due to the fact the ink could go
that concepts might appear to which I am unable
to attribute aspect, form,
a signifier which does not fit into my process
in any of the languages I know and that sometimes
I act on the unspeakable impulse to
let myself fall into the arms of a mother that is not mine:
I must read more about the relationships
between subject, rejection, object.

The comfort of an apposite technique,
the repetition of movement,
the necessary recycling of the problem, the errors,
turn them into refined changes of pace,
counterpoint, premeditation, evolution,
I put myself into the labyrinth and there I killed god,
angel and even friend.
Afterwards those ladies of cotton appeared
that left the mark of their breath
on the wrinkles of my groin,
surplus phonemes I have left over
or that I do not know how to articulate with precision
and that underground passed the currents
of the Homeric subjects of which once
I was enamoured, rivers.
Because it was not theology that gave shape to my ethics
but rather the flow of electric charge,
repetition and permanence,
the contradiction in which they always obliged me to live,
symbol of the stateless and all of that which they know
that is creole, fruit of a different direction:
I am willing to analyse my pieces.

BIO

Isaac Xubín is an award-winning poet, writer and translator born in A Coruña (Galicia) in 1978 and based in Sheffield. He holds a degree in Galician Philology and an MA in Language Policy and Planning. As a teacher and researcher he wrote a Galician-Basque dictionary and taught Galician Language and Culture in University College Cork. He is currently writing his PhD, an approach to the relationship between Galician Literature and Gastronomy. His first novel, *Non hai outro camiño* (2016, 'There is no other way') was awarded in 2017 with the Spanish Critics Prize in Galician Language.

JANE YEH

A Short History of Migration

We boarded a seashell to ride across the waves.
The mythology of our passage involved dirt, sharks, a zeppelin, and wires.
We ate the same meal seventeen days in a row (pancakes).
We learned to say yes, please in four different languages.

Our fur-lined hats were useless in the fine September air.
The mystery of our parentage was a serape on our backs.
Out on the prairie, the locals usually took us at face value.
We learned about sturgeon, washing machines, ennui, and fake tan.

We joined a fruit-of-the-month club to widen our horizons.
The mastery of our foliage required an endless sea of mowing.
We attended bake sales with a suspicious degree of fervor.
We hindered our children with violins, bad haircuts, and diplomas.

Our names were changed to make them easier to remember.
The monastery of our heritage was repurposed into handy snacks.
We sold refrigerators to people who already had refrigerators.
We lived in suburban glory in our double-decker townhouses.

Our children were changed to make them meaner and fatter.
The memory of our verbiage was as a schnitzel in the wind.
We kept our money close, and our feelings closer.
In the event of an emergency, we kept a baseball bat prepared.

BIO

Jane Yeh is the author of *The Ninjas* (2012) and *Marabou* (2005), both published by Carcanet. This poem first appeared in *The New Republic*. She has lived in the UK since 2001.

ÁGNES LEHÓCZKY

Endnotes: On Paper Citizens, Disobedient Poetries and Other Agoras

1 In Lisa Robertson's *Occasional Work and Seven Walks from the Office for Soft Architecture*, the unnamed narrator spends a significant amount of time immersed in some kind of phenomenological derive, epistemological fog or otherworldly flânerie, drifting around the city of Vancouver, watching its civic space and soft, porous centre dissolve in the 'fluid called money'. Buildings disappear into newness. Her speaker, an urban vagabond, tries to 'recall spaces', but she can only remember 'surfaces', which are, from the viewpoint or angle she observes them, tarred with money. This drifting unnamed narrator, encountering her own melancholic metamorphosis/ dissolvement in the 'looking' exercise, realises that the act of noticing/ seeing has had an emotional impact on her and so decides to document this emotion, this tarred desire, through the series of drifts in both language and city, in which 'I' becomes multiple, in other words, in which people turn into 'money', a market, a place of cringing. A city made of soft composites; visible and invisible layers of both human creativity and human error, political loss, a place in which all those 'without paper' carry the civic emotion which she calls 'service' of the paperless. Robertson's heterotopian terminology becomes especially useful here, inasmuch as I want to define the genre of this book and reference it as documentation, or simply *notemaking* of a particular zeitgeist, cultural (i.e. thinking/feeling) milieu of the *now* and our own emotional response to it, manifested in the fluid movement of poetries, languages, others' (note)books assembled in here; movement *as* building of one's fixed/fluid environment, the fragmentary documentation of a bizarre building site of the present, always also retro-futuristic, at once synchronic and diachronic, a polis – always already *bordering* and border-breaching – in the making, which, often, with a singular term we call *home* or, in less emotional terms, 'accommodation' or 'housing', or even soft habitat. 'Soft', again borrowing Robertson's term, is not emotive decor: it simply refers to fluidity, the tangibility of movement of bodies, many bodies or that of the motioning of language and within that culture,

or *thought* itself. An environment or agora as *perpetuum mobile*, a centre of a public assembly, synchronically babelic, clandestine, labyrinthine, political, violated, liberated, in resistance, disobedient, underpoliticised, heteroglossic, palimpsestic in which poetry as rhythm, despite all gloom, unstoppably reinvents, rejuvenates, or reproduces itself. Theatrum mundi for art is both a hostile and a productive milieu in which poems vanish or survive, often in their countermotion. It is the conflict/friction of movements – of the static and the flux. And so let's imagine this heterotopian civic space of the book, the retrospective, the nostalgic, the melancholic, the progressive, the deviant, the nilling, the static city, the anthology, as a temporary accommodation, our alternative agora, (a planetarium, a glass house, an orangery, an amphitheatre, a labyrinth, an asylum, a sanatorium, a library, etc.) and catch the rhythm of simultaneity, synchrony, solidarity; the circular, the dialogic, and dialectic of this particular feeling of the paperless, the paper citizen. Catching a movement in interlocations (per/interlocutions) is paradoxical or frictional even. Where is the origo of motioning? What is the direction of thinking? Where have you come from? Who do you think you are? And there is, of course, the collective chronic disease: the forgetfulness, the dramatized, politicised amnesia. Just when you are about to capture it...So perhaps, or so I would like to think, this book is an attempt, not so much to capture, but to document, photograph, temporarily solidify the mobility of poetries within the pages of the communal, within the momentarily built municipality, the making of the building of the *solidaire*, which simultaneously, for now, in the form of this book, stands as our disobedient polis, or city of dissidence. Just when you think the world has reached the limit of its own resources, here come the next seven years of desolation. You find a secret well or passage to a surprise city of abundance, because there is immense creative potential in the building of a fluid temporal, insofar as one knows it remains temporal. Incomplete. Fragmentary. Others will come to resume, reconfigure or perhaps even complete the unfinished discourse and rebuild your own incoherent marginalia into a...

2 Paul Celan in his 1960 talk 'The Meridian', originally delivered for the German Academy for Language and Poetry and Literature on the occasion of his acceptance of the Georg Büchner Prize, a speech which since then has become one of the most important European manifestos on art, culture, history and poetics, evokes the figure of a solitary 'voyager', Büchner's Lenz, whose home region exists solely in language. A wondering, peripatetic, *estranged* self, musing, drifting in the world having 'heaven as an abyss beneath him' – in his self/cultural graveyard – who, searching for his own place of origin while simultaneously moving away from 'it', (before disappearing into the nothingness of the Alps), can only exist in and within the poem: which, Celan suggests, also always leads to 'encounters', the 'mystery of encounter', and where the only certainty is found purely in 'something as immaterial as language, yet earthly, terrestrial, in the shape of a circle which, via both poles, rejoins itself and on the way serenely crosses even the tropics'. In other words, he says, Lenz finds the 'meridian'. Celan never quite reveals what he means by this meridian, but there are plenty of references to 'circularity', dialogue, and conversation, 'desperate conversation', turn-taking even between I and you/other, 'encounter with' an absolute or wholly other, en

route to the desired I who does not exist. But here we might recall the image of Ágnes Nemes Nagy's fictionalised Rilke, the 'paperless' citizen, or perpetual vagabond, always on the go, whose 'house' is on his back, his bread on his chest: these are the people who really need a home, at least as much as is necessary. 'What else could he have done, the permanent guest of halls, friends, girlfriends and admirers? He made himself a home that cannot be abandoned, an intimate apartment, its roofs the covers of his books, his domestic objects, his poems'. There is a sense of solid identification in such seemingly elliptical/ephemeral displacements or deconstructions, or dismemberment of concepts such as 'home', selfhood, memory, one's alternative and private *status quo* or state of being in the world. It is because simultaneously there is a comforting tangibility/physicality in language or in the folios, in the construction of a book in other words, and so paradoxically, in the state of 'paperlessness' that is still immersed in the tangibility of writing, standing here, for now, in the form of our anthology or *note*book, with all its 'darkly confected scenes', recalling by analogy Lisa Robertson's *Nilling*, staging a 'speculative, temporarily striated polis', building or home, shelter of re-imaginings of oneself. The notion of homecoming inhabits the security that lies both in the struggle of naming and silence, Heidegger writes: and so as soon as one gives thought to this 'homelessness, it is a misery no longer.' If we, only temporarily, find solace in this premise, then it is true that what binds these works together is the attempt to fill in such elliptical constructions – silences, erasures, or more precisely the space or *lack* between appearances and disappearances – of 'arbitrary' reveries, peripatetic meanderings, off-track mobilities, from the experience of being lost in this motioning, dissipated in disappearing surfaces of structure, or in the 'reading' of the *note*book, one's 'notes on oneself'. Concerning some collective pursuit, a Homeric (but non-heroic) quest, and the resistance or disobedience to such searching or let alone to any settling down (into any name or place). *Discordia concors*. Give me the (language) postcode for the house of happiness (of such hobo habitat). 'I is for *ire* to go,' Alice Notley writes in *Disobedience*. Or, later in the book: 'I am origi', (her) voice says in a real dream.

3 While not at all convinced that language can secure a physical or even heterotopian home (or whatever real environments language does or can construct around one's floating, non-comforming, nomadic self or soul as one's private/public/virtual, hyperreal or even non-hegemonic *status quo* made of immaterial bricks or from the non-profit books make or bring as funding source to find and fund 'that' idyllic habitat), I suspect that perhaps bringing together perspectives, bodies of poetries, and encounters to name, document or take notes of our own collective *emotion*, triggered by such quests for a home or polis (collective inasmuch as it is a place or a country we have never been before, with country signifying less a specific 'place' than a zone of *time*, *thought*, *desire* or *experience*) does ease one's misery inasmuch it is a collective misery. Theoretically, and the poems stand here as evidence, language does help inasmuch as we become *beings made of* discourse, at the intersection with other heteroglossic discourses, which, if nothing else, is intuitively comprehensible as a language that feels 'ours'. There is an abyss between the language of passion and that of compassion. The emotion

of the *solidaire* (referring to [the offering of] 'whole sum/solid' support) is frequently invoked, but I prefer *compassionate* (feeling *for* and *as* another). And *disobedient* ('against being submitted to'). We may need to invent a word which embraces the amalgam of the three.

4 But the opposite is true, too, i.e. that one's main obstacle stems from the simple fact that we do possess, alongside our more fluid bodies, a physical ('fixed') body or quality (as Notley notes), which simply, biologically or physiologically, requires a concrete, solid shelter, refuge, and therefore space, since as Robertson writes again, watching the city of Vancouver dissolve in the fluid called money, 'everything wants to live; there is no such thing as utopia'. In other words, as our collective mother would say: you can't live on 'air' especially if we are not in the privileged Rilkean position of being surrounded by wealthy patrons and other generous celestials or saints who would put us up in the middle of our solipsistic meanderings, overwhelming and so nurturing us with overnight canopy and early morning breakfast and even with some viaticum before we take off, providing that in exchange of all goodness we pay back with good service, i.e. that we *will* write and that, if we do, we will do it well, in order to give something back to the world. A little while ago, I was asked by a literary journal to reflect on what my imaginary poet's house was like and if I could put down a short sketch of its fantastical parameters, architectural planning, image, shape, size etc. Thinking about it now, the question from the journal arrived at a time when I – and, in a ridiculously uncanny way, most of those close to me, my closest friends, boss, mother, colleagues etc. – seem to have been encountering a series of problems with accommodation, wishing to sell and buy, not possessing the right papers, being in the wrong market, struggling to find a habitat, being forced by my/her/their own recklessness to change postcodes every third or fourth month in the city where I had decided to semi-settle eight years ago. Secretly superimposing my ideal/childhood/nostalgic/imaginary city on this chosen new one, whichever civic space I attempted to settle, fills it with some kind of perpetual urge/angst to keep moving on/going off in a tangent, not sticking to conventional trajectories. As if one's own inner antagonist, obsessive vagabond or obnoxious non-conformist nomad – 'antisocial' even, a term borrowed here from Sam Solomon – had been epitomising, and thus carrying, and resisting, her own zeitgeist anxieties in her own Rilkean rucksack or survival kit, her own restless body or psyche in search of a hopefully final and ideal accommodation. Maybe it is the parable of the fool who has built his or her own house on quicksand, or on water. This notion of carrying your own mobility, leaving old contents, bric-a-brac of your 'rucksack' at various random houses, or just the concept of motioning in yourself, is what conjures up lots of questions and queries about the act of reading of the world through yourself, or reading yourself through the world always both fixed and fluid, always breaching borders – and so through language; some kind of temporarily written book of selfhood – the frustrating interconnection, inter-boundary (weird triangle) between book (by which I mean language), self and the world; all assembled in some mobile home, with your own self standing outside and inside it (yourself), at the threshold of yourself, not quite *inside*, not quite *outside*; this I or *I*, the paperless citizen – with a 'paper-self' – claiming the right *not* to have to be 'this or even that', the

I, the moving pen, the 'unbuilder', the 'deconstructor' of self-demarcations (as it goes along), parergonally – between the physical and the conceptual, private and public, social and anti-social, knocking on the door, pleading the book, the world, the economy to let you in into its domestic drama; or dramatic/dramatised domesticity to which you don't quite belong. The desire you carry in you is doomed to be paradoxical, a so-far nameless 'emotion': an amalgam of nostalgia for and phobia towards *being belonging to*. In other words: this so called paradox, often described as a hybridity, parergonality, or the cultural manifestation of it as a poetic, cultural, political or simply civic or even personal/private disposition – feeling and thought, our now's idiosyncratic cultural/civic emotion – perhaps has been one of the objectives to document or make present in this *notebook*. A series of documentations, or statements on things that matter to us or frustrate us. Or just worry us.

5 But the poet's house (our anthology, for now), or psyche, or as Notley writes in *Disobedience*, selfhood/soulhood, structured as a polemic, angry, baffling city moving in its own memory-stream in a perpetual present, or as Robertson suggests in *Soft Architecture*, drifting, appearing and disappearing *as* body – noticed/unnoticed – in an imaginary, hallucinatory metropolis, as desire; or as name floating against the logocentric, reconfigured, made superfluous, body *as* accumulation, caught up in and at a juncture in history, annihilated at the surface of a 'style or a politics', bio-power or hegemony, is also haunted by our diverse and varied past psycho-political/historical geographies (spectres), while simultaneously, in the mobile house of this book, moving towards a collective unknown future, collective inasmuch it is unknown yet always certain: because one's desired Ithaca embraces one's finality, of course, or simply because all subjects, like Büchner's Lenz, are always already walking over their zeitgeist graveyard – even though all graveyards, or as Alice Notley would have it, the 'shitcave[s] of the World', contain recyclable treasures, as Różewicz suggests in his 1996 *Zawsze fragment: Recycling* ('Always a Fragment: Recycling'). So the postcode I search for and desire is bound to metamorphose into a final resting place for this difficult, fixed body I carry around no matter where I come from, outside myself. And so, of course, why the worry, Derrida asks, in the documentary *Ghost Dance*, which he produced with Ken McMullen in 1983, staring at you into the camera – long dead, enacting an interview with French actress Pascale Ogier – who dies tragically shortly after the interview: Slow down. You are always already your own ghost, haunted by the *ineffable*, your own estranged, posthumous self. There is always the horizontal gaze, even during one's physical/everyday existence – (a bit like the sense of sudden uncanny surprise you are left with when you receive an email from yourself, having forgotten you'd send it to save work). That accidental and impromptu interpellation imposed upon you by yourself. And then of course there is no more ideal or idyllic home, the place of rest than the horizontality (or 'dying into / a...future I am leaving / that you can't change', says Notley) of the book; its shape, the rectangularity, its architectural planning, its own temporality and finality and singularity. 'What better than to get to be dead while simultaneously alive?' Denise Riley asked me recently, playfully, rhetorically, in an email. The journal never published my response to its commissioned task in the end, part of which was asking me to imagine home *as* posthumous, to recall dwelling places

of poets long gone. There were two concrete houses I thought of straight away at the time: one is a small house in a village called Balatonszárszó in Hungary at Lake Balaton, not far from the Southern Danubian Railway Line (which used to travel down as far as Fiume) where Attila József spent his last few months in the late autumn/winter of 1937. It is the house he walks out of in the dusk on the 3rd of December and never returns. Now the little village house is a museum thousands visit each year: much of the original furniture, gas stove, and somewhere in one of the rooms his blood-stained shirt remain on display (with one sleeve missing, or was just that my imagination?). The other is John Keats's house in Hampstead. A fascinatingly haunted/haunting place of my own private past and future losses. Wasn't it the pathogenic *bacillus* whose cure he had searched for all his life that killed Keats in the end, the poet physician? Or perhaps it's not the actual place itself at all? Keats's house was also the witness of an eerie phonecall I received during my visit, as I was standing on the top floor in the room of Fanny Brawne, informing me of some devastating news. My own private news, my own 'event', now public. So, the poet's house: is it the house, in the moment of entering it, which both gives you and leaves you...

6 And so, bringing together a multitude of perspectives and encounters to name or document 'civic emotion', whether it be compassion, disobedience, cultural anxiety, resistance, bafflement, claustrophobia, entrapment, socio-political, humanitarian or environmental crisis, or melancholia even, does ease one's misery. We have so many different words for border – boundary, limitation, margin, perimeter, demarcation, frontier, or even the re-appropriated concept or phenomenon of the *curtain* – each pointing at a physical structure (a construct), but each aleatorically and often frustratingly and blatantly and obnoxiously disputing or denying its own fluid 'contours', ephemeral, in its concrete solidity some brutalist artifice: thus rendering itself as prohibition. The cover, binding, or frame of a book is only a parergonal boundary for its content insofar as its inside and outside co-habit the same border. Horizon, space and boundary are semantically conjoined, since a boundary is not that at which something stops. Rather, as the early Greeks recognised, a boundary is that from which something begins its presencing. Instead, we have the concept of *horismos*, that is, the horizon, as un-prohibitive boundary. 'Space is in essence that for which room has been made, that which is let into its bounds,' Heidegger writes in his essay on 'Building, Dwelling, Thinking'. What makes it diverse and abundant, he continues, is that border, which is horizon, is simultaneously shared and approached from different angles by the 'neighbour', 'the near-dweller'. Actual physical borders seem like phantasmagoria – despite the fact that all sorts of walls, Hadrian-sized or larger, we all know, can be erected overnight and change our landscape. No need to go into the history of wall-building (and so much has happened over the last thirty years). But wall-experts dismiss the fact that horizon only exists as amalgamation: one's perception always fusing into the other's. The object's contours are only contours inasmuch as it blends in and so stands out. This is the object's 'outer horizon', which is 'indefinitely extendable' and embraces, as *mise-en-abyme*, one's environment. It is a vantage point from which one can view the other, by distancing yourself from yourself. Inasmuch as we move and inasmuch as movement is progress

of thought. Our exilic panoramas somehow ease our obsession with fixities, finalities, conclusiveness, irrevocability, or control of all these: Borges spent most of his writing years outside Buenos Aires writing about the city (his posthumous self ending up buried in Genova). When my father died, my mother bought a family tomb within the National Panthenon's 56-acre parkland in Budapest. The cemetery had been opened for public use after the fall of the Iron Curtain and, coincidentally, is inhabited by the country's famous/infamous politicians, artists, writers, actors and actresses, architects, academics and so on. I suspect, somehow, every time I stand above my father's spectre, that, once I am dead, my little rectangular nook down there, resting place, assigned to me, will remain empty, unoccupied.

7 In *The Rings of Saturn,* Sebald's unnamed narrator, suffering from some kind of perpetual gloom, in and out of hospital, sick of an incurable, unshakeable melancholia, spends a large chunk of time rummaging along the East Anglian shoreline, picking up remnants, random objects, photographs, moths, forgotten books, maps, seemingly irregular and arbitrary things and people who lived or live quietly in adversity, 'the shadow of annihilation always hanging over them', those of *Le Strange*. Via these at times hallucinatory, phantasmagorical meanderings and phenomenological reflections, he shows us history, the physical and political texture of trauma, human error, and in all that human connectedness suggesting that most disparate things are each other's 'neighbours', near-dwellers, or predecessors even, 'relatives' no matter which side of the 'border' we stood or stand on, publically, privately, or otherwise. There is a lot of creative energy in Sebald's gloom, in the recognition of such unification, even if what unites us is error. This notion of interconnectedness is essential in the making of this book too, as documentation, a re-appropriated Sebaldian map. The method we employed is phenomenological insofar as it approaches the realm of cultural *mise-en-abymes*, synchronic or parallel horizons within horizons, unseen cities within the superficial, one's 'neighbours' among the citizens of *Le Strange*. Employing Sebald's concentric circling, we have found a labyrinthine city within a city, a city maze, the maze of the civic emotion beyond what feels otherwise sanitized and/or hegemonic. Excavating, and so moving within those concentric circles, we discover here an entire network not only entwined, coexisting with and so neighbouring one another('s horizons) in various parts of London or across the UK, but reaching out, like Socrates' atropos, his giant, universal insect/human, or like Sebald's imaginary map, reaching/breaching into various parts of Europe, Asia, Africa, North and South America and so on. Jèssica Pujol's *Our Home: In Solidarity with 'One Day Without Us'* reading in solidarity with non-British poets in the UK was one nucleus from which our research began, a four-hour poetry event organised in London in a tiny café *Iklektik* in Old Paradise Yard in Lambeth in February 2017, some mobile toilets attached to the building outside and a tiny little bar and café inside selling foreign lager and strange biscuits. There were at least a hundred poets, Brits, no Brits, there, from London, The British Isles, various parts of Europe, America and elsewhere, gathering together in response to the post-Brexit landscape-storm we woke up to on the morning of 24 June 2016. I recall it was a grey Friday. J.T. called and asked if we should get to work on the book we had been planning.

And there were other concentric circles, threads that fed our searching, archives and journals such as *Archive of the Now* edited by Andrea Brady, *Blackbox Manifold* edited by Adam Piette and Alex Houen, SJ Fowler's gigantic *The Enemies* and *Camarade* Projects, and some forerunners to this anthology's vision in the form of other anthologies such as, inter alia, *Dear World and Everyone In It*, ed., Nathan Hamilton, (Bloodaxe 2013), *OUT OF EVERYWHERE 2: Linguistically Innovative Poetry by Women in North America & the UK*, ed. Emily Critchley (Reality Street, 2015, after part 1, edited by Maggie O'Sullivan, Reality Street, 1996), *Atlantic Drift*, eds. James Byrne and Robert Sheppard (Edge Hill University Press & Arc Publications, 2017), *Liberating the Canon*, ed., Isabel Waidner, (Dostoyevsky Wannabe, 2018). Likewise, various reading series, such as the soon to be closing down (or in fact to be closed down by the time this anthology is born) *The Other Room* run and in its anthology format edited by Scott Thurston, Tom Jenks and James Davies in the heart of Manchester, along with those series J.T. and I co-ordinate in York and Sheffield. And then of course, there were the concentric circles of word-of-mouth, a chain of collegial recommendations. The response from every poet was overwhelming – this sense of collegiality, heart-warming, empowering, and so essential in the building of this book. Needless to say, how fortunate we were to find a great ally in Nathan Hamilton and his Boiler House Press.

8 [Note to oneself: Sebald's *The Rings of Saturn* ends with a giant sand storm in the East Anglian forest, in which the protagonist, our unnamed narrator, temporarily gets lost. What remains, Sebald writes, is absolute silence: no birds singing, no human noise, only whitened tree trunks erected in the ashened air. I realise the view in this section – following the 1987 hurricane, which swept through East Anglia, leaving a desolate landscape behind – becomes an apocalyptic vision, and there is a point where we can't differentiate between the fact and fiction of this episode. And it is this threshold, I think, between the two, where the energy or nucleus of the narrative unfolds. That split second, the chance of a *thought* to come, before the cataclysm. But we all know that progress is another 'storm', propelling consciousness towards some uncanny future landscape, while the pile of debris behind us accumulates. Are we recoiling, back to where we started, back to Benjamin's 'unending cycle of despair', as time, or Celan's 'desperate conversations'? Or: 'You think such / a vision of the century, of the future is extreme? (Notley)]

9 We all know the premise by heart: language is the house of being, a home in which one dwells. We are touched by it, reassured, even moved or humbled. But also confronted, baffled, irritated, frustrated by its ephemeral promises of comfort. Because at times Fredric Jameson's 'prison-house' analogy (as J.T. reminded me) rings more true and serves this comparison/allegory game more adequately in our aporia, its absurdity or paradox is understood here *as* experience. And what happens when I begin to become, Judith Butler writes elsewhere, 'that for which there is no place within the given regime of truth?' ('What is critique?', 2001). Or because, as Celan claims, this 'me' does not exist, 'can't exist'. Or because: 'Mother Fuck', Notley writes, 'I scream!/ There is no language for this!!!' Because who do we think we are? 'Is this the same origination shit myth and apple', Notley's *I* asks in another dream.

In other words, what if it is *language*, one's most obnoxious foe, which denies access to places, groups, privileges? And why the need for such (any) book for the discourse of identity, the non-identity, the parergonal identity, the mobility self, who is not quite ever inside, nor outside? This, a book joining and making space for conversation, within the broadest of all churches and dominating the history of 20thC philosophy on the national, private, non-, extinct, exilic, erased, trans-, eco-, hybrid, non-binary, etc. Isn't language philosophy somehow always the philosophy of the (crisis of the) self, a discourse which sometimes races ahead of us, sometimes struggles to catch up with us, with our racing/peripatetic/retrospective understanding of the self that is fantastical, imaginary, adrift, 'fixed' yet 'remaining fluid' (Notley)? To settle in the 'right' discourse or language is paradoxical, a psycho-linguistic cul-de-sac not only because 'each and every act of identification is fantastical' but because the 'name' we are assigned to is 'often profoundly politicised' or even 'arranged by language' (Riley, WoS). A language, my posthumous 'tomb-choice' imposed on me by a given system of utterance. And what if, Denise Riley asks, one does not wish to claim to be 'something-or-other' exactly because of language's flaws and shortcomings? This is a defence of claims, *our* claims, not to be either this or that; a defence of those who have got 'nothing to say for themselves'? There is a clearly recognisable tendency today of 'not' wanting to belong to a name, Riley writes in *The Words of Selves*, which firmly 'decides that hesitations in inhabiting a category are neither psychological weaknesses nor failures of authenticity or solidarity' because even 'mutating identifications, sharpened by the syntactical peculiarities of self-description's passage to collectivity, decisively mark the historical workings of political language'. Now, this is the real cul-de-sac. How not to fall into the grave of any names? Is addresslessness the new, alternative and most ideal postcode? Some are more than content with the stigma of the paperless, the illegitimate. Deviance (dissidence, disobedience or decadence) is empowering. *Esprit de corps*.

[Note to oneself: In many ways it would have been appropriate to have these poems published authorless, nameless, biog-less, past-less, faceless, paperless even.]

10 But there is almost as much need or desire to be seen as to remain in anonymity, to reconfigure or secure a 'place' and therefore a name in language. Violation, Butler asserts in a recent talk on bio-power, does not necessarily have to involve a 'physical blow'. Violence can manifest itself by the simple act of 'unseeing' various groups or masses of people, 'soft surfaces' of the world, or our environment itself, segments of it not in direct closeness, and thus this deliberation can and does produce masses of disposable 'names' (and species) whose identity or presence can be erased or discarded to violence, i.e. intentionally, and also internationally, not safeguarded against. Who or what gets 'noticed'/registered, overlooked or seen? Who or what has the right or who has no legitimacy to live? The central setting of China Miéville's *City and the City* is an unnamed polis, perhaps in Central-Southern-Eastern Europe, in which there exists a parallel city (or multiple cities), a city within the city, a metropolis (embracing its acropolis): the setting of the narrative is the cohabitation of the seen and the unseen, which are nonetheless aware of each other's presence, through visible and invisible surfaces of the civic

in an unknown, dystopian, yet rather painfully recognisable future zeitgeist. Citizens of both cities perform on the daily act or routine of seeing or unseeing the 'other', whichever city they belong or unbelong to, so live their lives in seemingly perfect harmony, symphony, cacophony, always making sure they don't breach the gaping 'invisible' border, like an intangible psycho-political/geographical no-man's land between the two parts of the same and only city. Because *as long as we are ok...*

11 ...in one of the series of *Walking Cities*, a new literature program that connects contemporary voices from Canada and the UK to exchange on ideas related to identities, places and territories, Canadian writer Dionne Brand and poet Vahni Capildeo feature walking, drifting in some impressionist reveries in and around Bloor Street West in Toronto, lost in conversation in a part of a city which was offering itself to the viewers as a seemingly open book, all of its vibrant micro life readable, decipherable. During their walk, the two poets talk about literature, poetry and art and discuss in detail the city's palimpsestic construction, the multiplicity of languages – e.g. Hindi, Italian, French, Spanish, English, Ukrainian, just to mention a few out of the 100–200, the city as heteroglossia, as accumulative place, its significance of corners, its layering of past and present, its tautologies, and in them the hidden surfaces, its repetition of colonial memories and structures in the architecture of the polis' civic space, while standing at the corner of the street both turning towards this city panorama of the now. It's a heart-warming and energetic dialogue. But what excites me about their conversation are the breaks, the pauses, the silences between the two flâneurs, the turn-taking in which there are a number of significant gaps. So this lack. As pars pro toto. Because palimpsest, our palimpsest here, De Quincey's appealing metaphor, is graver than what it appears to be because it is a structure, a layeredness , or an abyss even, which both conceals and reveals, accommodates, violates, annihilates.

12 It's true that almost all writers whose work I rate prefer anonymity. Or they are simply used to it after decades of being silenced, ignored, marginalised. And I know that's old hat, too. There is a need or desire to be seen, to hold a name, to belong yet, paradoxically a resistance to it; once recognised, one has given up one's freedom or privilege (or destiny) to drift. This anthology gives shelter to this friction, to this 'threshold'. Or so J.T. and I would like to hope. Inasmuch as unorthodoxy does not become the norm, that is, orthodoxy. But then...

13 Because one's horizon is another's. And so the power of language *is* documentary and documentation. In other words, Notley writes, dreams are real. We are passionate about this book, our impromptu building for disobedience and compassion, which is possibly not the book in any shape or form J.T. and I had been planning to put together for the past four years. Perhaps that book exists only in the future house, 'always better built lighter and larger than all the houses of the past' inasmuch as it renders continuity to the discourse of dreams and dreaming. 'Maybe it is a good thing for us', Gaston Bachelard writes, 'to keep a few dreams of a house that we shall live in later, always later, so much later, in fact, that we shall not have time

to achieve it'. There is a recent book project, *Uncommon Building*, edited by friend and former colleague Honor Gavin, a collaboration between writers and architects published by Spirit Duplicator (a recent-ish press), a project somewhat akin to Benjamin's *Arcades Project*, on a much smaller scale, configured from fiction and non-fiction, in which the collaborating writers reconstruct a non-existent part of Sheffield through an imaginary architectural design or planning. In other words, in my understanding, they not only configure a place that does not exist and talk of it as something concrete and existent, but also create a voice, a self, an identity, an imaginary civic emotion of an equally imaginary *I* through art who nostalgically and melancholically remembers its surfaces, carrying in him or herself as a response some kind of compassion for a part of the environment which had never been there, a building or a tower block made of the cement of imagination, imaginary emotion, non-selves, non-history as place and history, yet one which affects the book's readers, its components made from other texts, of political philosophy, art, architecture and economy, a self-theorized historico-social building, reflecting on its own being-built, built of fiction which reads with the conviction of non-fiction. Deceptively, playfully, the book itself turns into a stunning handbook, a reading of its own meta-structure in the making, carefully and cleverly built into something concrete and tangible as from nothing. The project, in a less sanguine sense, reminds me of a much more concrete architectural plan of an almost future Arts Centre in Sheffield, which was soon destined to be, despite having been designed by architects, having funding prepared to support its foundation, and objectives laid out – to offer a 'building', a civic heart to the city's creative arts practitioners and academics, musicians, poets, novelists, performance artists, architects, working within or affiliated to the University – destroyed, any phantom dreaming of it, soon erased, money used elsewhere. The remains of the grand project: an abandoned Henderson's Relish corner factory. So, we hope this book is not one of those phantom buildings of crushed dreams. There is a sense of the real produced, mimicked, imitated, in fiction, and comfort in this, a notion of homecoming in the simulacra architecture, which exists in all its tangibility, concreteness and therefore reliability as we *read* the book, respond to it, correspond with it and aim to 'break up', moving backwards, in retrospective re-order borders of old forms, paradigms, discourse, economies, while we also attempt to reconfigure and 'forsee the unforeseeable', moving forward, ploughing on. The promise of any creative prospect is in this 'broken down', re-erected 'absence', materialised, solidified nothing. The book offered here – despite all meandering reflections recorded above on spectrality, physical or linguistic homelessness, marginality, parergonality – is not an anthology about thanatology, except perhaps in the act of embracing concepts of dissidence, decadence and deviance, a celebration of all the unfinished, the temporal, the incomplete. And we can only hope that time spent building of and dwelling within this civic space, this disobedient polis, is not destined to complete destitution. It feels right to leave it incomplete, asymmetrical, impermanent, temporal. Maybe it's one of those houses which, as Sebald writes, the (good) traveller never leaves and never returns to. There will be others who continue the documentation, the notemaking, the conversation, with or without paper.

NOTES

Gaston Bachelard, *The Poetics of Space* (Beacon Press, 1992).
Walter Benjamin, 'Theses on the Philosophy of History' ([1940], in: *Illuminations*, Pimlico, 1999).
Judith Butler, 'Distinctions on Violence and Nonviolence,' (EGS, 2016).
Paul Celan, 'The Meridian,' [1960] in *Selected Poems and Prose of Paul Celan*, trans. John Felstiner (New York–London: Norton, 2001).
Jacques Derrida, *The Postcard: From Socrates to Freud and Beyond* (University of Chicago, 1987).
Martin Heidegger, 'Building, Dwelling, Thinking,' [1971] in *Poetry, Language, Thought*, trans. Albert Hofstadter (New York: Harper Colophon, 1975, Perennial Classics, 2001).
Martin Heidegger, 'Letter on Humanism,' [1947] transl. Frank A. Capuzzi in collaboration with J. Glenn Grey in *Basic Writings*, ed. David Farrell Krell (London and New York: Routledge, 1993, sixth reprint, 2004).
Ágnes Nemes Nagy, 'Rilke almafa,' in *Az élők mértana I. Prózai írások*, ed. Mária Honti (Osiris, 2004).
Alice Notley, *Disobedience* (Penguin, 2001).
Denise Riley, *The Words of Selves: Identification, Solidarity, Irony* (Stanford University Press, 2000).
Lisa Robertson, *Nilling* (Book Thug, 2012).
Lisa Robertson, *Occasional Work and Seven Walks from the Office for Soft Architecture* (Coach House Books, 2003, 2011).
W. G. Sebald, *The Rings of Saturn* (Vintage, 2002).
Samuel Solomon, *Lyric Pedagogy and Marxist-Feminism: Social Reproduction and the Institutions of Poetry* (Bloomsbury, forthcoming late 2018).
Uncommon Building, ed. Honor Gavin (Spirit Duplicator, 2017).
Walking Cities: Toronto, Adrian Smith and Jason Hopfner (Productions Spectrum, 2017).

Wretched Strangers
Edited by Ágnes Lehóczky & J. T. Welsch
First published in this edition by Boiler House Press, 2018
Part of UEA Publishing Project, Ltd.

Design and typesetting by Emily Benton
emilybentonbookdesigner.co.uk
Typeset in Arnhem
Printed by Imprint Digital, UK
Distributed by NBN International

ISBN 978-1-911343-38-7